Metallic Modern

Metallic Modern

Everyday Machines in Colonial Sri Lanka

Nira Wickramasinghe

berghahn
NEW YORK • OXFORD
www.berghahnbooks.com

Published in 2014 by

Berghahn Books

www.berghahnbooks.com

Library of Congress Cataloging-in-Publication Data

Wickramasinghe, Nira.
Metallic modern : everyday machines in colonial Sri Lanka / Nira Wickramasinghe. - First Edition.
pages cm
Includes bibliographical references and index.
ISBN 978-1-78238-242-3 (hardback : alk. paper) – ISBN 978-1-78238-243-0 (institutional ebook)
1. Industries–Social aspects–Sri Lanka–History. 2. Consumption (Economics)–Sri Lanka. 3. Civilization, Modern. I. Title.
HD60.5.S797W53 2014
338.095493–dc23

2013017853

British Library Cataloguing in Publication Data

A catalogue record for this book is available from the British Library

Printed on acid-free paper

ISBN: 978-1-78238-242-3 hardback ISBN: 978-1-78238-243-0 institutional ebook

Contents

Illustrations

FIGURES

MAPS

Preface and Acknowledgements

I have always liked short works of fiction. So, if one is to look for the origins of the idea of *Metallic Modern,* rather than in emblematic books of iconic scholars it is more likely to be found in my own youthful experience as a dilettante fiction writer. Growing up in Paris, my dream was to someday be the author of a book that people read casually while commuting to work in the metro. This was a time before e-readers and text messaging. My model was then Jorge Luis Borges's pocket-sized *Fictions* or *Labyrinthes.* But it was not only the convenient shape of his books, it was also what his concise text conveyed, a feeling both of uncertainty and escape distilled in erudite storytelling. In Clairefontaine coloured notebooks, like many of my generation I diligently composed similar stories full of maps, labyrinths, mirrors and libraries. After this embarrassingly imitative phase, in the wake of Francois Mitterrand's election victory, and immersed in the rebellious sounds of the Clash and the Stranglers, my teen-age political ideas sharpened. I tried my pen at Voltairian social satire critiquing vulgarity, prejudices and pomposity. This was the early 1980s and, yes, I wanted to be a journalist and change the world.

The content of this book is more recent than its form since it has been with me for a decade or so. From the moment I commenced my work on dress and the colonial body sponsored by SEPHIS, I was intrigued by the lives of things and machines as I sensed they could tell us something new and exciting about how colonized people lived the late nineteenth century and early twentieth centuries. A fellowship at the Davis Center at Princeton University in 2008–9 provided me with the testing ground for my ideas. During those quiet months I immersed myself in the Singer company papers, read widely across times and regions while trying out my ideas with my colleagues in lively discussions. My focus broadened from the Singer sewing machine to other machines – gramophone, tram, bicycle – while my problematic strangely returned to my perennial preoccupation with the fallacy of national belonging and the hazards of writing national histories. Events called for this framing. This was the last stages of the civil war in my country, when the Sri Lankan army was in the process of crushing the ruthless separatist Tamil Tigers inflicting civilian deaths on a scale we are yet to fully unravel. Issues of belonging and identification, of misery and pain insinuated themselves into my manuscript and remain there. These events convinced me that to move away from dusty written documents and look at objects and machines was salutary and would help me free myself from the caging of the nation-state.

I still would like to believe that what I write can contribute to creating a better world devoid of vulgarity, prejudices and pomposity among other ills, but after two decades of teaching in a public university in Colombo and my move to Leiden three years ago I am more than ever convinced that for a historian it is only through teaching young people in the classroom that any social transformation can come about. Eric Hobsbawm's life of teaching is exemplary in many ways and gives me sustenance in moments of defeat. Why do so few books today have the capacity to entertain and instil a sense of wonderment and curiosity or even surprise me? Our freedom to write fugues seems to be constricted in these very dispiriting times in which we live and work, forced as we are to obey the demands of the market and of intellectual fads. *Metallic Modern* is a moment of flight for me. I hope it takes readers on an unexpected journey across borders both intellectual and creative.

The process of writing took some time. Leaving Colombo and starting a new career and life at Leiden University stalled my research for a while, but Leiden, a kind of fairy tale town, was an inspiring setting and soon became a home away from home. I am very grateful to colleagues and friends who contributed to the making of this book by offering valuable comments on the manuscript or at talks, or by helping me find documents or pictures that I used in the book. I will only cite those directly involved and not all the others who made very sincere efforts to distract me from work and remind me of the other pleasures of life. I must apologize if I have forgotten someone in this very short list: Daniel T. Rodgers, Michael and Judy Laffan, Bhavani Rahman, Celia Applegate and Susan Pennybacker; Andrew Gordon; David Arnold, Andrew Godley; John Rodgers, Ranjith Nirmal Dewasiri and Janaki Jayawardena; Sanayi Marcelline, Sujeewa, Nadeera Seneviratne; Dileepa Vitharana, Harini Hamarasuriya, Athula Samarakoon; Idrees Kanth, Anup Grewal; Sujit Sivasundaram, Sandagomi Coperahewa; Marina Carter; Vilasnee Tampoe Hautin; Dilip Menon, Sunil Amrith; Francis and Coralie Pieterz, Anura Saparamadu, Sam Bastian. Three anonymous readers helped sharpen the chapters and I thank them for their close reading of my draft.

Many of my ideas were first tried out with students at Colombo University who followed my social history class and were more recently discussed with students at Leiden University who participated in my MA class 'History Theory Nation. Readings from the South.'

I am grateful to the staff at the Sri Lanka National Archives, and to the Wisconsin Historical Society Archives for allowing me to use and reproduce their material.

Thanks also to Marion Berghahn and Ann DeVita for their trust in me. Publishing a social history of colonial Sri Lanka is a risk that few publishers would have taken. Special thanks to my copy editor Kristine Hunt for her insightful comments and perceptive eye.

All errors of fact and interpretation that remain in the text are of course mine and I apologize to my readers in advance.

Finally a word of thanks to my family whose affection kept me going throughout the sometimes painful personal circumstances that accompanied the writing of this book: Amma and Thatha, Rapti and Joel, Maya and Anaelle, Susruta (also for the lovely map), Gameela, Arvind and Nangie and my two unconditional supporters who, I'm afraid, will still have to wait a little longer for the day when I finally write for them a book peppered with guns and tanks. Abhijit and Pratik, it is to you, I dedicate this book, with love.

Introduction

Exploring Sri Lanka's Modern

Multiple Loops of Belonging

A *BHIKKU* WRITES A LETTER

On 15 October 1912, a Sinhalese Buddhist *bhikku* (monk) from the village of Welipatanwila in the South of Sri Lanka[1] wrote a letter to his teacher, the chief monk of Sunandaramaya in the village of Thiranagama, addressing him with much devotion as *Waranaravinda* (excellent noble lotus) to inform him that a very special religious function had been held two days earlier. This letter has never been cited, to my knowledge, by any historian and it is purely by chance that I found its call number in the handwritten catalogue of the National Archives in Colombo. This letter is, however, of particular interest. It refers to a religious ceremony performed to bring merit to the deceased 'great king of Japan'. This was taking place in 1912 in Sri Lanka, then known by its colonial rulers as Ceylon, a Crown colony of the United Kingdom where at the time indigenous subjects had virtually no representation or voice in the governance of the country. Nevertheless, in this small southern village, residents had gathered on a full moon day to light lamps, offer flowers and incense and hear a religious sermon in order to transfer merit through a *prapthidanaya* (thanksgiving ceremony) to the deceased 'king of Japan', unmistakably Emperor Meiji also known as Mutsuhito. The bhikku signed his letter – entirely written in Sinhalese – in the English language and script.[2]

In Sri Lanka, at the end of the nineteenth and in the early twentieth century, a new space of experience was being forged and it was this new space – which I could call present-past – that would determine people's horizon of expectation and their future frames of reference.[3] This letter and many other written and material traces suggest that subject peoples were not prisoners in the cage of the colonial state or of empire but were a diverse and differentiated population who received and processed multiple messages in their everyday existence.[4] This quality of nonsynchronism, I will argue in this book, reflects the differentiated and fragmented nature of the category 'colonized' in Sri Lanka during the late nineteenth and early twentieth century.

The aim of this book is to describe how nonelite groups in Sri Lanka encountered modernity most directly through the encounter with machines – among them Singer sewing machines, gramophones, trams, bicycles and industrial equipment. It argues that the 'metallic modern' encompassed multiple worlds of belonging and imagination – from the United States and Japan, to a new conception of urban space in Colombo; it allowed also many different experiences of time to coexist. This book is not a history of everyday technology or of its adoption by local people but a reflection on the Sri Lankan modern that was, I hope to argue, created out of the mould of consumerism and commodification.

Sri Lanka's encounter with Europe was early and confrontational. After its maritime regions were occupied successively by the Portuguese in the sixteenth century and the Dutch from 1658 to 1796, the island was conquered by the British who first ruled the island from Madras and then from 1802, as a separate Crown colony. From the 1830s onwards Sri Lankan society underwent profound changes owing to the beginnings of an export-based economy, the abolition of *rajakariya* (corvee labour) and the introduction of the principle of a bourgeois and restricted public sphere where natives obtained limited representation.[5]

Few histories of modern Sri Lanka have been written outside the predictable frames of the Portuguese, Dutch or British colonial state, or the confines of an Indian subimperial system or empire.[6] Sri Lanka appears only as a 'figurant' in the theatre of the British Empire even when its spatialities are reinvented by new imperial historians, while the Sri Lankan island still reigns uncontested in self-indulgent nationalist histories that chart the glorious life of the nation-state past and present. All these studies whether colonial, imperial or nationalist have in common the fact that the nodal point from where everything begins is the political centre of authority and power. From there, sovereignty stretches and extends its tentacles, while the boundaries of the historian's gaze are determined by the extent of the area covered by the putative authority of the state, whether colonial or independent, or of empire that includes in its fold the kernel of power and its hinterland.

It is today imperative and politically urgent to move away from these given frames and attempt a history of how Sri Lanka was conceived and imagined in unbounded time and space by its own people, rather than persist in writing teleological histories that chart the political making of the state and its citizens.[7] Such a decentred narrative could take multiple referents – America, Siam or Japan, for example – rather than Colombo, and embrace Sri Lanka in a maze of territorial and temporal loops, thus deploying a kaleidoscopic gaze upon a people and a state that has until now been studied as one entity ruled by a single authority – colonial or national – in linear time. But just as we need to reconfigure space, we need to take issues of temporality seriously. Few historians have explored the way temporality was lived by common peoples. We are left with the colonial archive to read against or along the grain. Writing about the changes that were taking place in Sri Lanka in the early twentieth century, E.B. Denham, a colonial administrator in Sri Lanka, commented authoritatively in his encyclopaedic *Report of the Census of 1911* that 'the habits and wants of the natives have changed so considerably in the last hundred years that there is today a large and increasing demand for European goods.'[8] Denham argued further that notwithstanding their appetite for goods, 'the great mass of the inhabitants are quite unaware that any movement is taking place.'[9] He conceded that a colonized subject could become a consumer, yet he denied her the ultimate gift of temporal consciousness, something that he implicitly associated with market consumption. In fact, by asserting that consumption in Sri Lanka was not coeval with a new perception of time Denham could uphold both that time-consciousness harboured the possibility of freedom from colonized status and that Lankans were incapable of becoming modern citizens. Such opinions were integral to liberal imperial ideologies of the market, for they enabled a variety of empire-sponsored agents, missionaries and officials among them, to engage in a pedagogic exercise to teach inhabitants in the colony how to become proper modern, consuming subjects. As Timothy Burke's work on commodities in Zimbabwe shows in the case of Lifebuoy soap, consumers in places like Zimbabwe played an active role in the commodity's history. Their acts of consumption, their desire for soap redefined the use-value of Western personal care products.[10] Schooling a desire for commodities articulated the political project of colonialism to a market-driven vision of the modern. There is, however, something more at work. Consumers in the colony used commodities and their desire for commodities to define their own relation to the modern. The thrust of Denham's opinion on the inadequacies of Lankan consumption passes lightly over the opinion of a native chief headman recorded in the very same Census Report. 'Today', declared the headman, 'sewing machines and gramophones are the hallmark of respectability and wealth in the villages.'[11] Undermining Denham's reading of natives as people incapable of conceiving themselves as 'being in the world', these headman's words signal how the consciousness of contemporary lived experience of the 'now' was bound up with objects in colonial Sri Lanka. Perhaps Denham cited the headman as evidence that the isolated Ceylonese village had indeed changed with the penetration and spread of new technologies. But perhaps more than a confirmation of the diffusion of particular goods and the entry of the market in the lives of common people, the words index a consciousness of the new, encapsulated in the figure of two machines that embodied 'speed, shock and the spectacle of constant sensation'.[12] Had Denham considered commodity fetishism, he would have realized that in a world dominated by capital, freedom for the former colonized subject would spawn other chains, the chains that come with unlimited desires! The experience of the modern as desire installed through machines remains to be explored.

The eight chapters in this book compose a history at the margins of Sri Lanka becoming modern as its people enter the age of machines. They cast a pluriscopic gaze embracing the global, regional, urban and self all at once.

The life of machines in this book is not a way to track the diffusion of consumption practices or its representation. My approach departs from that of contributors to a recent issue of *Modern Asian Studies* on 'Everyday Technology in South and Southeast Asia' who try to 'understand the role of technology as instrument and agent in the transformations affecting everyday life'.[13] Rather the starting point of this book is an attempt to narrate the fashioning of a market imaginary, which indexed the modern as desire in Sri Lanka. This imaginary takes shape at the intersection of the business archive and circuits of communication that channelled goods. The colonial drive to constitute market society has been well studied, but less emphasis has been devoted to the international actors and circuits involved in these changes. An American company such as the Singer Sewing Machine Company functioned within a wider circuit of information flows beyond imperial circulation of goods, growth of trade and population movements. The spatial imaginary of the business archive, while attendant to imperial flows, also traversed the boundaries of politically and culturally demarcated regions. To wit, the Singer Company papers deposited at the Wisconsin Historical Society library contain boxes of correspondence between the headquarters and the agents arranged by region. The papers on Sri Lanka, then Ceylon, are not treated as a separate territorial entity but as part of the Indian market sector. The collapse of the distance between Bombay and Colombo welded once disparate spaces. At the same time, their conjoining allowed for the development of nationally differentiated commodity cultures.

The first chapter of this book follows the trajectory of the Singer sewing machine, a global object that moves from its site of production in New Jersey or Scotland to a small British Crown colony, and looks at the fashioning of a market in Sri Lanka outside the frame of empire. The second chapter focuses on the reception of the sewing machine to explain the creation of a market imaginary among a growing group of people through advertisements in the local press. The colonized subject insinuates himself/herself in the story of capitalist expansion not as a victim but as a player. Chapters three to five look at various overlapping circles or loops of history, to use a sewing metaphor. The Buddhist loop of the lost *chakravartin* (world ruler) shows a yearning for a Buddhist king mainly among the *sangha* (Buddhist monastic community) and perhaps a more dispersed desire for a figure of authority whose legitimacy comes not from a collective vote in his favour but from a right to rule. The American loop points to people's conflation of materiality and modernity through a growing need for new objects. The use of the gramophone in Buddhist preaching epitomizes the forging of a Buddhist modern. The loop that embraces Japan signals for the historian the singularity of Sri Lanka's approach to the 'modern' quite often misread as a *copie conforme* of India's modernity. The sixth chapter narrates people's encounter with everyday machines such as the bicycle, tram and car through a specific event, the 1915 riots between Muslims and Sinhalese, and tries to give a sense of the changes that followed in their relation to space and time. Users of these machines were not only physically more mobile but they could control and experience time in a way that was unthinkable before. The seventh chapter focuses on two users of sewing machines, tailors and women in the home, to reflect on the limits of the modern when confronted with national yearnings. The eighth chapter evokes the relations between labour and machines in the plantation factories and the persistence of rituals from the past in practices of the present. The conclusion reflects on the nature of the Sri Lankan modern born out of consumerism and commodification redefined as 'metallic'.

TOWARDS A STUDY OF A POPULAR UNDERSTANDING OF THE MODERN

This book emerges out of a conscious departure from a body of work on governmentality which for long structured the way power relations in the colony were framed and written about. I belong to the generation who began writing on issues of power in the colonized world in the wake of intellectual giants such as Michel Foucault, Edward Said, Benedict Anderson and the Subaltern Studies collective of historians.[14] The debt of my generation of scholars to Foucault's work in particular and that of his intercessors cannot easily be dismissed. James C. Scott compared works of great originality to a shipyard and suggested that a sure mark of influence was how many ships were launched from its dock. I have no doubt, to borrow Scott's words, that around the world thousands of ships have since sailed forth flying Foucault's pennant and others are still ready to sail away.[15] But with hindsight it is now clear that while Foucault unlocked a new world of interpretation, at the same time he gave us the hubris to think that we were the privileged ones who held the key.

For a scholar of colonialism whose archive was the Sri Lankan British colonial state, Foucault's work was an invitation to rethink the story told in the 1960s and 1970s by liberal and Marxist scholars alike about the nature of the colonial state – benevolent or extractive – and the relations between colonizers and colonized.[16] According to these master narratives the state was the privileged site of an immense power standing in opposition to a civil society – nested between state and market – imagined either as the absence of power or as the fulfilment of freedom. These works in the British empirical tradition were written in a theoretical void, divorced from the shattering developments in philosophy and social theory encapsulated in the term 'poststructuralism' sweeping through continental Europe. Foucault was at that time painstakingly tracking the emergence in early modern Europe of a new form of political rationality which combined simultaneously two seemingly contradictory modalities of power: one totalizing and centralizing, the other individualizing and normalizing. A decade later, however, scholars formed in American and European institutions began to question all the certitudes of Sri Lankan colonial historians. Cognizant of Michel Foucault's 1978 lectures on governmentality as well as of parallel radical trends emerging closer to home in India, they understood the circulation of power as a decentred process. Instead of identifying government with the centralized locus of state rule, this governmentality literature argued that governmental power operates through the production of discursive normalizations, political rationalities, and techniques of regulation that ultimately produce subjects who behave as they are expected to.

It has now become increasingly commonplace, even banal, to understand the circulation of power as a decentred process. The excitement of the 1980s and 1990s is gone. Today scholars everywhere are using Foucauldian frames to explore the production of colonial subjects.[17] In this book I seek to articulate a different approach to the operation of colonial power, one that has particular explanatory power in the Sri Lankan archive. My approach builds on a critical reading of the work of anthropologist David Scott.[18]

His influential piece, *Refashioning Futures: Criticism after Postcoloniality,*[19] set forth ways of understanding the political terrains that colonial power made possible: the new forms of subjectivity, society and normalcy that Europe's entry into the lives of the colonized organized and produced. Scott did so by working through one particular historical instance: what he called the 'formation of Sri Lanka's modernity' which he traced back to British Ceylon's Colebrooke-Cameron constitutional reforms of the early 1830s. These institutional changes, Scott skilfully argues, constituted a crucial break with the past, ushering in Sri Lanka's modernity by way of 'the introduction of a new game of politics that the colonized would (eventually) be obliged to play if they were to be counted as political'.[20]

David Scott's work is important because it moves away from the writing back at the West strategy of much of the work on colonialism, where what is at stake is the way colonialism as a practice of power works to include or exclude the colonized from the so-called epistemic violence of colonialist discourse. He tells us the story of Sri Lanka along the axis of the displacement of one kind of political rationality – that of mercantilism or sovereignty up to 1832 – by another, that of governmentality with the Colebrooke-Cameron reforms. These reforms introduced the idea of political representation, modern social institutions and a capitalist plantation economy. In Scott's book the move towards colonial modernity is described not in the language of modernization but read as a transformation of power, as colonial power adopting a distinct strategy and working on through different targets.

Yet Scott's work, however admirable, has its limitations. He argues that through the creation of a modern public sphere colonized subjects were recast as modern subjects, but this analysis of colonial governmentality addresses only those groups that the colonial state included in its path towards progress. Those people who were admitted to the enchanted realm of the colonial public sphere constituted about 5 per cent of the population. What then of the other? Their relation to the colonial state cannot be understood through the grid of governmentality. Their politics and voices, literate in the vernaculars or wholly illiterate, expressing their demands in various ways, are simply not heard.

Empirical archival work would have revealed to Scott another world beyond the text of the Colebrook-Cameron report. Such archives might reveal the presence in colonial Sri Lanka of particular ideas of improvement or progress to which people aspired; or they might show us people reacting to colonial structures with varying degrees of agency or acting with little concern for the traditional-modern divides or even outside that frame altogether.[21] My own work on colonial petitions that can be found in the archives provides us with a picture of 'colonial power' somewhat different than Scott's, a picture in which power was much less routinized and normalized, in which power was constituted by different and often conflicting forces and individuals.[22] The form of political action – the petition – adopted by the other 95 per cent had existed during Dutch colonialism. Then, typically, if petitioners did not succeed in obtaining their demands, they rebelled. They acted, in either case, outside the field of governmentality and remained there well into the twentieth century. The petition constituted the domain of those who were not yet ready for a 'civilized government', for the social groups that John Stuart Mill suggested were still under the control of gods, spirits and supernatural beings and who did not frequent the same spheres as the bourgeois. Since they had no civic rights they used the petition to express their demands and sentiments.

The petition, then, if one follows Partha Chatterjee, reveals the presence of a dense and heterogeneous time in the colony where the times of the modern – of the quasi-citizen and of the premodern, of subjects – were coeval.[23] Chatterjee used the term 'heterogeneous time' to describe the experience of native peoples at the turn of the twentieth century with reference to Walter Benjamin's critique of a concept of history based upon linearity, succession and homogeneity. Benjamin attempted to elaborate an alternative concept of history and temporality which he called the *Jetzzeit* or Now-Time.[24] Building on this idea Chatterjee suggests that a same historical period can be lived very differently by diverse actors, anchored in modernity or remaining in a premodern time nevertheless shaped by modernity.[25]

The letter from the bhikku cited at the beginning of this introduction also shows people thinking with little regard to the traditional modern polarities and indeed outside that frame altogether. It further testifies to how peoples in Sri Lanka were enmeshed – through ritual performances, language or travel as well as through imaginaries – in many global, territorial and temporal loops. All such loops transcended the frame of empire and subverted the authority of the colonial state, sometimes simply by ignoring it. The Matara poetic literature of early nineteenth-century southern Sri Lanka, for instance, makes no reference to British power, as though the presence or absence of colonial rule was irrelevant. For many people, more concerned with other forms of politics or other battles for power and distinction, colonial rule was only a shadowy presence in the background or on the margins of the more central aspects of their lives.[26] Looked at this way, the violence both of the colonial state and of what Achille Mbembe calls the 'postcolony' alert us less to the power of governmentality than to a failure of the disciplinary and governmental technologies of Western modernity – the failure to produce modern rational subjects.[27] But that said, the ways in which the people of Sri Lanka looked upon themselves and upon the world around them did drastically change with the advent of new influences and everyday machines. Through new practices people began to perceive themselves in different ways, both as individuals and as members of larger collectivities and spatialities. In a sense they inhabited parallel worlds that were constituted by a fluid interplay between spaces and their imaginations.

I would like to argue that in these parallel worlds, full of echoes, in these extended spaces of the imagination which are rarely encountered in archives and committed to paper, we find the lost politics of nonelite groups in South Asia. I am not pleading for 'grassroots history', which has acquired some disturbingly self-indulgent features. Neither am I engaged in an exercise in writing minor histories for the sake of retrieval or giving a voice to silenced peoples. As Marilyn Strathern advocates, 'We need to go precisely where we have already been, back to the immediate here and now out of which we have created our present knowledge of the world.'[28]

My modest intention is to intervene in the writing of major histories, creating a critical space where colonial, global and national histories are destabilized, reading anew the old tropes of power, resistance and nationalism, and newer ones of governmentality. My own work on colonial Sri Lanka has been haunted by the need to explore political imaginaries outside given frames of religion, nation, state or empire both in the colonial period and in the present. I hope to understand, through a foray into popular collective identities and other rituals of self as they were formed in the colonial era, how people can succumb to present-day politics of populism. To understand the politics of the flawed democratic present, I believe social historians need to confront and understand the past of those who did not shape history but were 'fires in the blood', as Tapan Raychaudhuri flamboyantly put it.[29]

MULTISCOPIC HISTORIES

I often wonder how explicit historians ought to be about methods, about how we write and the standards of evidence we uphold. This book inserts Sri Lanka within global, regional, national, domestic and individual loops and in so doing interrogates the notion of scale in history. What Blaise Pascal wrote centuries ago still stands: 'A city or countryside is a city or countryside from afar but as you get closer, it is made of houses, trees, tiles, leaves, ants, legs of ants, to the infinite.'[30] Since the scale of phenomena is not inscribed in reality, I would like to follow Jacques Revel when he reminds us that social reality is not the same according to the level of analysis or the scale of observation that one chooses … and that the choice of a scale of observation which is a choice of an instrument of analysis is not neutral.[31] A play on scales, a *jeu d'echelles,* entails transforming the content of the representation, a strategy rarely practiced as a heuristic principle in histories of South Asia but crucial, in my view, to understanding the heterogeneous times lived by colonized peoples.[32] If one moves from a smaller to a larger scale one sees that ordinary people in colonial Sri Lanka, be they shopkeepers, farmers or workers, lived different kinds of existence in different temporalities all at the same time. They were sometimes 'ignorant and hopelessly conservative', and as Leonard Woolf despaired, 'They positively hated anything new.'[33] But they were also consumers of goods from all parts of the world and readers of newspapers. Goods and newspapers together created an imaginary that encompassed everything from the Boer War, the Boxer Rebellion, and the Japanese victory over Russia in 1905 to the exemplary life of Harry Holst, a Dutch Buddhist in Chicago.[34]

As a second mode of inquiry, the chapters of this book pay careful attention to the limits of the colonial archive even read against the grain, along the grain or with the purpose of unmasking its technologies of reproduction of state power. Historians need to complement the 'pieces of knowledge' collected in the colonial archive with other types of sources gleaned from temple libraries or from material life. These are the kinds of evidence that have until now been read and used chiefly by other specialists – art historians, religious scholars or social anthropologists – but hardly at all by historians of Sri Lanka. There are many more letters like the one written by the bhikku in 1912. They have been used by scholars eager to understand religious debates of the day or renewed forms of religious practices but not by social historians with an eye for the everyday politics of the people. Other questions posed to these documents will elicit other answers. If we follow the idea of problem-spaces elaborated by David Scott,[35] we can fruitfully think of different historical conjunctures as constituting different conceptual-ideological problem-spaces and think of these problem spaces less as generators of new propositions than as generators of new questions and new demands. Propositions, Scott reminds us, 'are always answers to questions or interventions in a discursive context'.[36]

The prapthidanaya to the deceased emperor of Japan has never entered history books in Sri Lanka. It is nevertheless rich in historical meaning and can be read in many ways. It comes to us 'layered with the received account of earlier events and the cultural semantics of a political moment'.[37] It sends us many possible and different messages. Were Lankan villagers in the twentieth century still looking back to hierarchies and power relations of the precolonial era as models to emulate? The ideal of a Buddhist king was indeed an idea grounded in the past of the country where the king was the protector of Buddhism, the supreme ruler of the sangha which he constantly purified by expelling 'bad' monks from the established fraternities, introducing new ordination from abroad during periods of decline and circumscribing tendencies to Mahayana heterodoxy. In 1815, the demise of the king of Kandy, who had been the defender of the faith, led to a pervasive feeling of loss and widespread demoralization. By the end of the nineteenth century, Buddhists in Lanka began to see possibilities of redress for their grievances from Buddhist monarchs in other southeast Asian countries, Burma, Cambodia and Siam, an issue that will be dealt with in the third chapter of this book.

The political imaginary of the people in the village of Welipatanwila and their practice of a prapthidanaya to a deceased king of Japan could thus be understood as embodying a sense of loss for a Buddhist monarch, but it seems just as likely if not more that it was not the Buddhist monarch that was honoured but the emperor who ushered his nation into modernity, crushing the Western sense of superiority. If one adopts a wider scale of observation, Japan was now present in the imaginary of Sinhalese people as an Asian nation, modern and forging ahead under the spiritual guidance of its king. In honouring the dead king, the Lankan villager was honouring the harbinger of the new, of the *abhinava,* a word that translates (albeit badly) as modernity.

These were then the entangled political imaginaries of the vernacular-speaking social groups in Sri Lanka which would have co-existed with others more visible, because more intelligible, in the colonial texts used by historians. This book attempts to capture the multiple times and spaces that continued and coexisted over a colonial period and what ordinary men and women made and make of the political. The political I understand as a 'space of appearance' – I borrow this formulation from Hannah Arendt – where action and speech meet at particular moments to form an organization of people. This space is ephemeral and differentiated, and no man or woman lived in it all the time. It was there 'only potentially, not necessarily and not forever'.[38] The political, I hope to show, does not always appear in formal arenas but can be seen in people's life choices.

Retrieving the past of the subaltern is not a new enterprise in South Asia. Three decades ago, Ranajit Guha insisted on a world of Indian politics, conducted in Indian idioms, which survived the transition to colonialism more or less intact. There were, however, real political dangers inherent in the vision of separate cultural worlds and timeless primitivism. His central point captured in the title *Dominance without Hegemony* is a powerful one: the colonial state exercised 'dominance' primarily through coercion, but not 'hegemony'.[39] The coercive apparatus of the colonial state penetrated India and by extension Sri Lanka very deeply indeed, but the ideological apparatus failed to reach much below the higher levels of the Indian elite. Guha refers to the 'braiding, collapsing, echoing and blending' between the two idioms or paradigms, the two different political idioms, one based in liberal theory, the other Indian and often religious in its vocabulary.

My understanding of the politics of nonelite groups is somewhat different: I see their politics as something not confined to the religious sphere but as a 'complex field of social practices, moral judgments, and imaginative possibilities that were deployed in a time-space that continued over the period referred to as colonial rule' and after.[40]

I am less interested in representations even of liminal spaces than in imaginaries at the point of reception. On the consumption practices of ordinary people and their encounters with machines, information is, however, sparse. Successive volumes of *Ferguson's Directory* record the number of machines imported into the island but we do not know where these stocks of machines were sent and who actually bought them. Given how little is known about the lives of ordinary people during colonial rule, we lack the type of works mentioning tailors (*darzis*) which David Arnold has relied upon for his recent study on the sewing machine in India.[41] Furthermore, visual traces of the machine remain scant. We have neither drawings nor photographs of tailors or bourgeois women sitting in the comfort of their homes instructing seamstresses sitting on the floor as in the Indonesian record.[42]

My work moves away from a study of representation, and critiques of the politics of representation, to a focus on reception of ideas and practices of the self. A multiscopic approach allows the historian to apply a multiplicity of gazes, presenting often contradictory realities under different angles. A wider lens presents social and political imaginaries that extend outside the frame of the colonial state towards a Buddhist cosmopolis and a rising Asian power, but an even wider lens or a shorter lens would show us colonized subjects in other roles: as enthusiastic buyers of global goods, as users of new machines, as consumers and conscripts of modernity – issues I deal with in the chapters of this book.

In South Asia there is a literary device called *slesa* that lasted a thousand years where texts have double or multiple meanings; for example a text could co-narrate the two great epics the Ramayana and the Mahabharata.[43] This book is an experiment in parallels that are not textual or embraced in one poem but form a narrative that is demultiplied according to spatial scope: if we imagine for a moment looking at the island Sri Lanka as made of simultaneous depictions of the past, the preconceptions we may have about the birth of its modernity, the shape and nature of nationalism, the politics of its people dissolve and we are left with a richer yet more uncertain truth claim.

NOTES

1. When referring to the island I use the name Sri Lanka (resplendent island) that was adopted in 1972 when the country became a republic rather than its colonial name Ceylon. The term 'Lanka' was commonly used in the Sinhala language during the nineteenth and twentieth centuries to describe the island although many other names too were given to describe the island in Sinhala and in Tamil.
2. Sri Lanka National Archives, 5/63/150/ (7) letter (1912–8–15) written by Welipatanvila Deepankara Thero to Seelakkandha Thero on a ceremony held at a temple to felicitate and thanks giving (Prapthi Danaya) for a king of Japan.
3. R. Koselleck cited in A. Schinkel. 2005. 'Imagination as a Category of History: An Essay concerning Koselleck's Concepts of *Erfahrungsraum* and *Eerwartungshorizont*', *History and Theory* 44, 42–54.
4. See for example K. Malalgoda. 1976. *Buddhism in Sinhalese Society 1750–1900,* Berkeley: University of California Press, on the manner in which early missionaries were received by Sinhalese villagers: He shows that Christian missionary style violated norms of cultural decorum and produced laughter and derision in the village audience, 201. There was no active opposition of monks and, unlike the Brahmin, monks did not shun the company of Europeans. They even gave over the temple sermon hall to missionaries for preaching and were baffled when the missionaries refused to reciprocate, 211–13. Monks were used to tolerating animistic and Hindu practices and thus treated Christ like one of the Hindu gods subordinate to the Buddha.
5. See Chapter 1 in N. Wickramasinghe. 2006b. *Sri Lanka in the Modern Age. A History of Contested Identities,* Honolulu: University of Hawaii Press and London: C. Hurst.
6. See T.R. Metcalf. 2007. *Imperial Connections: India in the Indian Ocean 1860–1920,* Berkeley: University of California Press.
7. My previous book, *Sri Lanka in the Modern Age,* adopted a people-centred approach to identity politics but nevertheless remained a history of a place, namely, the island of Sri Lanka.
8. E.B. Denham. 1912. *Ceylon at the Census of 1911,* Colombo: H. Ross Cottle, Government Printer, 4.
9. Ibid., 193.
10. T. Burke. 1996a. *Lifebuoy Men, Lux Women: Commodification, Consumption and Cleanliness in Modern Zimbabwe,* Durham and London: Duke University Press, 214.
11. Denham, *Ceylon at the Census of 1911,* 173.
12. H. Harootunian cited in F. Cooper. 2005. *Colonialism in Question. Theory, Knowledge, History,* Berkeley: University of California Press, 128.
13. D. Arnold and E. de Wald. 2012. 'Everyday Technology in South and Southeast Asia. An Introduction', *Modern Asian Studies* 46(1), 1.
14. E. Said. 1979. *Orientalism,* New York: Vintage; B. Anderson. 1991. *Imagined Communities: Reflections on the Origins and Spread of Nationalism,* revised ed., London:

Verso; R. Guha and G. Spivak (eds). 1988. *Selected Subaltern Studies,* New York: Oxford University Press.

15. See foreword by J. Scott in R. Guha. 1999. *Elementary Aspects of Peasant Insurgency in Colonial India,* Durham and London: Duke University Press, ix.
16. On the Sri Lankan context see: K.M. de Silva (ed.). 1973. *History of Ceylon,* Peradeniya: University of Ceylon, vol. III.
17. As an approach that draws from Foucault's but departs from it see: A. Stoler. 2002. *Carnal Knowledge and Imperial Power: Race and the Intimate in Colonial Rule,* Berkeley and Los Angeles: University of California Press. For a critique of Dutch colonial historiography, see: J. Cote. 2009. 'Strangers in the House: Dutch Historiography and Anglophone Trespassers', *Review of Indonesian and Malaysian Affairs* 43(1), 75–94.
18. D. Scott. 1995. 'Colonial Governmentality', *Social Text* 43, 191–220.
19. D. Scott. 1999. *Refashioning Futures: Criticism after Postcoloniality,* Princeton: Princeton University.
20. Ibid., footnote 6, 28.
21. Frederick Cooper makes this point very cogently in his *Colonialism in Question.*
22. N. Wickramasinghe. 2006a. 'La Petition Coloniale. Objet de Controle, Objet de Dissidence', *Identity, Culture and Politics: An Afro-Asian Dialogue* 7(1), 82–97.
23. P. Chatterjee. 2004b. *The Politics of the Governed: Reflections on Popular Politics in Most of the World,* New Delhi: Permanent Black.
24. W. Benjamin. 1979. *Illuminations,* trans. Harry Zohn, New York: Shocken Books, 261.
25. P. Chatterjee. 2004a. 'The Nation in Heterogeneous Time', in *The Politics of the Governed. Reflections on Popular Politics in Most of the World,* New Delhi: Permanent Black.
26. See Wickramasinghe, *Sri Lanka in the Modern Age,* 11.
27. A. Mbembe. 2001. *On the Postcolony,* Berkeley: University of California Press.
28. Cited in A. Stoler. 2010. *Along the Archival Grain. Epistemic Anxieties and Colonial Common Sense,* Princeton: Princeton University Press, 31–32.
29. T. Raychaudhuri. 1979. 'Indian Politics as Animal Politics', *Historical Journal* 22(3), 76.
30. B. Pascal cited in J. Revel. 1996. *Jeux d'echelles. La Micro-analyse a l'experience,* Paris: Gallimard Le Seuil, 94
31. Ibid., 12.
32. Ibid., 19.
33. L. Woolf. 1963. *Diaries in Ceylon 1908–1911. Records of Colonial Administrator being the official diaries maintained by Leonard Woolf while Assistant Government Agent on the Hambantota District, Ceylon during the period August 1908 to May 1911,* London: Hogarth Press, 51. Leonard Woolf returned to England in 1911 and a year later married Adeline Virginia Stephen (later known as Virginia Woolf)
34. In 1911, 47.9 per cent of Low-country Sinhalese males and 36.4 per cent of Kandyan (Up-country) males were literate in their mother tongue (Sinhalese). The figures for females were still very low: 17.4 per cent of Low-country females

and 2.8 per cent of Kandyan females. Denham, *Ceylon at the Census of 1911,* 401; The Sinhala man of the early twentieth century was an avid reader of the *Maha Bodhi,* the journal of the Maha Bodhi Society which regularly featured Buddhist events in America; see T.A. Tweed. 1992. *The American Encounter with Buddhism 1844–1912. Victorian Culture and the Limits of Dissent,* Bloomington: Indiana University Press.

35. D. Scott. 2004. *Conscripts of Modernity: The Tragedy of Colonial Enlightenment,* Durham and London: Duke University Press, 7.
36. Ibid., 207.
37. Stoler, *Along the Archival Grain,* 34
38. H. Arendt. 1958. *The Human Condition,* Chicago, London: University of Chicago Press, 199.
39. R. Guha. 1997. *Dominance without Hegemony: History and Power in Colonial India,* Cambridge, MA: Harvard University Press, 6.
40. J. Spencer. 2007. *Anthropology, Politics and the State. Democracy and Violence in South Asia,* Cambridge: Cambridge University Press, 22.
41. D. Arnold. 2011. 'Global Goods and Local Usages: The Small World of the Indian Sewing Machine, 1875–1952', *Journal of Global History* 6, 407–29.
42. See J. Taylor. 2012. 'The Sewing Machine in Colonial Era Photographs: A Record from Dutch Indonesia', *Modern Asian Studies* 46(1), 71–95.
43. Y. Bronner. 2010. *Extreme Poetry. The South Asian Movement of Simultaneous Narration,* New York: Columbia University Press.

Chapter 1

Following the Singer Sewing Machine

Fashioning a Market in a British Crown Colony

We have to follow the things themselves.
– Arjun Appadurai, *The Social Life of Things,* 1986

The subjects of the British imperial world were not 'sealed off from the rest of the globe'.[1] Global webs of inspiration, imaginaries and materialities shaped the historical experience of peoples across the empire who lived through the nineteenth and twentieth centuries. The trajectory of the sewing machine, produced by an American multinational corporation as 'one of the first standardized and mass marketed complex consumer goods to spread around the world' cuts across the political boundaries of empire. Its story is better captured in the term 'transnational'[2] than in the frame of the transcolonial, but the creation of a market imaginary was spawned by many parallel dynamics. The widespread adoption of the sewing machine by colonized consumers in the Crown colony of Ceylon, known to its own majority population as Lanka, illustrates the potency of other ties between countries and territories. These ties invited people to think, live and identify with many spaces real and imagined, through their everyday experience of buying, touching and using imported consumer goods. In these modern times, many machines were made of steel, a material that became with the Bessemer process cheaper to produce from the mid-nineteenth century.

In colonial Sri Lanka it was the label Singer that was soon used to describe all sewing machines, foreign goods par excellence since they had their origin elsewhere, mainly Germany, Britain or the United States. This fact reaffirms more than any statistic that the global diffusion of sewing machines was predominantly the responsibility of a single American firm. Numbers confirm the popular designation: in 1912 Singer controlled 60 per cent of the market share of family sewing machines in America and 90 per cent in foreign markets.[3] Sri Lanka too became a market for this global object. Through the story of the sewing machine unfolds the story of how the market imaginary was made in a colony.

NETWORKS AND FLOWS OUTSIDE EMPIRE

The Singer sewing machine conquered the world at a time when distances were shrinking with steamships, railroads and telegraph cables ushering in revolutionary improvements in transportation and communication. Substantial technological changes had spawned new products that were taken away from their territories of production and nestled in every corner of the globe. The inauguration of the Suez Canal on 17 November 1869, opened the eastern trade for steamships. Distances were immediately cut. The trip to Bombay from Liverpool round the Cape of Good Hope – an 11,560 sea mile journey for a sail ship – was halved by a steamship that took the canal route. Steamships could carry larger amounts of cargo as coaling stops could be secured en route at places such as Gibraltar, Malta and Port Said. Steamers were soon adopted for trade between South Asia and the United Kingdom. American sewing machines entirely produced in a factory in Scotland were packed in wooden boxes and loaded onto British merchant iron and steel navy ships that traversed the seas and the Suez canal and then were unloaded in the bustling ports of Bombay and Colombo.[4] In 1904 a British steamship such as the *Torridge* covered the distance between Colombo and Suez in eighteen days.[5]

Conventional history tells us that in its heyday the British Empire governed roughly a quarter of the world's population, covered the same proportion of the earth's land surface and dominated nearly all its oceans. In Sri Lanka, which they conquered in 1796, the British were able to build on the foundation of earlier maritime empires. Portuguese rule from the sixteenth century and Dutch rule in the mid-eighteenth century had transformed the western and southwestern regions of the island: the growth of towns, a moving labour force, the spread of the use of money, the rise in production and the expansion of long distance trade had already broken the isolation and insularity of many of its people. For the British the path had been cleared and they found few obstacles among the islanders to their promotion of the free movement of goods, capital and labour. As in other parts of the empire the colony's growth was powered by commerce and consumerism. In the late nineteenth century 'of all nations, the one with the greatest foreign direct investment and the greatest number of overseas operations (1870–1914) was clearly Great Britain.'[6]

While there is an increasing scholarship on South Asia's global engagement, few histories of Sri Lanka recall that in the late nineteenth century other transnational trade networks emerged separate from those that linked the British metropolis to its colonies, inserting empire within a history of globalisation.[7] Some of these bridgeheads that originated from a former British colony, the United States, circumvented or even subverted British authority in its own empire. The connected history of Singer, an American multinational company, with a small tropical island under British rule epitomizes the need to move away from the given political frames of empire, nation and colony to understand the past in a less fractured and predictable manner. Such an approach is not a plea for ex-centricity. While precolonial networks were often restructured or disrupted as a result of British intervention, these newer networks essentially built on trade became entrenched in the former colonies, surviving the fall of empire and other political upheavals and shaping the multidimensional contours of the global modernity we contend with today. As Appadurai[8] suggests, transnationalism rather than 'empire' describes these movements of goods and conceptualizes the multiple intersecting spaces of the imagination and of material flows that continued over what is described as a colonial period.

The story of moving objects and colonial consumers belongs both inside and outside the British sphere, empire being a field of study that has recently been pulled apart, debunked, dethroned and rent asunder. Energized by the political insights of postcolonial and cross-disciplinary scholarship, 'new imperial historians' have critiqued the writings of earlier decades, beginning with the premise that imperialism is a construct sustained by culture, especially cultures of difference between 'us' and 'them'.[9] New geographers recast the relationship between metropolitan centre and colonial periphery into a more contested and mutually constitutive frame in order to examine multiple meanings, material practices, performances and experiences of colonial relations.[10] In British studies there came a rediscovery of the importance of empire in the British past and interest in methodologies of social and cultural history and criticism to address questions of identity and difference in imperial settings. A historian writing about the South would nevertheless find limitations in their approach which remains confined to the parameters of a 'British world'. Kathleen Wilson's focus on revising and conceptualizing 'Englishness' and 'Britishness' and categories through which colonizers and colonized are understood seems in many ways to be another attempt – albeit framed in different terms – at writing the history of the British in the empire.

If new imperial historians and geographers have raised important issues, others have eluded them. The need for historians to reconceptualise the colonial space has been emphasised but at the expense of investigating the multiple spaces and times that co-exist over a 'colonial period'. A narrative of the direct interaction of mutual influences between groups, peoples and territories included in and beyond the empire 'un-mediated by London' was needed.

Could a new history of the British Empire avoid replicating patterns of European dominance and reproducing the very hierarchies that critical histories of empire ought to reject? Scholars have responded to these issues in various ways. Burton for instance suggested a return to the idea of nation due to the inadequacy of the conceptual apparatus of cultural studies to study larger formations.[11] The need to overcome this impasse was especially well articulated by Cooper and Stoler, who urged us to pay more attention to problems of horizontal interactions between different elements rather than centre-periphery linkages and to the plurality of spatial linkages, a concern more recently asserted by 'global historians'.[12]

Interestingly, some of these issues were raised in the works of more conventional historians of empire and it is important to reread their works in a new light. The starting point was the ex-centric or centripetal analysis of Gallagher and Robinson where the expansionary initiative moved from the colonial edge of empire to the British centre.[13] With the collapse of the empire, traditional imperial history was faced with an inward turn where metropolitan concerns and capitalists took precedence. The work of Fieldhouse in the 1980s questioned the marginalization of indigenous people in earlier approaches to empire and searched for imaginative ways of reconstructing the core-periphery link by reconnecting race and nation with empire.[14] Darwin's problematic bridged the gap between accounts of British colonialism influenced by postcolonial theory and the more traditional positivist history out of which his own trajectory had developed.[15] He elaborated a networked or webbed conception of imperial space where multiple and contestatory 'projects' of colonialism were unfolding. What he too failed to conceptualize, however, was the existence of a multiplicity of metropolis and peripheries in the British world as well as bridgeheads between distinct colonies of the British Empire, such as Bombay-Colombo or Colombo-Cape Town. Thomas Metcalf's recent book shows that a colony such as India and not just metropoles spun webs of empire, creating what he calls subempires based on the export to other colonies of a variety of goods and services ranging from legal systems, labour and armed forces.[16]

Other studies reconceptualised the British Empire as made of structures as well as processes: indeed at times, people and places had nodal relationships and at other times, or even simultaneously, they had peripheral relationships. These could be fleeting or ephemeral links, like patterns in a kaleidoscope.[17]

Colonies were clearly parts of other webs, based on religious, cultural or commercial ties. The insightful work of Ghosh and Kennedy has moved the debate beyond the standard model of a bilateral circuit between imperial centre and colonial periphery and highlighted instead the web of transcolonial and transnational networks that spread across and beyond the empire, operating both on its behalf and against its interests and working to 'de-centre' empire.[18] The aim of this excellent volume was nevertheless to 'provide a richer, more integrative approach to *the British imperial experience*', thus remaining entrenched in a positionality that precluded looking at the colonial experience from the perspective of the colonized space.[19]

THE SINGER SEWING MACHINE IN COLONIAL SRI LANKA

The first shop and office of the New Jersey–based American firm Singer Manufacturing Company was established in 1877 in Colombo, the capital city of Sri Lanka, then called Ceylon, at 27 Main Street, in the Pettah, a populous commercial area of Colombo. It was, however, eleven years earlier, in 1869, that the first Singer sewing machine had been brought to Sri Lanka (Figure 1).[20]

The island of Sri Lanka was conquered by the British from 1796 onwards, and the fall of the Kandyan Kingdom in the Central Highlands in 1815 meant that for the first time a European power was in control of the entire island. When the first American sewing machine found a home in Sri Lanka, the island had been ruled by Britain for more than sixty years and had undergone radical changes from the 1830s as a result of the Colebrooke-Cameron reforms. These reforms heralded on paper a new relationship between colonized subjects and colonial rulers based on the Benthamite spirit of improvement.[21] The reading of the Colebrooke-Cameron reforms as the crucial moment in an approved journey of progress has been questioned recently by scholars such as Scott who argued that the difference between the pre- and post-1832 colonial power resided elsewhere, in the displacement of one kind of political rationality, that of mercantilism or sovereignty, by another, that of governmentality.[22] While governmentality was a component of colonial rule, the issue of inscribing the colonized into modernity as a well-defined intentionality and the representation of society as a network of

Figure 1. Singer Sewing machine. Undated (ca.1890). Historical Mansion Museum, Galle Fort (Author's collection)

omnipresent relations of subjugating power are questionable. It is difficult to believe that colonial rule in Sri Lanka was always equally intrusive, although it may have been felt very deeply at times of crisis and emergency, litigation or raising of taxes. Most of the time, however, the terms upon which people cultivated their paddy land, worshipped their gods, spoke their language in the confines of their home and ate their local foods was as much related to the colonial rule of law as to unchanging relations of power between peasant and landlord, bhikkhus, teachers and the people, and remained set within the frame of rigid patriarchal family structures. Imaginaries were shaped by these forces of custom and place but constantly refigured by new influences: there is plenty of evidence that ordinary people consumed migrant goods from all parts of the world and experimented with the new technologies that were penetrating their everyday lives from the end of the nineteenth century.

The Singer company gained early visibility in Sri Lanka through the establishment of shops and offices. The earliest record of a person in the employ of the company looking after the Colombo operation can be traced to 1885. Indeed a statement of 'Defalcations by Employees in India' lists as an employee in Colombo in December 1885 a G. Cronon, described as having embezzled a sum of nine hundred rupees.[23] Branches were next opened in Kandy, the capital of the central province and the second largest city in Ceylon, and in Hatton, a small town in the hill country central to the tea plantation industry – on Bazaar Street. Opening a branch at Hatton where a captive plantation labour hailing from South India lived in a virtual enclave and whose basic needs for food and clothing had to be met within the plantation was based on a gamble that tailors and entrepreneurs would rush to buy sewing machines, seeing in them a potential mine to exploit.[24]

Capturing the market was not as easy as it might have appeared to the company directors in New York. There were many teething problems. In 1893, for instance, Singer had to file a case against the Sewing Machine Company, a joint stock company registered and incorporated in India that also carried on business in Colombo. Singer alleged that the Sewing Machine Company was using a sign board with the intention of deceiving peo-

Figure 2. Advertisement of Singer machine in Burmese. Enclosed in letter from E.M. Sang, 18 August 1883. Singer Papers, Box 89, Wisconsin Historical Society Archives

ple into believing that they were the authorized agents of Singer machines. It is reported that Singer filed a plaint and obtained an interim injunction against its rival requiring the company's agent – a person named J.K. Hormusjee – to remove the sign board.[25] The next decade saw a steady growth of the company. Newspaper advertisements help us trace the spread of Singer shops throughout the island. In 1899 the company had recruited reputed agents in E. Cahill and Sons who advertised regularly in the main English daily newspaper, the *Ceylon Independent*.[26] In 1899 one such advertisement for Singer sewing machines boasted that the company operated a hundred offices in India, Burma and Ceylon (Figure 2).[27] By 1906, another branch was opened in Galle, the second largest port in the island and a commercial hub in the Southern province – on 28 High Street, Galle.[28] Thereafter the Singer Manufacturing Company established branches in many other towns throughout the island. In 1915 an advertisement placed by the Singer company supervisor B.J. Keating and his assistant supervisor S. MacQueen claimed twenty-eight shops in Ceylon and more to open.[29] From the late nineteenth century the machines came in regularly to Colombo from Scotland where the company had established factories to serve the European and Asian markets in steamships travelling via the Suez Canal, the entire journey taking about twenty-six days on the Harrison Line.[30]

SPREAD AND RECEPTION

There is no doubt that the peoples of Sri Lanka were receptive to sewing machines which they bought with a far greater zeal than their counterparts in India or China. In the early years of the company when offices had just been opened, in 1886 and 1887, figures for Singer sewing machines sold in the island were included under the category Madras and Depots, namely, Bangalore, Bellary, Cocanada, Colombo, Conoor, Seecundrabad, Trichinopol and Trivendrum. All the depots were located in Southern India except for Colombo. The Madras office sold 558 machines and the depots 726 machines, which is still a very small figure. The Colombo office sold 81 machines in the space of twelve months (1886–7).[31] While we do not have figures for Singer sewing machines in use in Lanka at given periods since trade lists do not make a distinction between sewing machines of different brands, one can still get an idea of the penetration of machines in general in Lankan society. One can for instance estimate the number of sewing machines in Sri Lanka in 1930 as 113,309, given the fact that machines are durable items – thus a machine bought twenty years before would still be in use – and assuming that Singer captured 90 per cent of the market.[32] Following Andrew Godley's method of assessing diffusion, the number of machines per household can be calculated with some accuracy. In a total population of Sri Lanka amounting to 5,312,548, if each family is constituted of 4.7 members[33] the number of families would be 1,130,329. The number of sewing machines per inhabitant can then be tallied to 1 for 47 persons (2 per cent of the population) and 1 for 10 families (10 per cent of households). As mentioned earlier, the diffusion of machines in Sri Lanka offers a huge contrast with the Indian market, where in 1916 only 1 per cent of households owned a machine, and is more comparable to the figures in Turkey and Greece, where over 10 per cent of households owned a machine before the First World War.[34]

It is not possible to prove beyond doubt that all these machines were Singer machines although the Singer supervisor in 1915 admitted that 'at present with an imperfect selling organization our weekly sales average 150 machines', which amounts to 5,000 machines a year.[35] He hoped to increase sales to 10,000 sewing machines in 1916. (This figure is probably exaggerated as it exceeds the number of machines imported into Sri Lanka, but it reflects Singer's domination of the market and its ambition to expand exponentially.) The American trade consul in Ceylon confirmed the visibility of the Singer machine in all parts of the island:

> I may first make reference to the fact that American sewing machines were noticed … in every native district visited. Practically all the sewing and tailoring in this island, a large part of whose people are engaged in various industries requiring the use of the needle, is done on American sewing machines, introduced here by persistent and systematic work of direct agencies. It was most interesting to watch in front of open bazaars, in even the most remote villages, American sewing machines hard at work sewing up simple cotton garments for the native population whose chief tangible assets are the very humble clothes they possess.[36]

MR SINGER AND HIS SEWING MACHINE

The first Singer sewing machine was conceived in the early 1850s as a partnership between a mechanical genius, Isaac Merritt Singer, and a lawyer, Edward Clark.[37] For a number of years Singer moved from job to job as a machinist, actor and occasional inventor until August 1851 when he patented an early improved sewing machine with continuous stitching that had the following features: 'lock stitch; eye-pointed needle; shuttle for second thread, vibratory or double pointed; continuous thread from spools; horizontal table; over-hanging arm; continuous feed, synchronous with needle motion; thread or tension controls, giving slack thread as needed; presser foot, and ability to sew in other than straight line'.[38] The early history of the company, I.M. Singer, can be read as a maze of patent grabbing by a number of inventors – Howe, Grover, Baker, Wilson and Singer were the most prominent – and subsequent litigation.[39] No owner of a single patent could make a sewing machine without infringing on patents of others. Clark was instrumental in the creation of the Albany patent pool where the holders of these key patents agreed to forego litigation and to license their technology to one another. The American sewing machine industry was virtually controlled by Singer, Elias Howe and two other manufacturers who earned a regular income from license fees. This also led to a rapid development of the industry. That same year Singer began demonstrating and servicing its products in its own domestic sales rooms and selling on instalments. Three years later it had fourteen branch sales offices in the United States.[40]

The 1851 prototype was adopted by industry and interestingly underwent very few significant design changes in the following decades even after the introduction of electricity. The working parts, structure and formal features of the modern sewing machine were there: 'The arm was horizontal, in a frontal position with respect to the operator, and parallel to the work surface; the needle was located on the left-hand side in a vertical position; and on the opposite side was set the mechanism of cogs that transmitted the movement.'[41] Electricity brought a considerable improvement in the quality of the work, and the practicality and manoeuvrability of the machine. As early as 1852 Singer had introduced the pedal and belt drive which was a huge improvement with respect to the previous handwheel. In 1856 a smaller, lighter-weight machine, the turtle-back, designed for household use rather than the garment industry, was introduced. The first electric machine was the 15K model marketed by Singer in 1889. The electric-powered motor was housed in the hand wheel at the side and was simply added to the existing body without altering its overall appearance. In a country such as Sri Lanka where electricity was still a luxury it was the manual model that was marketed. This model destined to find a home in a small tropical island was produced not in the United States but in the Singer factory in Glasgow.

SINGER'S OVERSEAS INTERESTS

The Singer company showed an early interest in the foreign side of the business. By 1864 it was exporting 40 per cent of its output and by 1912 controlled 90 per cent of foreign markets.[42] Seeking foreign markets was not then the norm among American businessmen and Singer did not benefit at the outset from any American government assistance. But among sewing machine producers there was an early interest in overseas activities, initially in technologically underdeveloped Europe where they saw a wide market and where they hoped to acquire capital for the establishment of factories.[43] The Civil War in the United States had led to losses among Northern sewing machine manufacturers and this situation provided an added incentive to establish depots, sales rooms and agencies in Europe.

In the next few years the company sold machines abroad using independent franchised agents in countries such as Mexico, Canada, Cuba, Germany, Venezuela, Uruguay, Peru and Puerto Rico and employed a salaried representative in Glasgow and in London. The importance of developing foreign marketing organizations similar to the American operation led to the appointment of two general agents in London and Hamburg whose offices were responsible for all countries with the exception of Canada and North America. George Woodruff who had been in charge of the Boston sales office was dispatched to London in 1864, while a year later George Neidlinger was made general agent in Hamburg. Their offices became the headquarters of the company's European, African, Asian and colonial business until the 1890s when New York started regaining control of the foreign business.[44] In 1879 Singer's London headquarters had twenty-six central offices in the United Kingdom, and one each in Paris, Madrid, Brussels, Milan, Basel, Capetown, Bombay and Auckland. Each central office in turn had suboffices under its control. By 1890 Singer was selling eight hundred thousand machines per year, three-quarters of all sewing machines sold in the world.[45] Russia was by far the most important market after the turn of the century while demand was growing from the Philippines, Japan, the Ottoman Empire and South Africa from 1914, and these countries collectively accounted for a quarter-million machine sales in 1919. This growth is best understood as a result of the saturation of the American market from 1870s. By 1879 two-thirds of all US households had a sewing machine.[46]

The British Empire was in a sense being conquered by its former colony, a feeling that resonated among many Europeans who were then apprehensive of the seduction of American machine-made goods and their 'invasion' of Britain.[47] Furthermore for American global companies Britain, the colonial centre, offered a number of advantages that ranged from infrastructure availability, labour, access to adjacent markets and capital incentives.[48]

FACTORIES

By the 1870s Singer's resources were focused on overseas sales and far less on production. Like many multinational companies of the nineteenth century it employed twice as many workers in marketing compared with its production operations, but soon the need for factories in Europe was felt. The growing productivity of the US economy led such American companies such as Singer, General Electric, Standard Oil of New Jersey, Otis or International Harvester to expand overseas. Sewing machines, harvesters and later mass-produced automobiles flooded European countries especially after the First World War when increasing protectionism in international trade with high tariff walls generated an unprecedented transfer of manufacturing to foreign markets.

The first Singer factory in Europe was established in 1867 in Scotland for a number of reasons. One of these was to circumvent the freight and duty charges on the heavy cast iron sewing machine stands. Another was the growing demand for sewing machines in Europe that exceeded the available stocks produced in America. There were furthermore very practical reasons: many of the machines shipped to Europe arrived in bad condition after the long sea journey and needed repairs. Glasgow in Scotland was selected as the site for an initial workshop as it offered 'such obvious economic advantages as an iron smelting industry, cotton thread companies, and an active ship-building and steamship business with worldwide trade and shipping connections'.[49] There was also plenty of available cheap labour, an important consideration given the fact that American labour costs were high.[50] McKenzie, the general manager of the firm, remarked that cheapness and docility of labour were the deciding factors for the choice of Scotland.[51] The irony of the labouring poor of the metropolis producing American goods to be sold to subjects of the colonial empire was lost on the purely profit-oriented businessmen in the Singer company.

A first workshop was established at 1 Love Loan, High John Street. Machinery was shipped over from the United States and a small number of workers started work in October 1867. By the end of the year, thirty sewing machines were being assembled every week. Due to an increase in the demand Singer expanded its operation in 1871 with the Bridgeton factory that grew into a four-storied building containing 147,000 square feet of floor space, becoming the largest factory in the United Kingdom. By 1881 Singer employed over two thousand people in Scotland alone. As demand was still growing faster than machines could be produced, it was decided to build a brand new factory at Kilbowie, nine miles west of Glasgow, which was completed in the summer of 1885, six months ahead of schedule. This factory was the largest sewing machine factory in the world. It could produce ten thousand machines a week and employed over five thousand persons. The US management were so pleased with the performance of the Clydebank factory that they set up the Singer Manufacturing Company Ltd in 1905, a wholly owned subsidiary of the Singer company.[52]

THE SINGER SEWING MACHINE COMPANY IN ASIA

It was during George Ross McKenzie's era at the helm of Singer (1882–9) that the company turned its eye towards Asia. This was not an unprecedented move but a somewhat early and innovative one as the rush to invest in Asia gathered momentum in the last decade of the nineteenth century. Asia had been, since American independence from Britain, conceived in the American imaginary as a land of exotic wealth. In the eighteenth century the map of Asia encompassed a massive, vaguely defined area that included India, China or the Arab world. For businessmen Asia was shaped into a succession of tempting markets: China, Japan, Korea and the Philippines. It had made its debut in the national imaginary as a space of convergence between economic fact and fantasy. Asia was the space of romance.[53]

Singer's understanding of Asia differed somehow from the American imaginary in that it continued to include India and the Middle East as potential markets. In 1883 as a response to a global economic downturn the general manager of Singer felt Asia would be 'a commercial safety valve' to combat slow sales and to unload his warehoused stockpiles. The reason for an all-out incursion into Asia was therefore described as purely practical.[54] The Asia where Singer sewing machines were marketed was composed of India, Ceylon, China, Japan, Burma, the Straits Settlements, Java, the Philippines and Australia, exemplifying a 'general expansionist behaviour' of the New York office. A Singer company publication advanced more noble but less convincing reasons for expanding overseas, when it stated that whenever people substitute a machine for direct physical strength 'they are so far uplifted in scale of being because they are enabled to make their lives more interesting as well as more productive … and a Singer sewing machine is one of the most conspicuous examples of this kind of invention which … elevates human nature.'[55]

In 1895, after Russia seized Taiwan and Germany captured the port at Kiachow, various segments of capital in the northeast formed the American Asiatic Association in order to educate Washington and the public on the importance of expanding exports to China, in order to relieve both the crisis of overproduction and the social crisis that was thought to result from that surplus. Eperjesi situates the formation of the American Asiatic Association within a historical moment in which a consortium of merchants, bankers and farmers successfully forged a consensus around the belief that opening markets abroad might ameliorate a broad range of domestic economic crises. China was envisioned as a vast market for overproduced goods.[56]

Ten years earlier the Singer company had calculated that if one sewing machine was sold for every two thousand inhabitants in the twenty treaty ports of China this would amount to huge sales figures. Information on the openness of the Chinese population to the sewing machine was sought from a missionary, Rev. John McIntyre, who was spending his sabbatical in Manchuria. The assessment was that although the Chinese were shrewd businessman and the tailors hostile to change, there was a good chance of success. The initial results were, however, very disappointing. The agent for Brussels, Edward M. Sang, was sent to China to open a central office in Shanghai. But even after advertisements were placed in Chinese-language newspapers and a tailor hired to demonstrate the sewing machines, sales results were disappointing. Only 2,216 machines were sold between 1884 and 1887.[57]

In 1888 London's chief inspector John Mitchell wrote a forty-four page report on the 'oriental market' where he concluded that the main problem was the style of clothing of the Chinese people who used loose seams. The report's negative conclusions were damning and led to the closure of the Shanghai office in June 1888. In China, after five years of attempting to capture the market, the company had to acknowledge that it had failed.[58] The reasons for the failure continued to be sought: the disinclination of wealthier Chinese to permit their wives and daughters to use machines, which led to the adoption of Singer sewing machines mainly by tailors and shoemakers, was mentioned in American consular reports.[59]

Another attempt in China was made in the 1890s, a period of economic downturn in the United States. This was prompted by encouraging signs following the visit of His Excellency Li Hung-Chang to Singer's Kilbowie works in 1896. The 'iron tailors', as the machines were known in China, found their way into industrial schools started under the auspices of the empress dowager. The question was how to create a general consumer demand in this country of 400 million people.

In 1897 Russia, France, Japan and Britain had acquired spheres of interest in China, a situation that led a year later to the formation in Washington of the American Asiatic Association as the main interest group concerned with 'Far East' policy. In the association's journal, China was a metonym for Asia and represented as a land of former greatness on the path of modernity.[60]

In 1904 a sales subsidiary called the Singer Sewing Machine Company with a new Oriental department was established, headed by Charles H. Pierce. Pierce introduced a chain stitch sewing machine to deal with the fact that Chinese clothing was loosely sewn and often dismantled in washing. He also started free company sewing schools open to everyone, unlike the earlier schools that were only for Singer customers. Sales picked up but never reached the expectations of the Singer directors. Furthermore as a protest over the American Alien Exclusion Act of 1904 the Chinese boycotted American goods, and in Hong Kong sales dropped to one machine sold per week.

The situation changed with the revolution of 1901 which introduced foreign clothing for students, soldiers and the police and made the lock stitch machines marketable. But after an encouraging start sales levels were not sustained. With hindsight the vision of limitless fields for American markets in China at the turn of the century belonged to the domain of economic fantasy rather than realism. The contrast with industrial Europe where markets were actually present was clear. Only limited areas of China were open to trade, while lack of transportation, widespread poverty and resentment of foreigners by many officials constituted serious obstacles. China never became the world market opportunity dreamt of by the first Singer directors, a dream embodied in the rhetoric of the American Asiatic Association members.[61]

JAPAN

The Singer Sewing Machine Company entered the Japanese market in 1900 approximately at the time its directors were giving up hope of conquering China.[62] Although Singer's penetration of Japan can be considered a relative success story, the diffusion of the machine never reached the rates that prevailed in the Philippines, South Africa, the Balkans and the Ottoman Empire. After 1930 local competitors in Japan were indeed able to answer the needs of the consumers better than Singer.

The Japanese market had quite early shown positive signs with the move to Westernize norms that followed the Meiji restoration. After the unequal treaties were signed with the Western powers in 1857–8, foreigners were given extraterritorial privileges in the treaty ports but were prohibited from doing business, owning property, travelling or residing outside designated ports and settlements. Under these conditions and until 1899, the Singer Sewing Machine Corporation was unable to lease property for its retailing operations.

The overthrow of the Shogun regime and the Meiji restoration from 1868 onwards witnessed attempts to both 'accelerate and control social change' through the creation of new legal norms.[63] Dress reform was a crucial element in the government-led modernization process and included policies determining what constituted the proper attire to interact with Westerners and policies over hairstyle, nudity and how much clothing to wear. The adoption of Western dress by factory workers was pragmatic since long-sleeved kimonos might get caught in industrial machinery, causing accidents.[64] The empress set the example in 1886 when she adopted Western dress in public and initiated a 'court circular' that asked her attendants to follow her in their dress style. This circular set the trend for women who 'aspired to high social status'.[65] With the spread of Western dress among Japanese people the Singer company found a new mass market. The process started in 1884 with a law that entitled women to wear European clothes, and when European-styled uniforms were adopted in the armed forces and in some government departments. In the 1920s debates were still raging about the merits of machine-made Western dress versus hand-stitched kimonos.

Singer's corporate headquarters were moved from Yokohama to the port of Kobe in 1924 following a devastating earthquake the year before, and moved back to Yokohama in 1933. Singer divided the country into regions each supervised by a central office, at Yokohama, Kobe, Osaka and Seoul. Seoul for instance oversaw operations in Korea and Manchuria, two areas under Japanese control. American capitalism was clearly not concerned with issues of political sovereignty. Between 1903 and 1935, 950,000 household-type machines were sold in Japan, amounting to a household penetration rate of 7.5 per cent.

The *mishin,* as it became known in Japan, soon became an emblem of industrial technology. It actually entered the Japanese market in earnest only in 1900. Singer's practices – its pioneering monthly instalment sales and its network of stores and salesmen – were adopted by local competitors by the 1930s and sometimes presented as a peculiarly Japanese practice. One practice was to take in old machines of any brand and offer new Singer machines. All the old machines were destroyed in order to eliminate any source of spare parts for the competition. Singer salesmen visited homes frequently in the hope of building a long-term relationship and left a machine for a free trial, which meant a very detailed inventory had to be kept. In the early 1920s women teachers (*onnakyoshi*) were used, who were often trained at the Singer Sewing Academy in Tokyo which opened in 1906. There were also smaller Singer Sewing schools located on the second story of many of the retail stores around the country. In 1907 the company began to offer instalment credit. The repayment period was usually two years at approximately 12 per cent annual interest. A Singer machine accounted for about two months' wages for an ordinary salaried man.[66] Instalment sales proved successful. The sales system introduced by Singer in Japan was very close to the modular system in place in America and in Britain, unlike in Russia where the two functions of canvasser and collector were merged due to the huge distances that needed to be covered. The only change made was that the company structured its instalment payment plan monthly rather than weekly as white collar workers were paid monthly wages.

According to Carstensen the company's goal was to keep expenses to 45 per cent of sales.[67] From 1921 onwards Japanese operations were able to produce results in line with worldwide expectations. The household penetration rate of Singer machines between 1903 and 1935 was 7.5 per cent. And using Godley's method the diffusion rate in 1935 was 15 machines per thousand, a figure still far short of the Philippines, South Africa and the Ottoman Empire.

'Singer', it has been argued, 'was exporting a protean vision of modernity, both prudential and pleasing, in Japan as around the world.'[68] Indeed Japanese women's magazines encouraged women to switch over to Western clothes and use a sewing machine for this purpose. Furthermore the machine promised women more freedom of movement in Western clothes. The purchase, ownership and uses of the machine were steps in a complex process which gradually – if unevenly – integrated families of diverse economic means into a common culture thus helping reconstruct a Japanese collectivity.

SINGER AND THE INDIAN SUBCONTINENT

Policy makers at the Singer headquarters in New York treated India, Burma and Ceylon as one single region. In this they followed the general approach seen in American consular reports where Sri Lankan companies were often but not always listed under the India heading.[69] The fact that Ceylon was a distinct Crown colony ruled separately from the British raj did not concern them, as for all intents and purposes the geography of business did not follow geopolitical boundaries.[70] This was the case not only in Asia but also in Europe where 'the Market Empire much preferred to have as its main interlocutor not the national state, but a generic entity called Europe.'[71] The Singer Sewing Machine Company was in that sense no different from other manufacturers who looked overseas for market opportunities.

The Indian market had been developed in the early 1870s by the general agent for Britain and its colonies, George Woodruff, who had divided the Indian subcontinent into a southern district to be controlled by Bombay – Ceylon would come under this – and a northern district to be worked from Calcutta. The imagined map of India on the part of Singer was quite distinct from the political map of the British administration. The Singer Company devised its own divisions in India which were clearly not based on any political template: Bombay, Ahmedabad, Allahabad, Belgaum, Calcutta and depots, Delhi and depots, Karachi, Lahore and depots, Madras and depots, Poona. Colombo was one of the Madras depots not distinct from Bangalore, Bellary, Cocanada, Consor, Seeundrabad, Trichinopoly or Trivendrum and was perceived as another subdistrict of Madras (Figure 3).[72] In 1905–6 the

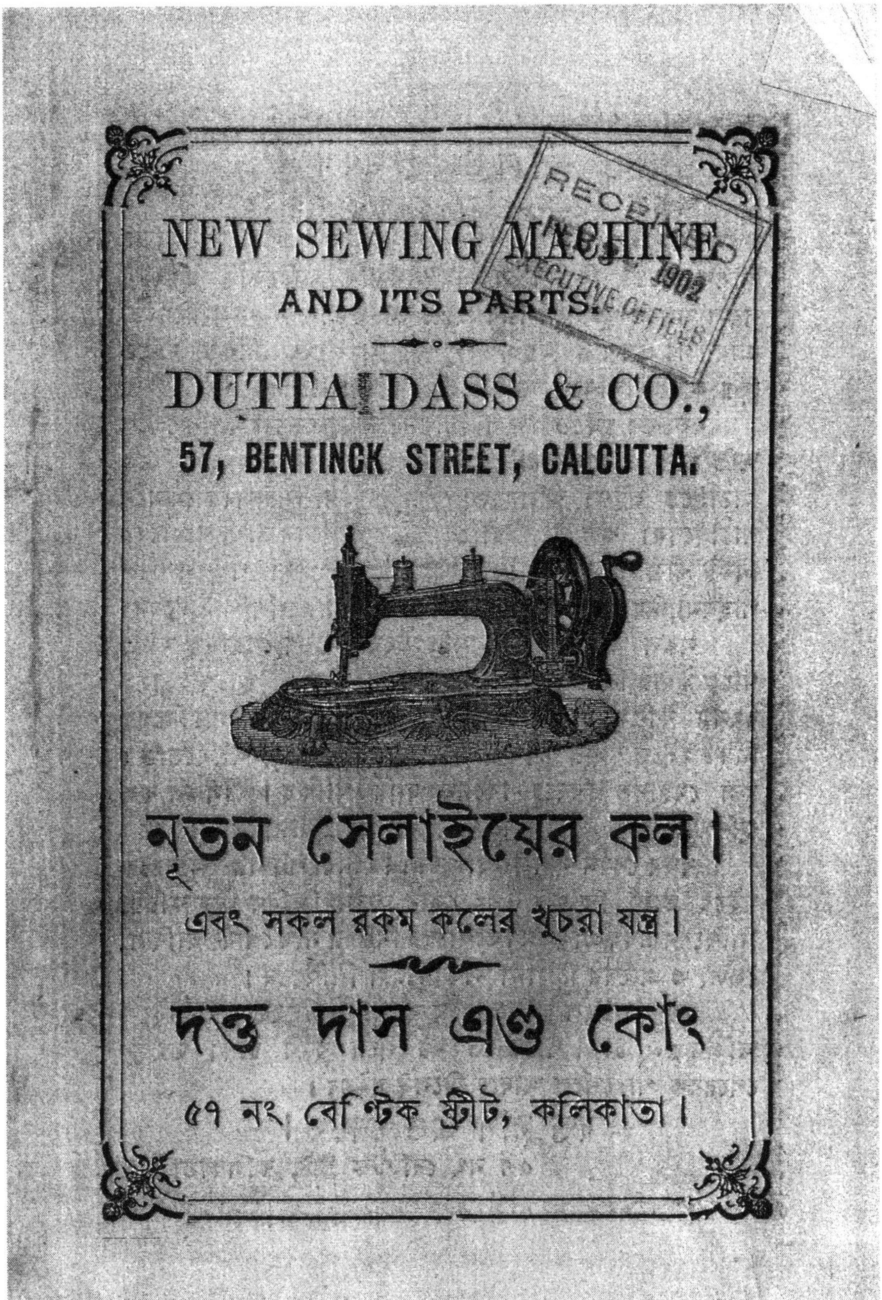

Figure 3. New sewing machine and its parts, Calcutta. 1902. Singer Papers, Box 89. Wisconsin Historical Society Archives

district offices grew in number. The list offers a peculiar mix of important cities such as Aden, Allahabad, Bombay and much smaller townships such as Belgaum, Jubbulpore, Indore or Secundrabad. More than business opportunities or political boundaries, the criteria for the selection and opening of offices seemed more likely to have been dependent upon the whims and fancies of the Singer agent in India: Nusserwanjee Merwanjee Patell (Figure 4). With this single individual who forged and sustained a human link between

Figure 4. M.N.M. Patell. Report of the Proceedings at the Presentation of an Address to N.M. Patell, Agent for India, Burmah and Ceylon, The Singer Manufacturing Company on His Retirement, 1911. Smithsonian Institution Libraries, Trade Literature.

America, India and Sri Lanka, a history that transcended boundaries of state and empire appears in the interstices.

The relative failure of Singer in India has been explained by Davies as related to India's culture: the caste system, the seclusion and widespread illiteracy of Indian women, the inaccessibility of homes to canvassers, the popular preference for cash sales and a style of clothing that did not require a sewing machine stitch.[73] But Davies attributes too much to structural issues and not enough to flaws in the office in Bombay solely run by Patell. It seems that sewing machines as early as 1883 were popular, a fact pointed out by a Singer employee visiting from New York: 'When walking in the native quarters of the town, I was struck with the number of machines in use (the people always working at the open doors) but scarcely any of ours, something more must evidently be done.'[74]

Another reason could be Patell's inability to cope with the effect of climate on stocks and his use of doubtful selling methods. When Edward Sang went to inspect the operations in Bombay and Calcutta he noted with dismay the state of the stock. He suggested the use of nickel plating as a measure against dampness and deplored the 'skeletons of machines rusty and stripped of parts' that he discovered in the warehouse. The selling techniques of Mr Patell were also problematic since he was described as not having 'the necessary patience' especially with 'those of a lower caste'.[75] Nor had he managed the stock-keeping in a methodical way. Patell was warned not to advertise the sale of damaged items as this would create the idea that Singer sold old machines returned by hirers and would weaken the confidence of the public in the goods.[76]

If one follows Davies's argument to understand why Lankans consumed more sewing machines than Indians, certain cultural differences may be put forward: the caste system was not as entrenched except in relation to marriage, and there was seldom exact correspondence between caste and occupation – thus tailoring was not considered a job only fitting for certain communities; in a predominantly Buddhist country literacy of women was higher than in India, and women of the Sinhalese community enjoyed a relative freedom of movement; this allowed them to engage in sewing work in common; homes were more open and more accessible to travelling salesmen or canvassers. Due to the influence of the Portuguese and the Dutch, the style of clothing was already Europeanized or combined sewn clothes with draped clothing in many cities and coastal areas. Finally, Sri Lanka had a less harsh climate which mitigated problems of wear and tear of the material. But common approaches to credit make up another important factor behind the different response: the people of Sri Lanka already had formed a habit of borrowing from Chettiars suggesting their familiarity with the idea of interest and instalment purchase.

The absence of any written communication between the Singer Colombo office and the Madras district office seems to suggest that there were virtually no relations between the two. Was there a reluctance on the part of Madras staff to intervene in Ceylon, a territory ruled separately as a Crown colony or did cultural and language divides between the Hindu Tamil-speaking south India and the Buddhist Sinhala-speaking southern Sri Lanka preclude any close ties? For whatever reasons the flexible boundaries that prevailed in the business world did not apply and Colombo continued to function in a quasi-autonomous fashion. In spite of having mapped Sri Lanka/Ceylon and Rawalpindi in Punjab as parts of a subcontinental market empire, the company seems to have given these fringe territories separated by natural borders a deliberate space of freedom. Any difference in the success of instalment payment in India and Sri Lanka is also difficult to pinpoint. Instalment payment relied on disciplined households that could make regular payments while rationally budgeting and saving. In many ways the planners in the United States were quietly subverting or ignoring the 'geographies of empire'. Ironically while the British were demarcating their geographical zones according to carefully constructed alliances and policies of caste, class and region, the Americans either in blissful ignorance or perhaps willingly playing a trick on the British constructed equally absurd but to them pragmatic ways of envisioning an 'Asian' market which in effect can be seen as a counterreality – a capitalist 'empire' operating as a counterflow to the political construct of empire.

NOTES

1. G.B. Magee and A.S. Thompson. 2010. *Empire and Globalisation. Networks of People, Goods and Capital in the British World c. 1850–1914,* Cambridge: Cambridge University Press, 26.
2. For a critique of the notion of transnational see C.A. Bayly, S. Beckert, M. Connelly, I. Hofmeyr, W. Kozol and P. Seed. 2006. 'AHR Conversation: On Transnational History', *American Historical Review* 111(5), 1441–64. http://www.historycooperative.org/journals/ahr/111.5/introduction.html.
3. A. Godley. 2006. 'Selling the Sewing Machine Around the World. Singer's International Marketing Strategies, 1850–1920', *Enterprise and Society* 7(2), 266–7.
4. M.E. Fletcher. 1958. 'The Suez Canal and World Shipping 1869–1914', *Journal of Economic History* 18(4), 556–73.
5. 1904. 'Ceylon: Cholera on Steamship Torridge at Colombo', *Public Health Reports (1896–1970)* 19(53), 2676–7.
6. M. Wilkins. 1988. 'European and North American Multinationals 1870–1914: Comparisons and Contrasts', *Business History Journal* 30(1), 14.

7. See D. Gosh and D. Kennedy (eds). 2006. *Decentring Empire. Britain, India and the Transcolonial World,* New Delhi: Orient Longman, 2, where a call is made for the need to go beyond metropole and colony and 'extend our analytical focus to the multiple networks of exchange that arose from the imperial experience, networks that connected colonies to one another as well as to Britain and stretched across the geographical and political boundaries that normally delimit such inquiries.'
8. A. Appadurai. 1996. *Modernity at Large: Cultural Dimensions of Globalization,* Public Worlds series Volume 1, Minneapolis: University of Minnesota Press.
9. K. Wilson. 1994. *A New Imperial History: Culture and Identity in Britain and the Empire 1660–1840,* Cambridge: Cambridge University Press.
10. For example C. Hall (ed.). 2000. *Cultures of Empire: Colonizers in Britain and the Empire in the Nineteenth and Twentieth Centuries: A Reader,* Manchester: Manchester University Press, has written extensively on notions of race, class and gender that connected Britain and Jamaica; and M. Sinha. 1995. *Colonial Masculinity: The 'Manly' Englishmen and the 'Effeminate Bengali' in the late Nineteenth Century,* Manchester: Manchester University Press, has explored the discourses of manliness and feminism that linked India and Britain.
11. A. Burton (ed.). 2003. *After the Imperial Turn: Thinking with and through the Nation,* Durham and London: Duke University Press.
12. F. Cooper and L.A. Stoler (eds). 1997. *Tensions of Empire: Colonial Cultures in a Bourgeois World,* Berkeley and London: University of California Press; see S. Hazareesingh and J. Curry-Machado. 2009. 'Editorial: Commodities, Empires and Global History', *Journal of Global History* 4, 1–5.
13. J. Gallagher and R.E. Robinson. 1953. 'The Imperialism of Free Trade', *Economic History Review,* 2nd series 6(1), 1–15; A. Lester. 2006. 'Imperial Circuits and Networks: Geographies of the British Empire', *History Compass* 4(1), 125.
14. D. Fieldhouse. 1984. 'Can Humpty-Dumpty Be Put Together Again? Imperial History in the 1980s', *Journal of Imperial and Commonwealth History* 12(2), 10–23.
15. J. Darwin. 1997. 'Imperialism and the Victorians: The Dynamics of Territorial Expansion', *English Historical Review* 112(545), 614–2.
16. Metcalf, *Imperial Connections.*
17. Lester, 'Imperial Circuits and Networks'.
18. Gosh and Kennedy, *Decentring Empire.*
19. Ibid., 5.
20. On 7 September 1967 a Mrs F. Subramaniam was presented with a Singer cabinet model sewing machine at Ratmalana for winning a competition for owning the oldest sewing machine in Ceylon. Her machine was made in 1869. Twenty-five other entries were received for machines made before 1877. 'Singer 90th Anniversary – A Supplement issued to commemorate the 90th anniversary of the Singer Sewing machine Co in Ceylon – Oct. 1967'.
21. Scott, *Refashioning Futures,* 41–42.
22. See introduction for a summary of David Scott's argument.
23. Wisconsin Historical Society Archives, Singer Papers, Box 89, John Mitchell to Singer Directors in London, Bombay 20 April 1888.

24. Ibid., Box 89, Folder 7, List of Offices in India, Burmah and Ceylon, 1904; and List of Offices in India Burmah and Ceylon 1905.
25. *The Ceylon Law Reports – Being Reports of Cases Decided by the Supreme Court of Ceylon* v. 1–3 (1887–1897), Ceylon Examiner Press, 1897.
26. *Ceylon Independent,* 2 September 1899.
27. Ibid.
28. Wisconsin Historical Society Archives, Singer Papers, Box 109, 2m3605, Directory of Shops for the Sale of Singer Sewing machines throughout the World, revised January 1906, 5.
29. Sri Lanka National Archives (SLNA), *Amicus Annual,* 1915.
30. *Ferguson's Directory,* 1926. Advertisement, Colombo: Ceylon Observer Press, 1013.
31. Wisconsin Historical Society Archives, Singer Papers, Box 89, Letter from John Mitchell to head office in New York, 20 April 1888.
32. SLNA, Colombo, Ferguson's Report, 1900, 1910, 1926, 1930.
33. Denham, *Ceylon at the Census,* 366.
34. A. Godley. 2001. 'The Global Diffusion of the Sewing Machine, 1850–1914', *Research in Economic History* 20, 22.
35. SLNA, *Amicus Annual,* 1915.
36. Department of Commerce, Special Consular Report – No. 72, 1915, 614.
37. The goal of mechanical sewing had been tackled by British and German inventors since the middle of the eighteenth century. Like most other machines it was not invented by one person but must be seen as a series of inventions and patents: from the needle with a point and eye on one side (around 1755) to an abortive breakthrough by the son of a tailor Barthelemy Thimmonnier of Amplepuis, near Lyon, France. Thimmonier's invention made of wood which produced a tambour stitch (a single thread chain stitch) using a barbed needle like a small crochet hook, was patented in 1830. It was never, however, a commercial success and in 1841 his eighty machines used for stitching army clothing in a workshop drew the ire of and were eventually destroyed by a mob of Luddite tailors who feared his machine would bring their work to an end. During the first four decades of the nineteenth century, the basic features such as the eye-pointed needle, the combining device to form the stitch and the feeding mechanism were developed in Germany, Austria, Britain and France. In the 1840s these ideas were converted by American engineers into a commercially viable machine. See B. Bonnier. 2003. 'Barthélémy Thimonnier et le machine a coudre, 1793–1857', in Institut des Etudes regionales et des patrimonies (eds), *Creations et solidarities dans la grandevilleouvriere,* Saint Etienne: Université de St Etienne, 155–221; N.L. Green. 1994. 'Art and Industry. The Language of Modernisation in the Production of Fashion', *French Historical Studies* 18(3), 730.
38. F.V. Carstensen, 1984. *American Enterprise in Foreign Markets. Singer and International Harvester in Imperial Russia,* Chapel Hill and London: University of North Carolina Press, 14.
39. Elias Howe Jr. (1819–1867) of Cambridge, Massachusetts, patented the lockstitch made by an eye-pointed needle and a shuttle in 1846. Howe was a journeyman mechanic in Lowell, Massachusetts, when he conceived and developed

his first sewing machine. He patented his second machine but found it aroused little commercial interest. He sent his brother Amasa Bemis Howe to London with his third machine, and finally a corset manufacturer, William Thomas, purchased the machine for £250 and registered an English patent for it in his name. Elias came to London to work for Thomas and adapt the machine to sewing corsets. When he returned to America in 1849 he found that others had developed lockstitch machines and some were in small-scale production. In the years that followed new elements were added including an improved shuttle and the four-motion feed, and Howe claimed not without reason that all these new machines infringed his patent. Having recovered his patent from London, Elias Howe Jr relentlessly pursued rival manufacturers such as I.M Singer and Co., the Wheeler and Wilson Co. and the Grover and Baker Co. See J.M. Gregory. 2006. 'A History of the Sewing Machine to 1880', *Transactions of the Newcomen Society* 76, 127–9.
40. The history of the firm has been well covered in the following: M. Wilkins. 1970. *The Emergence of Multinational Enterprise: American Business Abroad from the Colonial Era to 1914,* Cambridge, MA: Harvard University Press; R. Davies. 1976. *Peacefully Working to Conquer the World,* New York: Arno Press; R. Brandon. 1977. *A Capitalist Romance: Singer and the Sewing Machine,* Philadelphia and New York: J.B. Lippincott Company; D. Bissel. 1999. *The First Conglomerate. 145 Years of the Singer Sewing Machine,* Brunswick: Audenreed Press.
41. R. Riccini, 1998. 'History from Things: Notes on the History of Industrial Design', *Design Issues* 14(3), 57.
42. Wilkins, *Emergence of Multinational Enterprise,* 39; Davies, *Peacefully Working,* 303; Godley, 'Global Diffusion', 267.
43. Davies, '"Peacefully Working to Conquer the World"', 302.
44. Ibid., 307.
45. Ibid.
46. Godley, 'Global Diffusion', 276, 277.
47. See F.A. McKenzie. 1901. *The American Invaders: Their Plans, Tactics and Progress,* New York: Street and Smith, cited in Davies, 'Peacefully Working to Conquer', 299. For the spread of the 'consumerist empire' in the early twentieth century see V. de Grazia. 2005. *Irresistible Empire: America's Advance through Twentieth Century Europe,* Cambridge, MA: Harvard University Press.
48. P. Scott. 1998. 'The Location of Early Overseas Multinationals in Britain 1900–1939: Patterns and Determinants', *Regional Studies* 32(6), 489–501.
49. Davies, *Peacefully Working to Conquer,* 44.
50. Wilkins, 'European and North American Multinationals'.
51. Davies, 'Peacefully Working to Conquer', 316.
52. http://www.singermachines.co.uk/faq/singer-sewing-machine-company-history/.
53. K. Moon. 2005. *Yellowface: Creating the Chinese in American Popular Music and Performance, 1850–1920s,* New Brunswick: Rutgers University Press, examines depictions of Chinese and Chinese Americans across a variety of popular musical and theatrical conventions.
54. Bissel, *The First Conglomerate,* 107.

55. Singer Sewing Machine Company. 1914. 'Mechanics of the Sewing Machine', *Monograph 5*, National Education Association, New York: Singer Sewing Company, 42, cited in Davis, *Peacefully Working to Conquer,* 97.
56. J.R. Eperjesi. 2005. *The Imperialist Imaginary. Visions of Asia and the Pacific in American Culture,* Hanover and London: University Press of New England.
57. Davies, *Peacefully Working to Conquer,* 190–91.
58. Ibid., chapter 6.
59. Monthly Consular and Trade Reports, September 1905, no. 300, Department of Commerce and Labour Bureau of Manufactures.
60. Eperjesi, *Imperialist Imaginary,* 86–99.
61. Davies, 'Peacefully Working to Conquer,' 323–24.
62. This section draws heavily on the pioneering work of Andrew Gordon on the Singer Sewing Machine Company in Japan and particularly on his article of 2008, 'Selling the American Way: The Singer Sales System in Japan, 1900–1938', *Business History Review* 82 (Winter), 671–99, and his book, A. Gordon. 2012. *Fabricating Consumers: The Sewing Machine in Modern Japan,* Berkeley: University of California Press.
63. P.J. Katzenstein. 1998. *Cultural Norms and National Security. Police and Military in Post-war Japan,* Ithaca: Cornell University Press, 48.
64. M. Roces and L.E. Roces (eds). 2007. *The Politics of Dress in Asia and the Americas,* Eastbourne: Sussex Academic Press, 82–85.
65. Gordon, *Fabricating Consumers,* 20.
66. This is comparatively higher than in Sri Lanka where a skilled worker earned approximately Rs 3 as a daily wage or Rs 60 monthly wage, and a Singer machine cost Rs 66.
67. Carstensen. *American Enterprise in Foreign Markets.*
68. Gordon, 'Selling the American Way', 681.
69. Consular Reports, U.S. Bureau of Foreign Commerce, U.S. Department of Commerce and Labour GPO 1905, 8. For a separate listing of Ceylon see Special Consular Reports, U.S. Bureau of foreign Commerce, U.S. Department of Commerce and Labour, U.S. Bureau of Manufactures, GPO 1900, 123.
70. V. Tampoe-Hautin has shown in her Ph.D. thesis that American film companies too in the early twentieth century saw territories as made of potential consumers rather than discrete subjects of different empires. 2009. 'Cinéma, Colonialisme et Identité : naissance et évolution du cinéma au Sri Lanka (1896–1966)', Ph.D. diss., Université de la Réunion, St Denis.
71. V. de Grazia, *Irresistible Empire,* 8.
72. Wisconsin Historical Society Archives, Singer Papers, Box 89, Letter from Mitchell to Singer Manufacturing Company Directors, 20 April 1888.
73. Davies, *Peacefully Working to Conquer,* 174.
74. Wisconsin Historical Society Archives, Singer Papers, Box 88, Letter from Edward Sang to Mackenzie, 10 August 1883.
75. Ibid.
76. Wisconsin Historical Society Archives, Singer Papers, Box 88, Letter from Edward Sang to Patell, 17 April 1888.

Chapter 2

Creating a Market Imaginary

The popularity of the Singer sewing machine suggests that changing social and spatial conditions bred new expectations and desires in the late nineteenth century and contributed to fashioning a market imaginary among the people of Sri Lanka. The sewing machine and a number of other household appliances that were transformed into discourse by fledgling advertising campaigns appear to have been seamlessly integrated into the fabric of everyday life. Advertisements in newspapers and magazines were not, however, the only way to market goods to customers: storefront displays, word-of-mouth promotions, door-to-door travelling salesmen were other valuable strategies employed by companies. But how did new colonial consumers receive the messages produced by advertising? Probably with some circumspection. Just as they questioned and defied the way the colonial state defined for them what was tolerable and intolerable, they would have questioned the value of a product before consuming it.[1] The colonized urban dweller was not an unconditional follower of new state rules policing the fluid spaces where communities were accustomed to meet. The market and its logic of commodification would have been received with similar suspicion.

The positives of the market were, however, demonstrated and demonstrable. People witnessed fast and visible transformation of the living environment in the cities through technology, especially electrification and the new forms of mobility that came with it. There were also the lessons learnt as children in school about the spread of the great trading companies of the past and the prosperity and advancement of the nations that followed in this path. All these underlying forces created a fertile terrain for the arrival of the instrument of market propagation par excellence that was advertising.

It was not only the anglicised middle classes who underwent an 'education of desire' but the ordinary man and woman whose lifestyle was shaped anew by the entry of imported consumer goods into their home and lives. If one accepts that what separates the traditional consumer from the modern counterpart is his view that the novel is to be feared, if not actually regarded as the embodiment of evil, the ordinary man or woman in Sri Lanka had entered the modern age at the turn of the twentieth century. Just as in any market place, the consumer in colonized Sri Lanka would be easily attracted to a product read about in a newspaper before even seeing it in its materiality. Of the origin of his or her wants and choices we have only tentative answers, but sales figures suggest that he or she was seduced into walking into a shop and letting the salesperson take over the task of selling. The Singer company offers an ideal entry into the process involved in the making of a market imaginary as it tried out a number of possible selling strategies on indigenous people.

THE LOCAL SALESMAN

Of the Singer salesmen who manned the shops in Colombo and other cities in Sri Lanka from the early stage onto the 1930s, little is known.[2] The Singer trade card of a native salesman in 1893 is the only pictorial representation available. A few names recorded in the letters that went to and from Colombo to Bombay tell us shards of a story. The Colombo office had in 1888 a canvasser in charge named Rastonji Nasserwanji who was paid thirty rupees as a monthly salary and collected a 2 per cent commission on sales. The visiting representative from the London office felt a 2 per cent commission was not sufficient and even advised introducing a bonus to encourage canvassers to perform better.[3] Also employed was a porter who was paid six rupees as a monthly salary. The fact that the employee in Colombo was a Parsi shows the influence of R.M. Patell, the Singer agent in Bombay, in the selection of the staff.[4] The growth and development of the Singer Sewing Company in Sri Lanka was indeed closely linked to one exceptional individual, Nusserwanjee Merwanjee Patell, until the beginning of the twentieth century.

Patell left a deep imprint on the first thirty years of the history of the company in India as well as Ceylon. He was appointed as Singer's agent in June 1875, based in Bombay but visiting his suboffices on occasion and communicating with Colombo quite frequently. Patell related the way in which he was recruited in the address he made at his retirement ceremony:

> One afternoon in 1875, when I was going to my father's office, I happened to pass by a show-window containing some Sewing Machines. Being of an inquisitive nature, I stood to look at them, when a gentleman named Mr Leonard

> Cohn came to me and requested me to walk in. I did so reluctantly, because I had to attend my father's office and never meant to buy a machine. I inspected the machines and while leaving, I was asked if I was willing to take up buying agency. He was much after me and gave me all favourable terms as I wanted and I signed the agreement in 3 days.[5]

His account suggests that his recruitment was purely by chance and it simply may be that Mr Leonard Cohn was immediately taken with the Westernized and eloquent young man. Patell's career spanned nearly four decades; he did not retire until 1911. In 1881 Singer president Edward Clark gave Patell charge of the whole of India which included Ceylon/Sri Lanka. During this time Patell was entirely responsible for developing the Indian market. As the general agent he had to remit the net weekly proceeds to London after 'deducting all rents, salaries, advertisements, and other business related expenses'. His salary amounted to £3 a week plus a 5 per cent commission on net cash proceeds up to £6,000 with an additional 2.5 per cent commission on all monies remitted in excess of that amount.[6] Three years later he was granted a guaranteed yearly salary of £500.

The Singer corporation followed the British colonial usage of appointing a member of the English-speaking minority as their representative, but in this case instead of relying on Eurasians Singer selected in Patell a member of the Parsi community. Patell in turn chose his own cousin as his cashier. Notwithstanding the almost quasi-European status ascribed to Parsis, it was claimed that Parsis were not so well considered and integrated into society in Calcutta and Madras as in Bombay. The suggestion was that the Calcutta and Madras operations were large enough to have 'a good European management', but the issue was clearly one of race: 'Would a European work under a Parsee as general manager?' Edward Sang advised having separate districts dealing directly with London as the country was deemed too large to be under one single management, but his recommendation was not adopted.[7] Patell remained solely in charge.

For a time he did not follow the Singer model of selling that had been adopted all over the world. The canvasser-collector system used by Singer was the key innovation of the company all over the world. Canvassers were based in the retail stores, but they also approached the public directly in their homes to demonstrate the sewing machines and collect signed orders. To check on the work of the canvassers, Woodruff, the British office director, created a separate cadre of collectors while the retail branch manager doubled as the sales manager. Each canvasser was allocated a district and his responsibility was to knock on the door of every house every two years. He was supposed to befriend the family, offer advice and solicit introduction and if necessary service the existing Singer machines. The collectors intervened only once new accounts were opened: they delivered the machines and made the subsequent requests for the weekly instalments to complete the purchases for up to two years. This was a very expensive method of selling and a few years later salesmen-collectors replaced the separate cadre of canvassers and collectors. This system was expanded globally. By 1905 Singer employed 61,444 people in 4,552 branches throughout its global selling organization.[8]

In contrast Patell succeeded in recruiting one canvasser and only for a short time. The former canvasser then proceeded to join Singer's main competitor! After that no canvassers were used in India. Another reason was that the terms offered were so low that 'no Europeans for canvassing among the people resident here, could be found on these terms.'[9]

After a brief fall from grace due to a financial scandal, Patell was reinstated in 1887 and John Mitchell, the chief inspector with the London office, introduced a change of strategy after his visit to India. He authorized the appointment of resident commission agents who would advertise, secure orders, and collect market information which would be used by the occasional traveling canvassers from city offices.[10] This change was based on the observation that local customers preferred to buy at a shop and pay in cash rather than make use of the hire purchase system. Often customers would pool their resources to buy a machine. Patell was authorized to sell at a lower price for cash. In 1917 the Bombay price for a Singer sewing machine was 93 rupees cash ($30 gold), or 106 rupees on instalment ($34 gold).[11] Adapting sales methods and management styles to India paid off but never quite matched the sales expectations Singer had for a country of 200 million people. Patell on the day of his retirement described the growth in the number of offices, up to 1880 – one office, in 1890 – 52 offices and in 1900–1901 – 200 offices.[12]

Just as in India, Parsis in Sri Lanka – who numbered 184 in 1911 – were engaged in trading and played a prominent role in public life as active members of the community and philanthropists.[13] The clock tower that still marks the entrance to the Pettah market in Colombo was built by the Khan family of Bombay who also owned the Colombo oil mills and other business interests.[14] There were close contacts between Parsi families across borders, a fact which the American corporation exploited to its benefit by relying on ties based on blood and trust for consolidating its business.

People in Sri Lanka had begun to buy sewing machines on instalments, as Patell would discover during his visit to the island in 1901. His visit was motivated by the need to check on the Colombo office and their difficulties in controlling affairs in the suboffices. He soon found out that his feelings were well founded. The manager in the Central Province city of Kandy, after misappropriating about Rs 1,000 by selling stock, had disappeared. Patell referred the matter to the police, aiding their work with photographs he had secured of each and every manager with their signatures at the back.[15] After visiting Kandy, Patell used also informal networks – the elderly mother of the defaulter – to try to recover the losses. 'The old woman came to my hotel at about 10 pm at night with her relatives and beg[ged] forgiveness.' He also announced a reward of Rs 100 for any information. Finally his mother brought over the defaulter and Patell was able to go through the books with him. He found that Rs 988 were missing and that the first instalment payment on 8 machines had been misappropriated.[16]

The New York office encouraged Patell to be inflexible:

> We are naturally glad when we can avoid resorting to extreme legal measures, but in the case of dishonesty, if we are to protect our interests we believe that the only course we can pursue is to press the prosecution of the offender as a warning against any attempt at similar speculations.[17]

In 1888, however, Mitchell's report on the state of affairs in India advocated a more centralized system with Bombay occupying a pivotal place:

> The subs have in fact in many cases more resembled district offices for the influence exercised over them by the office under which they were nominally working has been almost nil, and in the case of Rawalpindi in the North and Colombo in the South there is reason to believe that their results would have been at least as good if their reports had been sent direct to Bombay, instead of passing through Lahore and Madras respectively.[18]

The account of the attempt on the part of the Singer Kandy manager to steal from the company belies the accepted view that sellers of the Singer machine played a key role in bringing system and reputability to the job. At an early stage at least there was no highly managed form of salesmanship in Sri Lanka and probably resistance to the imposition of managerial discipline. This episode relating to the defrauding of the company by the Singer manager in Kandy also reveals that canvassing was used to attract clients, but on the extent of the practice and the way in which canvassing was adapted to the habits and customs of the peoples little is known.

INSTALMENT PAYMENT

The episode in Kandy shows, however, that people had enrolled in this form of payment scheme and probably would have continued had there not been embezzlement. Local people were accustomed to dealing with moneylenders reclaiming dues or pawning jewellery when necessary, hence the idea of paying on instalments would not have been totally novel to them. Afghans, Arabs and Europeans were involved in lending money to Lankans in the colonial period. Chettiars furnished capital to the more traditional parts of the economy and the British dominated modern banking.

Although the data is insufficient to vouch for a wide appeal of instalment payment in the pre-1930s period, the evidence suggests that this was the preferred mode of payment for sewing machines since Sinhalese people were not easily given credit from banks.[19] The practice of buying on credit atomized products such as a few grams of sugar in small village stores in rural areas where the shopkeeper kept a book of accounts for each of his clients was common. There were no indigenous practices of instalment payment, however, similar to Japan in the 1880s and 1890s where in the lacquer industry goods were sold on credit to rural households and later businesses evolved into 'instalment department stores' selling additional household goods such as furniture, bedding, tatami, and clothing.[20] Apart from the sewing machine there were a few attempts to introduce instalment plans for other products with more or less success. Pianos from America marketed by a firm based in Chicago could be obtained on the hire-purchase system and old pianos were frequently taken over in part payment for new one.[21] An American agency in the second decade of the twentieth century undertook to sell a few cars as an advertising expedient, on an instalment plan. The U.S. consular officer in Sri Lanka described the 'native buyer' as 'so unreliable' that severe terms were introduced: the cars were sold for one-half the purchase price down and the remainder would have to be paid in 'five equal monthly payments with interest at 10 per cent a month'.[22] Clearly the 'native' was not seen as a disciplined consumer at least for large items such as cars.

ADVERTISEMENTS

What did the average consumer in Sri Lanka read about the Singer machine? What did Singer consider persuasive advertising? Scholarly analyses of Singer advertisements and business strategies have relied on a close reading of the visual message in trade cards. For example, Mona Domosh's work, which is based on five American international companies including Singer, has relied solely on one particular type of material, the trade card (see Figure 5).

Figure 5. Singer trade card, Ceylon. 1892 (Author's collection).

The trade card was the result of a new technology called chromolithography which replaced the wood and copper engraving illustration used in the early nineteenth century. It could provide an almost limitless supply of the same prints from one set of prepared stones. Just like the sewing machine that it advertised, the trade cards, produced and distributed out of large lithography firms in New York, Boston, Cincinnati and Philadelphia, were a product of the modern world predilection for replicable serials.[23] During the presidency of Frederick Gilbert Bourne (1889–1905) the company invested in a new advertising department that introduced Singer calendars, handouts, posters, thimbles and tape measures bearing the trademark red "S." National trade cards were introduced at this time. The cards, according to the Singer company, served two purposes: they provided the salesmen with 'talking points' with prospective customers, and they provided an educational service by furnishing 'something of a high order that shall appeal to the best element in the Homes'.[24] From this limited data Domosh infers that there were representational differences between 'civilising' through colonization and civilizing through the sale of commodities.[25] America's companies, she wrote, 'produced a temporally fluid view of culture and place, a narrative of progress, within which all peoples were potential consumers and all nations potentially modern.'[26] Domosh's analysis rests upon a textual analysis of Singer trade cards.[27]

What is noteworthy is that consumers in Sri Lanka had little if any access to trade cards which were essentially aimed at American consumers and collectors in the United States. What local people did read were advertisements produced by the company and published in local newspapers, a genre of literature that has not been consulted in Domosh's work. The near obsessive urge to understand how the native was 'represented' in a more general sense gives us only part of the story, however compelling it might be. I would like to argue that what the local consumer received and was more directly touched by was a different message, one which emanated from local knowledge producers who were embedded in a known cultural and political background.

The content of advertisements insofar as they are formulated to interact with a background constituted of tacit knowledge, intersubjective meanings and a form of life sheds light on the worldview of the potential buyer. Advertisements for Singer sewing machines can be found in the English press in Sri Lanka and less frequently in the Sinhala language press, a fact that belies the assumption that because Singer invested so heavily worldwide in a selling organization it had no need to make investments in advertising, the 'official art of capitalism'. But in fact, as the business archive shows in countries such as India and Lanka, the usual canvasser-collector system selling method had not worked. The Singer company had to use various other methods and strategies to sell its products in India, Burma and Ceylon. Among these was the production of a 'Singer Guide to India Ceylon and Burmah'. Twenty thousand guides were printed in 1901 including nineteen thousand paper bound and one thousand cloth bound. It contained the complete illustrated catalogue with prices and the history of the sewing machine. Patell planned to sell the book 'through book sellers, or at the book stalls on railway stations or some good firms like Messrs Thomas Cook and Sons'.[28]

Advertisements were the main strategy to reach potential clients. John Berger has suggested that advertising works in terms of wish fulfilment. It creates images of happiness and then tries to convince buyers that they can achieve that happiness through possessing the advertised product. In effect advertising works by setting up convincing metaphors in which two terms are given symbolic equivalence through their semiotic linkage.[29]

It is generally believed that the colonial attitude to advertising was one of disdain for a practice that was deemed vulgar and that in colonial times the inner logic of advertising entailed a kind of intrusiveness into the natural order of things that was uncalled for. Citing the words of the first manager of the Ceylon *Daily News,* Kemper paints a society displaying a complete lack of interest in advertising:

> Advertisers felt (in the first years after World War I) that they were conferring a favor by advertising in a newspaper. To many of them money spent on advertis-

> ing was money thrown down a drain. The Pettah shops especially took years to learn the value of press advertising. The large British business houses were the hardest to tackle. They were content to advertise in the newspapers owned by Europeans.[30]

It is certainly true that in villages provision shops where people bought all their foodstuffs and first encountered foreign tinned food had little use for advertising. But house inventories of the early twentieth century tell another story. In Kalutara a villager's house contained pictures of the Buddha published and sent out by the Mellin's Food Company as an advertisement of their foods, together with a portrait of the late John Kotalawela. Religious memorabilia reproduced en masse was fast becoming for commercial companies a useful means of promoting their goods for mass consumption.[31]

In the city British families and elite local groups are believed to have formed a world of steady and unadventurous consumers of products found at Elephant Cold Stores. There was no need to advertise for such clients. This reading of a passive colonial consumer can be cast in doubt by the regularity of advertisements in Sinhalese-language newspapers. Advertisements might have appeared, as Kemper flippantly suggests, confined to tombstone ads[32] but after that they had a new lease of life. Soap advertisements in particular frequently appealed to local buyers representing figures of the local either as Oriental women in all their splendour as in the Wana Ranee advertisement or as a Kandyan Sinhalese upper-class woman handing over soap to the lower-class dhobi man (Figure 6 and Figure 7). These advertisements produced during the last decades of colonial rule reinscribed everyday life distinctions between classes and confirmed the nationalist reading of the woman as embodying tradition through her dress and demeanour. Between

Figure 6. Wana Ranee. 1917. www.vintagepostersofceylon.com, Vintage Posters of Ceylon—Courtesy Anura Saparamadu, 2011.

Figure 7. Snow White Soap. 1940s. www.vintagepostersofceylon.com, Vintage Posters of Ceylon–Courtesy Anura Saparamadu, 2011.

1915 and 1940, however, the female figure of advertising had acquired a certain independence and moved from being a purely passive object of desire to a determined-looking and thrifty housewife.

Advertisements for the sewing machine were either purely textual or if a picture was included, it did not represent the user of the machine, thus keeping the machine open to any type of buyer, man or woman, rich or poor (Figure 8). The consumer was not expected to inhabit a cultural form produced by the advertisement. Advertising in these early years did not create an image of the machine that could instil sentiment, emotion or shock unlike the dream images that Walter Benjamin alluded to in his reading of advertisements as capable of inspiring emulation and imitation.[33] The English press advertisements, unlike trade cards, did not draw on issues of race or civilization although there was a clear appeal to women as users of the product:

> If you wish to reduce your tailoring expenses
>
> If you wish to save your time
>
> If you wish to see your family neatly dressed
>
> If you wish to see your ladies engaged in useful and intelligent work at home.[34]

The appeal was clearly to the housewife as consumer and displayed a conventional perception of what constituted a useful occupation for the women folk of the country. The native stockist and buyer were, however, positioned as male, as the term 'your ladies' indicates. Indeed at that time, urban upper-middle-class women were becoming involved in Victorian leisure activities – such as piano playing – which were not considered useful by many nationalist critics. The sewing machine reinscribed colonial Victorian templates of female respectability – such as confinement to the home, caring and looking after husband and children – and reproductive labour in the private sphere of the lower middle classes. But unlike other products from foreign countries

Figure 8. Advertisement of Singer sewing machine. *Ceylon Independent*, 5 November 1898

such as cigarettes, perfume or liquor that were advertised in the English press with figures of Western women and men consuming these products, there was no obvious attempt to represent a modern lifestyle through the sewing machine. The reason was quite clear: the sewing machine was sold not as a modern machine but as a machine that could morph into any household or culture. It was culture blind.

This explain why more often in both Sinhala and English, it was the efficiency of the machine that was proclaimed. For instance one advertisement claimed that Singer products had won fifty-four first prizes at the world's fair, 'the largest number of awards obtained by any single manufacturer and more than double the number of all the other sewing machine companies'.[35] An advertisement in the Sinhala paper *Lakmina* warned against imitations and stressed the after-purchase servicing as well as the easy payment scheme.[36] The language was more of business than of culture. Advertisements were informative; they indicated the name and address of the shops where machines could be purchased and sometimes information was given on the different purchasing options, either cash or on hire, and on after-purchase service: the availability of repairs, duplicate parts and reminding that accessories like needles, oils, cottons were always in stock.[37] But the dryness of the language was clear. Perhaps Singer, advertised as 'under European management', as it was,[38] was less immersed in the cultural idiosyncrasies of the indigenous peoples.

'We have new heavy competition and I must say mean competitors,' wrote Patell in 1901.[39] Competing with Singer were other brands essentially European such as National and Pfaff, the former of which regularly advertised its product in the Sinhala papers:

> New National sewing machine
>
> No home is complete without this machine.

Singer's main competitor, the German company Pfaff whose agent was P.F. Goonesekere, a Sinhalese merchant, advertised in widely read Sinhala newspapers such as the *Sinhala Bauddhaya* and appealed quite openly to the cultural values and traits of its readers.[40] Pfaff sold the machine as an ideal Christmas present – paradoxically in a Buddhist paper – or wedding present. The sewing machine would gradually become a central part of the dowry of a middle-class woman in postcolonial Sri Lanka.

Although its machines were 35 per cent cheaper than Singer,[41] Pfaff never succeeded in seriously threatening Singer's domination of the market. It was at some point embroiled in a serious affair with Singer. It all started with an advertisement placed in the local newspaper, the *Ceylon Independent,* by a company called Sewing Machine Company. The advertisement for machines manufactured by Pfaff were described as 'The Perfect Singer best for ladies and for tailors Pfaff's oscillating machine is most efficient.' (see Figure 9)

Figure 9. The Perfect Singer, Colombo. Singer Papers, Box 89. Wisconsin Historical Society Archives.

The Sewing Machine Company had previously been in litigation with Singer in Colombo about displaying a Singer sign in their shop. The head office corresponded with Mr G.M. Pfaff about the wrongdoings of his agent. Pfaff immediately repudiated any liability in the matter and condemned the advertisement. He promised to write to the Sewing Machine Co. and request them to alter the advertisement.[42] Now it appeared that he was persisting in 'writing vulgar advertisements' and attempting 'to lower down [the] late Mr Singer in the eyes of the public by calling him German'.[43] The Singer directors advised that the matter should be ignored 'as anything we might attempt to do legally or by way of counter advertisement would only have the effect of further advertising our competitor and would not in the end be of benefit to us'.[44] There was also competition from within the company itself. Individual buyers in Sri Lanka would sometimes buy a machine directly from the Kilbowie plant as in the case of a machine supplied to Messrs Alexander Miller Bros and Co. at a 40 per cent discount, that is, Rs 60 cheaper than the price of a machine sold in Colombo. Patell wrote a vehement protest to the London office calling the discount of 40 per cent 'terrible'.[45]

Competition finally came from the department stores that were beginning to appear in the city. Among them Cargills was the most prominent. Cargills Ltd Universal Providers was the first department store in Colombo. It sold machines that competed with the Singer dealer, according to a list compiled by Patell. In 1901, the estimate was a sale of 10 machines a month but Patell suggests the figures are purely conjecture since imports from Singer by Cargills were only of 26 machines in 1898, 57 machines in 1899 and 29 in 1900, an average of 4 a month.[46]

Thus the Singer corporation through its local advertisements was not trying to project a certain idea of progress or civilization to a backward gendered people, but was treating them as universal consumers. It assumed that the people who read advertisements in the newspapers and visited the showrooms displaying the different models of the machine had an open-ended notion of wants unlike the conventional vision of the native as a person stuck in tradition and the belief that all desired goods were in fixed quantity. The Lankan example begs us to question the reading of commodification as inhibiting critical awareness and understand culture in the way Walter Benjamin predicated it, as the aestheticisation of politics.[47] Whereas in North America Singer advertisements sold the idea of civilizational difference, in Sri Lanka it beckoned the buyer into the aura of universal bourgeois consumption. This invitation to consume into the world inadvertently gave them a type of liberty, which can be defined as the freedom of making a rational choice. It was made available to a much large section of the population than those who by 1904 had the right to vote under colonial Ceylon's limited representation structures. You could consume even if you could not vote.[48]

CONCLUSION

The global engagement of Sri Lanka's people with the market in the nineteenth century comes to us through anecdotal and limited traces. There is, however, evidence of the presence of immigrant objects and their widespread reception by the people in the statistics we glean in the business papers of the Singer company. The sewing machine acts as an eponymous object that talks for all other everyday machines that were imported in the same period. One of the main difficulties in writing a history of consumption in colonial Sri Lanka is, indeed, the lack of data available about local consumers. How and why colonized people consumed global products in the age of international capitalism is a question few historians have addressed. The consumption-production dichotomy between colonizer and colonized permeates the field of economic history. Even Sidney Mintz's *Sweetness and Power* that captures so well both the openness of local history and its conditioning by larger scale structures reinforces the distinction between the South as site of production of sugar and the North, in his case Britain, as a space of consumption.[49]

There is a practical reason for the lack of work on colonized peoples as consumers. We have only shards of information on their practices. One is left with a few fragments in newspapers, colonial administrative reports and novels to piece together in order to construct a history of the reception of the machine. But the Singer archive constitutes the main invaluable resource if one combs these sources in a manner different from the business historian. A social history of the manner in which a market imaginary spread to a colonized society has yet to be written for South Asia.

NOTES

1. See the contest over space during the Kotahena riots of 1883 and the 1915 Muslim-Buddhist riots in Wickramasinghe, *Sri Lanka in the Modern Age,* 114–20.
2. Unlike their Japanese counterparts who left biographical accounts, salesmen in Lanka have left no written traces of their years as employees of Singer, or if they have these have not survived. A. Gordon, in his 'Selling the American Way', 671–99, deploys an array of sources which include an 1922 photograph of salesmen and teachers employed by Singer; a 1903 report filed by Hata Toshiyuki, occupying a managerial post in the Singer company; and a retrospective account of the life of a salesman: Osaka Tsuhsho Sangyo-kyoku (ed.). *Mishin Kogyo* [The Sewing Machine Industry], Osaka: Mishin Geppo-sha, 1951 (cited in Gordon, 'Selling the American Way', 676).
3. Mitchell to Patell, 17 April 1888.
4. Wisconsin Historical Society Archives, Singer Papers, Box 89, Mitchell to London directors, Bombay, 20 April 1888.
5. *Report of the proceedings at the Presentation of an Address to R.M. Patell, Esquire JP, Agent for India, Burmah and Ceylon,* Singer Manufacturing Company, On His Retirement, 1911 (Smithsonian Institution Libraries), 15–16.

6. See Wisconsin Historical Society Archives, Singer Papers, Box 88, Folder 8, Patell's contract.
7. Wisconsin Historical Society Archives, Singer Papers, Box 88, 1992/83, letter from Edward Sang to G.R.M. Mackenzie, 10 August 1883.
8. Godley, 'Selling the Sewing Machine,' 281–85.
9. Wisconsin Historical Society Archives, Singer Papers, Box 88, 1992/83, Letter to G.R. Mackenzie, 10 August 1883.
10. Davies, *Peacefully Working to Conquer,* 184.
11. S. Garland. 1917. 'Sewing Circles Round the Globe', *Journal of the American Asiatic Association* 17, 40.
12. *Report of the Proceedings at the Presentation of an Address to Mr R.M. Patell Esquire, JP, Agent for India, Burmah and Ceylon,* Singer Manufacturing Company, On His Retirement, 1911 (Smithsonian Institution Libraries), 18.
13. Denham, *Ceylon at the Census,* 241–42.
14. J.R. Hinnels and A. Williams. 2007. *Parsis in India and the Diaspora,* London: Routledge, 193.
15. Wisconsin Historical Society Archives, Singer Papers, Box 89, folder 6, 7 November 1901, Patell to Singer Manufacturing Co., NY.
16. Wisconsin Historical Society Archives, Singer Papers, Box 89, Folder 5, Patell to Singer Manufacturing Co., 15 November 1901.
17. Ibid., NY office to Mr. Patell, 13 December 1901.
18. Ibid., Mitchell to Mr. N.M Patell, Agent at Bombay, 17 April 1888.
19. See W.S. Weerasooriya. 1973. *The Nattukottai Chettiar Merchant Bankers in Ceylon,* Dehiwela: Tisara Press. From the Dutch period onward, a variety of Chettiar groups worked in Sri Lanka. All were Tamil, and most were Hindu. Some worked as labourers but the caste became identified with trade in general and finance in particular. In South India Nattukottai Chettiars had once been a localized salt-trading caste. By the end of the eighteenth century, however, they had gained control of the pearl fisheries in Sri Lanka, then moved into coastal trade between South India and Sri Lanka and eventually controlled the import of rice from Thanjavur and Bengal to the island. By the late nineteenth century they had become financial intermediaries in Burma and Malaysia, transforming themselves into merchant bankers across the Bay of Bengal. Their reliability and long-distance connections soon made them rich.
20. A. Gordon. 2006. 'From Singer to Shinpan: Consumer Credit in Modern Japan', in S. Garon and P. Maclachlan (eds). *The Ambivalent Consumer. Questioning Consumption in East Asia and the West,* Ithaca and London: Cornell University Press, 139.
21. Ibid., 615.
22. Department of Commerce, Special Consular Report – No. 72, 1915, 580.
23. M.M. Mehaffy. 1997. 'Advertising Race/raceing Advertising: The Feminine Consumer (-Nation), 1876–1900', *Signs* 23, 137–38.
24. Bissel, *The First Conglomerate,* 116, cited in Davis, *Peacefully Working to Conquer,* 99; Wisconsin Historical Society Archives, Singer Papers, General Circular No. 33, Box 159, from S.M. Colema to agents, 26 July 1892.

25. M. Domosh. 2006. *American Companies in an Age of Empire,* New York and London: Routledge. On the idea of 'civilising mission' in U.S. foreign policy see A. Kaplan and D. E. Pease (eds). 1993. *Cultures of United States Imperialism,* Durham and London: Duke University Press; H. Fisher-Tine and M. Mann (eds). 2004. *Colonialism as Civilizing Mission. Cultural Ideology in British India,* Wimbledon: Anthem Press. On the idea of imperial governmentality see A.L. Stoler (ed.). 2006. *Haunted by Empire. Geographies of Intimacy in North American History,* Durham and London: Duke University Press.
26. M. Domosh. 2004. 'Selling Civilization: Towards a Cultural Analysis of America's Economic Empire in the Late Nineteenth and Early Twentieth Centuries', *Transactions of the Institute of British Geographers* 29(4), 464.
27. Singer's set of nation cards, all identical in format, all showing people posed around the Singer machine with similar colour schemes, were originally issued as a set of 12 cards, then increased to 24 in 1892 and 36 in 1893. Ceylon was one of the thirty-six nations depicted in 1893. The context is important. The cards were issued at the World's Columbian Exposition held in Chicago to celebrate Columbus's 'discovery' of America, aptly described by A. McClintock. 1995. *Imperial Leather: Race, Gender and Sexuality in the Colonial Context,* London: Routledge, 32–33 and 210–13, as the first 'commodity spectacle' of American imperialism, the staging for America's move from nation-state to imperial power.
28. Wisconsin Historical Society Archives, Singer Papers, Box 29, Folder 6, Patell to Singer Manufacturing Company New York, 10 October 1901; Patell to Singer Manufacturing Company, New York Executive Office, 6 January 1900.
29. J. Berger. 1972. *Ways of Seeing,* London: BBC and Penguin Books, 132.
30. Cited in S. Kemper. 2001. *Buying and Believing: Sri Lankan Advertising and Consumers in a Transnational World,* Chicago: University of Chicago Press,103.
31. Denham, *Ceylon at the Census,* 160.
32. Ibid., 104.
33. W. Benjamin. 2002. *The Arcades Project,* Cambridge, MA: Harvard University Press.
34. *Ceylon Independent,* 6 February 1904.
35. Wisconsin Historical Society Archives, Singer Papers, Box 29, Folder 6, Patell to Singer Manufacturing Company New York, 10 October 1901; Patell to Singer Manufacturing Company, New York Executive Office, 6 January 1900.
36. *Lakmina,* 4 January 1896.
37. *Ceylon Independent,* 17 September 1898 and 2 September 1899.
38. SLNA, *Amicus Annual,* 1915.
39. Wisconsin Historical Society Archives, Singer Papers, Box 89, Folder 6, Patell to Singer Manufacturing Company, 20 June 1901.
40. *Sinhala Bauddhaya,* 5 May 1936.
41. Godley, 'Selling the Sewing Machine', 288.
42. Wisconsin Historical Society Archives, Singer Papers, Box 89, folder 6, Patell to Singer Manufacturing Company, NY, 24 October 1901; G.M. Pfaff to the Singer Manufacturing Co., 7 September 1901.

43. Ibid., Letter from Patell to Singer Manufacturing Company New York, 21 July 1902.
44. Ibid., Douglas Alexander, 2d Vice-President to Mr N.M. Patell, 17 May 1902.
45. Ibid., Letter from Patell to Singer Manufacturing Company London.
46. Ibid., Folder 5, Letter from Patell to the Singer Manufacturing Company New York, Colombo 7 November 1901. Cargills Ltd was a development of the firm of Milne, Cargill & Co. which started business in Kandy in 1844. The firm grew and prospered throughout the coffee industry days and then went through vicissitudes after the failure of the coffee trade. The firm survived and eventually became one of the leading distributors of tea. In 1896 'it was converted into a private limited liability company, under its present title. The principal departments, wholesale and retail, are ladies drapery, dressmaking, millinery, household furnishing, wines and spirits, groceries, horse-feed, gentlemen's tailoring and outfitting and drugs and dispensary.'
47. I borrow these ideas from A. Rajagopal. 2001.'The Violence of Commodity Esthetics. Hawkers, Demolition Raids, and a New Regime of Consumption', *Social Text* 19(3), 91.
48. In 1904 the voting population was 3,013 as only literacy in English was recognized as a qualification for civic rights. In 1921 and 1924 when the constitution recognized literacy in the vernacular, the voting population rose to 54,207 and 189,335.
49. S.W. Mintz. 1985. *Sweetness and Power: The Place of Sugar in Modern History,* New York: Viking.

Chapter 3

Paths to a Buddhist Modern

From Siam to America

From news snippets in the vernacular press of the first decades of the twentieth century emanate imaginaries that reached beyond the sandy beaches of the island and far across its emerald seas: at times these imaginaries drew and withdrew from India as a mother country, home to Buddhagaya; at others they encompassed a wide arc of territory that stretched from Siam to America. The embrace by Lankan peoples of foreign consumer goods such as the sewing machine is understandable only in the context of a people engaged in multiple translocal relations who were confidently aware that it was possible to emulate countries other than colonial powers on the path to progress.

This chapter will show how in colonial Sri Lanka first a few men from Buddhist monastic communities and then larger and more diverse groups were enmeshed through ritual performances, language or travel as well as through imaginaries in many global territorial and temporal loops that transcended the frame of empire and subverted the authority of the colonial state sometimes by simply ignoring it. Through new practices they began to perceive themselves in different ways, both as individuals and as members of larger collectivities and spatialities. The parallel worlds they inhabited were constituted by a fluid interplay between spaces and their imaginations.

How can these parallel worlds help the historian who casts a multiscopic gaze upon a reality that has always been shown as one to understand what ideas, values, issues and questions inhabited the minds of the people who did not make history but whose erstwhile trajectory and choices are shaping the present?

This chapter will trace the different stages that foreshadowed the eventual embrace of a 'modern' linked to Buddhism and congruent to a market imaginary. This sense of being modern inhabited people when they drew from changing Buddhist practices, looked outwards to the Indian subcontinent and beyond while distancing themselves from colonial models. These geographies of belonging in the space of a few decades moved from a period dominated by ties and affinities with a wider Buddhist world that encompassed Siam and other Theravada Buddhist countries or sites like Buddhagaya to an emulation of America, the epitome of the noncolonising modern (Map 1).

BUDDHIST LOOPS: IMAGINING A COMMUNITY BEYOND THE COLONIAL STATE

The late nineteenth and early twentieth century was the time when Sri Lanka, Burma and Siam moved even closer to each other through the combined effect of new technologies and transport and a more vibrant Buddhist monastic politics in these countries. An idea that was gaining currency among the monastic communities was that Sri Lanka, without a religious head since 1815 when Britain conquered the kingdom of Kandy and deposed the king, needed a supreme Buddhist authority. This dream of retrieving a Buddhist monarch for Sri Lanka from an existing Buddhist country by members of the Buddhist community suggested a concept of sovereignty that did not differ in substance from the British claim to toleration of separate political, economic and religious domains. By forging closer links with other Theravada Buddhist countries through diplomatic missions, pilgrimages, visits of monks to and fro and ties with the royal courts of Burma, Cambodia and Siam, Buddhist leaders were redefining their relation to the colonial state by affirming a sphere of being where religious authority was vested in a translocal sovereign.

A PARALLEL BUDDHIST WORLD

The Buddhist world of the late nineteenth and early twentieth century was a space that functioned in parallel to the colonial imperial system. The traffic between the monastic worlds of Sri Lanka and other Theravada countries was related to the emergence of a 'tightly linked global Buddhist culture that had gained momentum in the late nineteenth century'.[1] While the colonial state counted, taxed and disciplined its subjects, ideas and individuals circu-

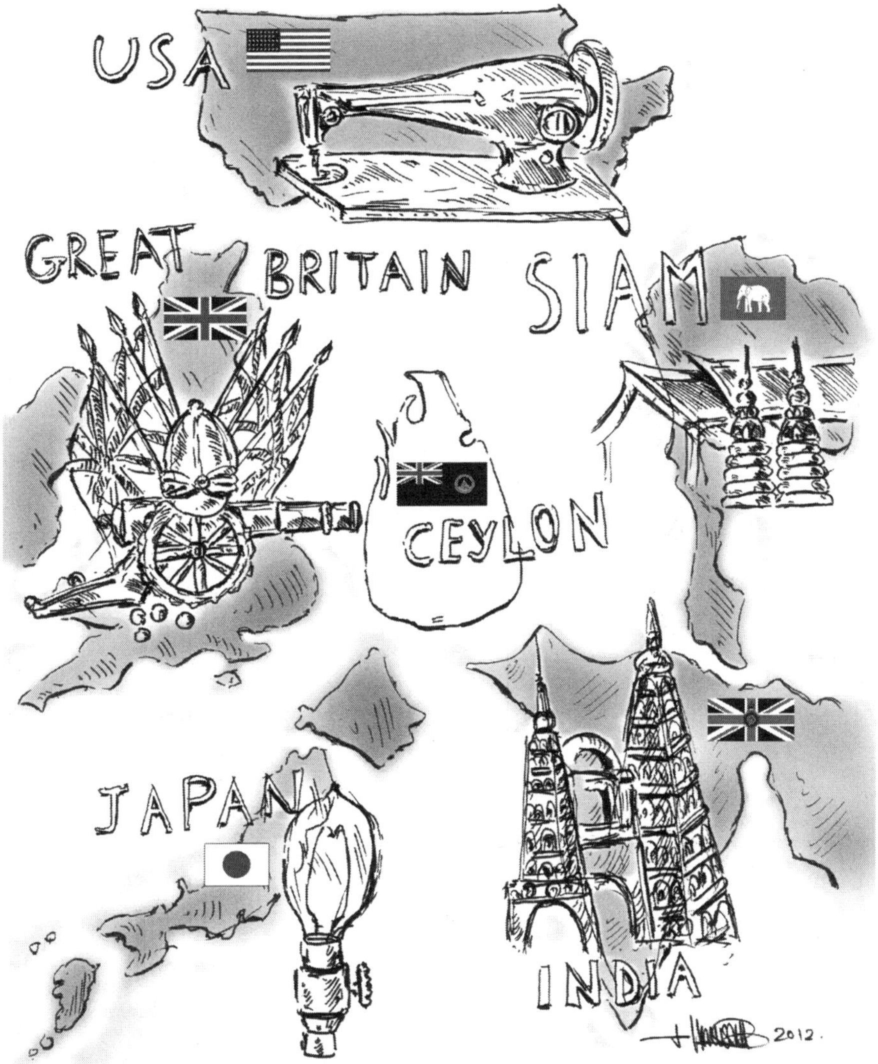

Map 1. Global loops. Artist: Susruta Samarasinghe

lated freely between Buddhist countries. There were, in the words of Prasenjit Duara, 'complex global loops' through which ideas were transmitted.[2]

Theravada Buddhism had spread from Sri Lanka to Southeast Asia, and relations between monastic communities continued over the centuries and took various shapes from exchanges in art and architectural forms to monastic missions. In the fifteenth century monks from the Thai kingdom of Chiang Mai travelled to Sri Lanka to be reordained and upon their return founded a Sinhalese sect. This was followed by a revival of the doctrine and the sacred language Pali as well as a resurgence of the faith among the people. Sri Lanka occupied a central place in the collective consciousness of Thai local leaders who vied for the Phra Sihing Buddha statue that was brought from Sri Lanka and became a symbol of their legitimacy to rule.[3]

Southeast Asian monastic communities had been formed through ordination lineages from Sri Lanka. More than in Siam, the concept of valid ordination and *parampara* (monastic ordination lineage) were central tenets of Lankan Theravada Buddhism. They implied 'pupillary succession and links through time between the ordainer and his disciples'.[4] In the eighteenth century a Buddhist monk called Weliwita Saranankara persuaded the king of Kandy to appeal to Siam to revive the Buddhist order in Sri Lanka by bringing in monks to reinstate the *upasampada* ordination (higher ordination) in Sri Lanka. Apart from creating a new monastic order called the Siyam Nikaya, which was caste based in spite of doctrinal views to the contrary – it remained the preserve of Goyigama caste bhikkus – this episode demonstrated the firm ties that existed between Buddhist countries throughout the colonial period through the notion of valid ordination. Other groups in Sri Lanka followed suit in the early nineteenth century. In 1799 a group of laymen from the maritime provinces who belonged to wealthy lower-caste groups sent a monk of the Salagama caste and novices to Burma to gain higher ordination. Upon their return they held an upasampada ceremony on Vesak Full Moon Day under the most senior Myanmar bhikkhu who accompanied them. The new fraternity came to be known as the Amarapura Nikaya, from the then capital of Burma.[5] This fraternity clearly drew from the Mon-Burmese model in terms of ordination procedure and style of wearing the robe and resembled in many ways the practices of Mongkut's reformist fraternity.[6]

These relations continued and have been charted in Siamese accounts of visits of Sinhalese monks to Siam and visits of Siamese monks to Sri Lanka during the reign of Rama I. Novices from Sri Lanka were received in the royal monasteries and given higher ordination. In 1815 a mission consisting of seven Siamese monks and some Sinhalese monks started on a journey from Bangkok towards Sri Lanka in order 'to renew the former good relationship between the Buddhist countries, for Ceylon had just then come under a non-Buddhist rule'.[7] The description of their arrival in Sri Lanka provides an interesting glimpse of relations of the colonial power with other Asian countries. It is reported for instance that the 'British customs officer treated them with civility when he learnt that they had been sent by the King of Siam.'[8] In Kandy British authorities placed no obstacle in the path of the visitors and the mission was allowed to visit all the famous shrines and holy spots for a period of twelve months. Sinhalese peasants were also curious about the party and 'farmers on learning of the nationality of the pilgrims called to neighbours to come and have a look at the foreigners.'[9]

Even more interesting is the manner in which the Sinhalese monks used Pali to converse with the Siamese monks, thus cementing the notion of a global community (in the present) through a literary and liturgical language. The monk Dharmapala in Anuradhapura greeted them with 'Avuso kuto agata' asking them from where they had come, to which they replied 'Bhante, Ayodhyapuraramna agata' – that they had come from the city of Ayodhya.[10] Pali, which has been called 'an artificial language or an ecclesiastical written koine',[11] thereby constituted during the late nineteenth and early twentieth century a linguistic bridge between Theravada Buddhist monks in Asia; its significance and extent is, however, unclear. Pali *gathas* (verses) were certainly commonly known and recited by Buddhists. Pali *suttas* (discourses) were recited at various occasions in the everyday life of people such as the Angulimana *paritta/pirith* (chanting) which blessed houses with pregnant women. Pali verses punctuated the life of Buddhist people creating a community of faith that stretched beyond territorial boundaries. These practices gesture towards the idea of a Pali cosmopolis that transcended the immediate ritual community and described a sense of being translocal through cultural and religious networks.

PALI AS AN INTERNATIONAL LANGUAGE OF MONASTIC COMMUNITIES

In the mid-nineteenth century King Mongkut of Thailand revived the knowledge of Pali among monks in order to enable them to read Buddhist texts rather than rely on commentaries. He created a monastic lineage called the Dhamma yut which meant literally 'in accordance with the *dhamma* [teachings of Buddha]'. It is reported that this allowed monks who used the language to converse with Sri Lankan monks who visited the country, thus creating a community of Pali-speaking Buddhists. King Mongkut also invented an alphabet for the Pali language which he called *Ariyaka* to replace the commonly used Khmer script for writing Pali.[12] The term 'Ariyaka' means the Aryan people, referring to the lineage of the Buddha. There was clearly an attempt to standardize Pali as a language for all Theravada Buddhists. Moreover, evidence also proves that the Ariyaka was not only used among King Mongkut's group in Thailand but also by Sri Lankan monks to write to them. There are many letters in Pali dating around 1885 written between Sri Lankan monks from Sri Lanka and abbots of Wat Bovoranives in Thailand in the Ariyaka alphabet which testify to the place of Pali as a bridge language. There is a possibility that Sri Lankan monks studied this new Pali alphabet at Wat Bovoranives when they visited King Mongkut. The history of Wat Bovoranives records that 'King Mongkut was often visited by Sri Lankan monks and there was a dedicated residence for them called "Khana Lanka" in Wat Bovoranives.'[13] In 1862, King Mongkut sent a gift of a lithographic press to the Sri Lankan sangha for them to publish Buddhist books with perhaps the intention of helping them compete with missionaries in Sri Lanka or exclude them from their circle of understanding with his new Ariyaka alphabet.[14]

Clearly ties continued in the decades that followed with Sinhalese monks visiting Siam and Siamese monks visiting the island with the intention of obtaining copies of the *Tripitaka* (sacred canon of Theravada Buddhism written in the Pali language). In 1844 thirty-five Sinhalese monks – among them Varapitiye Sumitta, the founder of the Ramanna Nikaya Buddhist fraternity in Sri Lanka – went to Siam. Parts of the *Tripitaka* that were lent were returned to Sri Lanka in 1852 by a mission sent by King Mongkut.[15]

CAKRAVARTI FOR SOUTHERN BUDDHISTS

The feeling of loss and the need to seek a ruler for all Buddhists beyond the shores of the island would have seeped down slowly from the sangha to the people of the island after the fall of the Kandyan Kingdom in March 1815. With the signing of the Kandyan Convention by its chiefs and Brownrigg on behalf of the British, the Buddhist religion was first not seemingly affected. A promise was made that Buddhism would be maintained and protected by the new rulers who replaced the Nayakkars, a concession necessary to secure the support of the bhikkus and chiefs. A British resident was substituted for a Kandyan king. In 1817–18, however, the realization that British rule was there to stay and nostalgia for the restoration of an indigenous monarch ignited a rebellion that spread to the remote Kandyan provinces of Uva and Velassa. A pretender appeared claiming blood ties with the Nayakkars and princely status. The tooth relic, the possession of which gave legitimacy to a Buddhist king to rule the island, was taken away by bhikkus from the Dalada Maligawa (Temple of the Tooth in Kandy).[16] Eventually the rebellion was crushed with the help of troops dispatched from India and the peoples of Sri Lanka had to resign themselves to the sombre reality of a land without a king. From the late nineteenth century to counter the feeling of loss and demoralization that followed the demise of their king and defender of the faith, Buddhists in Sri Lanka, mainly members of the sangha, began to look to Buddhist monarchs in other southeast Asian countries.

In Theravada Buddhism the monarch or *cakravarti* is the secular equivalent to the Buddha. The king is expected to protect the *sasana* (community of bhikkus) and give leadership to the Buddhist people of his land. His status is elevated to a point that words used to denote the Buddha are also used for the king. In essence, 'The king is a bodhisattva [a being dedicated to helping other beings to achieve enlightenment] on whom the sangha bestowed kingship in order that he may defend the bowl and the robe.'[17] In 1862 a group of monks from Galle wrote to King Mingdon of Burma to intervene with the 'great queen, ruler of all the English' after a group of foreigners had insulted Buddhist monks. They wrote in the name of 'the inhabitants of Sihala and of monks in the Buddha-sasana who are completely weakened'.[18] Thus the idea of a community that they projected was not an inclusive one since it explicitly referred to Sinhala peoples in a land where many other ethnic groups lived. The ideal of a Buddhist king was one grounded in the past where the king was the protector of Buddhism, the supreme ruler of the sangha which he constantly purified by expelling 'bad' monks from the established fraternities, introducing new ordination from abroad during periods of decline and circumscribing tendencies to Mahayana heterodoxy. Attempts were also made in the 1880s to explore possibilities of Cambodian patronage to Sri Lankan Buddhist activities. The Khmer royal power was, however, closely controlled by the French military and although there were high-level contacts between Cambodia and Vidyodaya *pirivena* (monastic college) there was no real possibility of any further patronage. When in 1885 Burma fell completely under the control of the British, there remained only the kingdom of Siam as a possible patron for Buddhists of Sri Lanka.

After his enthronement, in testimony of the aura he wanted to project as a king for all Buddhists, King Chulalongkorn of Siam presented the Sinhalese sangha with gifts and a monetary offer to restore the Mirisaveti *cetiya* (monument containing relics of the Buddha) in Anuradhapura. In so doing he acted outside the authority of the colonial state as though their rule was an irrelevance of a sort. He visited Sri Lanka from 19–21 April 1897 and was warmly greeted by the people of Colombo with a banner that proclaimed him 'the protector of our religion'. Although the Pali spoken by the welcoming party of Sinhalese monks was not well understood by the king, it was a real attempt to converse in a language that excluded the colonial.[19] In Kandy, however, while the welcoming party addressed the king in Pali, the king responded in English (Figure 10).

His visit was an occasion for many Buddhist leaders in Lanka to encounter and interact with the only Buddhist monarch who had remained

OF CEYLON, WEDN

D. M. C. C.

A general meeting of this Club will be held at the Darawella Pavilion, on Saturday, May 1st, to receive the report of the Committee appointed to consider the removal of the Tennis courts from their present position.

THE VISIT OF THE KING OF SIAM TO CEYLON.

LAST NIGHT'S DINNER AT QUEEN'S HOUSE.

The names of those who dined with the King of Siam last night were the same as those published as having been invited in our issue of yesterday, with the addition of Mr. S. D. Young. The Volunteer Band attended and played a programme of music, beginning with the British and ending with the Siamese National Anthems. There were no toast.

DEPARTURE FOR KANDY.

His Majesty the King of Siam left Colombo for Kandy this morning. Leaving Queen's House at 8-30 a.m. he drove to Maradana Terminus in company with the Lieut. Governor, the Maha Mudaliyar, Mr. S. D. Young, and a large retinue composed of Princes and officials. At the station he walked along a carpet which had been laid down in his honour, and was saluted by a Guard of Honour composed of a hundred of the Loyal North Lancashire Regiment, under Capt. Stable, with Lieutenant Woodward, and Lieutenent Berkeley bearing the colour. He then entered the saloon which was constructed for the Prince of Wales upon the occasion of the visit of His Royal Highness. This was attached to the special train for the King of Siam because the Governor's saloon was being used for His Excellency to journey from Nanu Oya to Kandy at the same time in order to meet the King there. His Majesty started for Kandy at 9 o'clock, accompanied in the saloon by the Maha Mudaliyar, and Mr. S. D. Young, together with his sons, brothers, aide-de camps, chamberlains, and private secretary. Another saloon followed in which were about thirty members of his suite, and there were also in the train Mr. Cantrell. Acting Manager of the Railway, Mr. Byrde, Assistant Traffic Superintendent, and Mr. Clarke, Railway Engineer. His Majesty was timed to arrive in Kandy soon after midday, and H. E. the Governor, coming down from Nuwara Eliya to meet him, was expected to arrive shortly before him.

Messrs. W. L. H. Skeen & Co. photographed His Majesty the King of Siam this morning at Queen's House. They got two fine negatives of the King alone, and two of himself and suite.

TO-MORROW'S [illegible]

Figure 10. King Rama's visit to Ceylon in 1897. *Ceylon Independent*, 21 April 1897

aloof from British and French designs in Southeast Asia. Ven. Hikkaduve Sumangala was among the party that had planned the visit of the king. He and others were 'strongly invested in a vision of Siamese patronage for Sri Lankan Buddhism and, indeed, for Siamese oversight of the Lankan monastic world'.[20] They hoped the king would form an ecclesiastical council encompassing Siam, Burma and Sri Lanka that would have supreme authority and that the king would unite the higher ordained monks of these three countries within a single monastic order.

If Siam seemed the only possible source for the unification of the sasana and 'ecclesiastical' leadership for Buddhists of the south by Sri Lankan monks such as Hikkaduve, its appeal to lay people is more difficult to fathom. Newspapers did make frequent allusion to Siam, even in nonreligious issues as for instance in July 1900 in a news item relating how the king of Siam was trying to do away with the slave trade[21].

The close relationship between Buddhism and kingship is epitomized in Sri Lanka in the worship and protection given to the tooth relic kept in the Dalada Maligawa in Kandy. The tooth relic sanctioned the king's right to rule over the kingdom, and the fusion between Buddhism and kingship was illustrated in the fact that palace and temple shared the same space, the landscape proclaiming this close relationship. This palace/temple complex could be read as an 'earthly version of Mount Mandara where Sakra and the Tooth Relic of the Buddha dwell'.[22] From the eighteenth century onwards the *perahera* (procession), which honoured the tooth relic contained in a golden casket by displaying it to the Buddhist people in a procession in Kandy, was revived by King Kirti Sri Rajasinha. The public worship of the tooth relic played a central role in reinforcing the authority of the king and in ritually presenting the hierarchy of social status in the Kandyan Kingdom.[23]

Some people were aware of the visits of the Siamese royal family to Sri Lanka to visit the tooth relic in Kandy as they were able to read about it in newspapers such as the *Sarasavi Sandarasa* and *Lakmini pahana.* We know also that there were more than five hundred Buddhist monks present at the king's visit to the Temple of the Tooth in Kandy who would have shared their experience through preaching to the lay people. But of this process of dissemination there is no historical record. To what extent did Buddhists of the late nineteenth century and early twentieth century feel bound to the courts of Southeast Asia? Visits of Burmese pilgrims increased after the fall of Burma to the British and one can imagine that the presence of seven hundred to eight hundred Burmese visitors staying at Vidyodya for the viewing of the tooth relic in 1899 would not have gone unnoticed among the peoples of the area. Sri Lanka and the tooth relic represented for Cambodia and

Burmese Buddhists a place where they could take refuge from the shattering sense of loss that had come with colonial intrusions.[24]

The king of Siam was recognized by the British colonial administration as being the king of all the Buddhist subjects of the empire, thus bestowing him with a kind of moral authority that overrode that of the colonial state. Indeed in 1897 when relics of the Buddha were discovered at his birthplace in Kapilavastu the British viceroy Lord Curzon went to Bangkok and offered them to Rama V whom the British considered the only remaining Buddhist monarch. The condition was that he would share them with Buddhists of the empire, namely, in Sri Lanka and Burma.[25] Colonial policies in a curious way acknowledged the existence of other sovereignties.

In parallel to this turn towards the east, Lankans' perception of India too was undergoing changes and during this period fractured into a number of different and conflicting visions: an idealized mythic and spiritual vision of India as the land both of the Buddha's birth and of unwanted immigrants from its southern regions in search of work in the city or in the highlands. At times India was the non-West and looked upon as the mother country by Sinhalese and minorities alike united in their moderate opposition to British rule. It was not the same India all communities looked towards for inspiration and support. For the Sinhalese community pride of place was given to northern India. India was quite different in the imaginary of the Tamil peoples who shared cultural and linguistic ties with the southern areas of India.

BUDDHAGAYA AND A FRACTURED INDIA

India was present in ordinary people's imaginary in many forms, through the old myths of foundation energized by the Tower Hall theatre, through travelling performers who used gramophone recordings of plays to reach out to the hinterlands, but also through peoples travelling to India on pilgrimage or for education, and peoples from Southern Indian villages moving to Sri Lanka to work in the city factories or toil on the tea plantations in the highlands. There were also the performances and writings of Ananda Coomaraswamy and Rabindranath Tagore who dreamt of a mother India and an ideal Asia at the heart of which would reign not the India of the raj but an India that loomed large in peoples' stories and myths. But the place of India in the articulation of nationalism in Sri Lanka underwent, as we have suggested, significant changes. In the popular imaginary of the early twentieth century India as mother country faded away, gradually giving space to a territory imagined as swarming with cheap labour ready to swamp a smaller, vulnerable island. But if the real India was dismissed, the imagined India – land of the birth of the Buddha and of the *Jataka* tales (tales of the previous lives of the Buddha) – continued to permeate people's minds although the two maps functioned at different levels.

The two main ethnic communities of the island, the Sinhalese and the Tamils, then as now trace their origins to Indian settlers. In Sri Lanka's modern foundation myth, India is the mother country. The *Mahavamsa*, a sixth-century court chronicle, states that on the very day of the Buddha's death, Vijaya – an Indian prince and the founder of the Sinhala race – landed in Sri Lanka as if to bear witness to the Buddha's prediction.[26] The *Mahavamsa* was discovered and translated from Pali to English by George Turnour, a British civil servant in the 1830s, but early writers such as John Davy and Anthony Bertolacci suggest that the content of the *Mahavamsa* was already in circulation among the people even though they were not aware of its written version.[27] The written version of the *Mahavamsa* gave it increased value in the minds of a Sinhalese intelligentsia stirred in the late nineteenth century by anticolonial sentiments. Prince Vijaya was believed to have come from northern India, the Aryavarta as it was called in Sanskrit texts, so that the *Mahavamsa* gave credence to the Aryan origins of the Sinhalese in northern India.

In the late nineteenth century the awareness among Buddhists of a worldwide community beyond the southern Buddhist fold of their co-religionists was sparked by a movement spearheaded by a Sinhalese lay preacher called D.D. Hewavitharana, who in 1883 adopted the name Anagarika Dharmapala.[28] The movement aimed to protect and restore Buddhagaya, the site of Sakyamuni Buddha's enlightenment and the holiest Buddhist shrine in India.[29]

In 1891 during his pilgrimage to Buddhagaya (in the present state of Bihar) he became deeply convinced that his mission was to restore the sacred site to Buddhist control and unseat the Hindu monastic incumbent from the site.[30] The Maha Bodhi Society established in that same year had a clear pan-Buddhist approach. Dharmapala travelled the world to mobilize public opinion against the destruction of the holy site and according to his own writings even raised money from Lankan and Burmese Buddhists to purchase the Maha Bodhi village at Buddhagaya. He began correspondence with Buddhists of 'Ceylon, Burma, Siam, Japan, China, Arakan and Chittagong' for this purpose.[31] Buddhist monks were brought from Sri Lanka to Buddhagaya in order to establish a resident Buddhist presence at the site. The Buddhagaya movement was not, however, a success due to tensions with the British Indian government and the lack of support of the Buddhist monastic community in Sri Lanka and the King of Siam for Dharmapala's activities. To what extent people's consciousness of being Buddhist in a modern world was shaped by the outwardness of its new bourgeois propagators, such as Anagarika Dharmapala who travelled the country in an automobile to convey the message of Buddhism for the new age, remains difficult to fathom. He himself appears to have distanced himself from India through his battle with Hindus over the 'Buddhist Jerusalem' and felt it more urgent to define the identity of Sinhalese Buddhists in opposition to Hindus. The majority of Sinhala Buddhists, it has been suggested, 'remained indifferent to the "great tradition" of India'.[32] What is certain is that at least for a few this movement reinscribed India as a land close to the heart of the Buddhist community in Sri Lanka and encouraged a stream of pilgrims to the sacred sites. From being a purely mythic, imagined India it became a real territory that could be visited and fought over.

There were other competing visions of India. While India was the land of birth of Vijaya, it was also in people's consciousness the land of the Chola invaders who had conquered the capital city of Anuradhapura and reigned there until the Sinhalese hero Dutugamunu repulsed them. In the early twentieth century novelist Martin Wickramasinghe related how for the villager the world of folktales, of King Dutugamunu and Queen Yasodhara, constituted the real world, not a fantastic one.[33]

Some intellectuals under the aegis of Ananda Coomaraswamy represented India as the source of all things past and spurred a renewal of interest in Sinhalese and Tamil art. The *Ceylon National Review,* the journal he edited, emphasized the mental and spiritual kinship between India and Sri Lanka.[34] India was identified as the 'motherland' and the 'anglicisation of the East' was subjected to much criticism.[35] Coomaraswamy believed in uniting the 'Eastern races of Ceylon'.[36]

In the same way the Bengali poet Rabindranath Tagore, who visited the island on three occasions in 1924, 1928 and 1934, was a well-known critic of materiality who bemoaned the disappearance of moral values and beauty associated with the Orient. The 'East' he believed in was one from where it was possible to learn from the past.[37] During his 1922 visit to Colombo he spoke of 'all the different peoples of India'; he qualified this statement by saying, 'When I say India, I certainly include Ceylon in India.'[38]

In the text entitled 'To My Ceylon Audience' written after his first visit to the island, he expresses disappointment at the way people in Sri Lanka had 'drift[ed] into the vagabondage of imitation':

> It struck my heart with dismay, when I visited Ceylon, to find that the people there have lost the consciousness of their unity with their Indian kinsmen … A tree grows in its own shape and finds its fulfilment, but when cut off from its root it is, as timber, at the mercy of the dealers who turn it into toys of their fancy.[39]

He felt that Sri Lanka's 'subconscious mind, its racial mind, has unbroken connection with that of India'.[40] Rabindranath Tagore's indictment was based on the impression he had obtained from a minority of anglicised, urbanized peoples he had encountered during his trip who dressed in top hats and suits and spoke in English in their homes in a manner which was quite inconceivable in India. Tagore felt they were casting away their intellectual and spiritual links with India but did not understand that, for the majority of the vernacular-speaking educated youth, it was no longer a question of turning away from the West but searching for a model in the East that answered their twin need for authenticity and for technology, science and progress.

In the following decades it was no longer India but a specific geographic portion of India, the land of the Aryans identified as the province of Bengal, which was looked upon as the motherland of the Arya Sinhalas by the Sinhalese literati. There were also references to a pre-Aryan colonization of Ceylon contemporaneous with the original Aryan colonization of southern India. The myth of Ravana was invoked to sustain this interpretation of an ancient invasion. The story goes that Ravana, king of Lanka, hearing of the beauty of Sita, the wife of Rama (then in exile) carried her off to Lanka. Rama, having allied himself with the Aryan races of southern India, crossed over to Lanka, gave battle to Ravana, defeated them and recovered Sita. The *Lak Mini Kirula* claimed that Lanka was a powerful kingdom even prior to the advent of Vijaya and the mythical ruler Ravana had ruled the island in about 2837 BC with the assistance of a council of ten.[41]

For other Sinhala intellectuals Vijaya, the Indian prince, was not a hero but the arch enemy. In the 1930s and 1940s the Hela (Sinhalese supposedly free from Sanskrit influence) identity upheld by the Sinhalese scholar Munidasa Cumaratunga (1887–1944) amounted in effect to a denial of the Arya-Sinhala identity forged during the religio-cultural revival and to a refusal to acknowledge filiation to mother India.[42]

But neither the Hela theory of the origins of the Sinhalese nor the earlier incarnations of the Ravana myth succeeded in capturing the imagination of a large group of people. While the Hela theory was perhaps too literary and complex to be understood by nonliterate people, the Rama-Sita-Ravana myth which saw the king of Lanka ultimately defeated by Rama did not give Ravana a persona people could easily identify with. It was very much a myth for Hindus.

Indeed for Sinhalese living in the south of the island, India was much more remote than for the predominantly Hindu peoples of the north and the east who have been over the centuries linking and delinking with southern India. There were definite pan-Tamil feelings and cultural traits which surfaced with more or less vividness in the nineteenth century. British rule offered opportunities for scholars and poets to travel to India freely. In the last quarter of the nineteenth century the 'Jaffna School' dominated the literary scene in Madras. The more affluent Tamils visited India frequently: Arumuga Navalar (1822–79) travelled and preached in India for a great part of his life. Others too, such as C.W. Thamotharampillai (1832–1901) and V. Kanagasabhai (1855–1906) spent most of their lives in south India, holding positions in government service but returning to Jaffna on and off to found schools in their villages. Leading Tamil politicians from Jaffna such as the Ramanathan brothers received a greater part of their education in Madras.[43]

At a popular level there was in the nineteenth century a constant flow of pilgrims from India to Hindu *kovils* (temples) in Sri Lanka and Hindus from Sri Lanka crossing over to India to temples and other pilgrimage centres. A large part of the subcontinent was connected by a cluster of pilgrimage centres. Ashes were taken from Sri Lanka to Kasi by those for whom Benares was too far away. Often the travel was organized by members of the Chetty community.[44] The popular sense of belonging to a greater India was not expressed in word but practiced on foot by peoples who trekked for days before crossing the Palk straits.

While India was part of the social world of Tamil Hindus in Sri Lanka, Indians were viewed with less affection in the southern parts of the island. In the common perception they were either plantation workers working on lands that had been taken away from Sinhala peasants to create the tea plantations or they were city workers engaged in the labour that Sinhalese found demeaning; the more affluent merchants and traders became the targets of Sinhalese nationalists representing the interests of the incipient entrepreneurial class.

Colombo had grown into a bustling colonial centre with an urban labour force engaged in skilled and unskilled work in factories, public works and transport and an informal sector of vendors that serviced the working population. Only on rare occasions did workmen speak for themselves; one such was the Donoughmore sittings in 1927–8, another the Jackson Commission on immigration, ten years later. A group calling itself 'Ceylonese workers' sent a memorandum to the Donoughmore commission: 'We feel very keenly the menace to Ceylonese labour occasioned by the influx of foreign and especially Malayalee labourers.'[45] Indians were perceived not only as unfair competitors but also as inferiors since they performed tasks a Sinhalese would consider despicable. A worker appearing before the Commission on Immigration to Ceylon claimed that the Indian is 'cook, sweeper and everything himself and boils the water and makes the tea'; another said: 'A Sinhalese will sit on a stool, rather than weigh a tea chest which a Tamil or Malayalee puts on the scale.'[46] These sentiments increased when the world slump began to affect Sri Lanka from 1926 and throughout the 1930s. This created a mental distance between Sinhalese city folk who saw themselves as 'authentic' and part of a collectivity and the 'other' who came from across the Palk Straits. Although the village was never a secluded place, before the spread of newspapers it was mainly in the temple and through the preachings of the local monk that villagers received news of the world around them. For the monk it was for a long time a secure world ordered by religious time and lived in religious spaces of temples and pilgrimage sites in the island and beyond. But for the peoples he preached to the visions of the *sastras* (oracles) and traditional sciences conveyed by leading monks in the mid-nineteenth century were more and more at odds with the changes taking place in society. Not only lay people but the next generation of lay Buddhist leaders too turned away from Theravada Buddhist countries and India that were in their view intrinsically linked to the past. It is in this context that we need to understand the aura of America, a country that unlike Britain was not contaminated by dreams of expansion and appeared to be even welcoming to Buddhism.

THE LATE NINETEENTH CENTURY – IMAGINARY LOOPS: AMERICA'S AURA

In Sri Lanka in the late nineteenth and early twentieth centuries, America was best known for the Thomas clock and the Yankey stylo pen[47] and admired as the land that had given birth to an exceptional being, Colonel Henry Steel Olcott (1832–1907), an American theosophist who spent years in Sri Lanka, publicly converted to Buddhism and became a hero of the Buddhist cause. Olcott embodied America, an advertisement of good will and ingenuity. He exemplified the possibility of being white, turned towards the future while at the same time respecting the mores of the past of the colonized peoples. He helped create an environment where it was possible to straddle multiple beings. One could with ease be a devout Buddhist and use machines created in America.

Olcott was extremely active in his first stay in Sri Lanka. He not only popularized his ideas through a series of lectures, he also gave those ideas institutional form by founding a series of school and voluntary associations. Lay branches and one monastic branch of the Buddhist Theosophical Society (BTS) were established and Buddhist 'Sunday schools' affiliated to the BTS as well as secondary schools were founded. He became virtually a folk hero in the island as a result.

On his second visit to Sri Lanka in 1881 he travelled around the western province for eight months in a bullock cart of his own design. 'Villagers flocked, according to Olcott, to witness the mechanical wonders of this device, whose lockers for furniture and books, canvas roofs to keep out rain and cushioned central compartment with removable planks that could set eight for dinners or sleep four all testified to Olcott's Yankee ingenuity.'[48]

Machines made in the United States, a country recognized as friendly to Buddhism, seem to have been used by local peoples without any sense of anxiety. Writing in 1915, the American consul in Colombo underscored the significance of the sewing machine as a symbol of America:

> It is likely that these sewing machines have made the United States really famous to many of the uneducated Ceylonese who may otherwise have never heard of this country, except perhaps from noticing 'USA' on empty kerosene cases, which they find useful for many purposes.[49]

This was not entirely true. America had in fact been present in the cognitive map of the peoples of Sri Lanka for centuries. The first impact of America on Sri Lanka was related to the arrival of American Christian missionaries in the island in the early nineteenth century. After the British had conquered the entire island in 1815 they had practiced a policy of religious neutrality epitomized by the fifth clause of the Kandyan Convention as mentioned earlier in this chapter. Missionaries were accepted in the island on condition they confined their activities to the north and east, in areas where the population was mainly Hindu and Tamil. But after the 1830s, colonial administrators became convinced that Christianization would ensure social order and from then on opened up the country to Christian missionaries. Missionaries utilised the printing press and a network of voluntary associations to print and distribute Bibles, catechisms and prayer books and a host of anti-Buddhist tracts. In the 1880s of over 1,200 government-sponsored schools in Sri Lanka, only four were Buddhist. Missionary schools had largely transplanted traditional modes of religious education offered by Buddhist monks and in temples.

Sinhalese Buddhists responded to the evangelization and civilization of their island with a Buddhist revival movement that had roots in the eighteenth century with the transformation of Buddhism initiated by Welivita Saranankara. Saranankara convinced the Kandyan King Kirti Sri Rajasinha to bring a delegation of Thai monks to Kandy, revive proper ordination and reorganize religious life. He became the *sangharajah* of the Siyam Nikaya. Under his auspices corruption was rooted out, and Buddhist tradition preserved.[50] Opposition to the Christianization of Sri Lanka, which started as early as the 1820s, gained momentum with the creation of the Lankopakara Press at Galle in 1862. That same year the activist monk Mohotivatte Gunananda organized the Society for the Propagation of Buddhism, and another Sinhalese press began to issue a series of printed responses to anti-Buddhist pamphlets. A tract war culminated in a famous exchange between Mohotivatte and Wesleyan clergyman David de Silva at Panadura in 1873.

A renewed Buddhism fed upon the burgeoning print industry to reach out to the newly literate people and tear them away from the 'heresies' preached by Christian missionaries. The spread of literacy through the development of schools created a new reading public in Sinhala and Tamil – avid consumers of the culturally conscious press and writings of the day, breaking the monopoly of modern knowledge until then preserved by the Anglophone elites.

When the two prominent theosophists Colonel Olcott and Helena Petrovna Blavatsky arrived in Colombo in 1880, the Buddhist revival was already well in motion. The cross-fertilisation of ideas and practices between Sri Lanka and other Asian Theravada Buddhist countries were often defined against Christian missionary religious discourses and European understandings of Buddhism. The result was a transformation in the practices of Buddhism which in Sri Lanka has been described as Protestant Buddhism.[51] On 25 May 1880 at the Wijayananda Monastery in Galle, Olcott and Blavatsky publicly and formally converted to Buddhism. Kneeling before a huge image of Buddha they 'took pansil' by reciting in Pali the Three Refuges and the Five Precepts of Theravada Buddhism which involves the promise to dedicate oneself to the Buddha, the sangha and the dhamma. Through this act they endeared themselves to the Buddhists of the country by becoming the first persons of European and American extraction to publicly embrace Buddhism.[52]

Most previous American business undertakings in Sri Lanka had emerged from relations with India. The rigid trade monopoly imposed by the East India Company imposed many difficulties on American privateers until about 1811, but there was a thriving business between India, Sri Lanka and what was described as the 'Far East' which involved smuggling spices, opium, sugar, hemp, indigo and textiles. Ice was exported from Boston in New England, then the centre of American maritime trade, to the port cities of Colombo and Galle. The ice trade was initiated by Frederic Tudor, a scion of a well-to-do Boston family, in 1806.[53] The nearby lakes supplied the required amount of ice. Between 1834 and 1880 the Indian ice trade thrived as a joint venture. Frederic Tudor became known as the ice king and 'the first person in the post-Revolutionary United States to amass a million-dollar fortune'.[54] Calcutta constituted Tudor's principal market, followed by the presidency towns of Bombay and Madras where ice houses were built for storage. The East India Company provided special exemptions to Tudor's company such as allowing discharge of ice at night and exemption of sawdust accompanying the ice from import duty. The consumers were essentially the British residents of India and later a few natives: they used the ice for medical and essentially nonmedical purposes such as chilling their alcoholic drinks and preserving perishable foods. From the 1880s onwards the introduction of artificial ice manufacture in India compounded by other factors such as changes in global maritime transport economics and natural environmental change in New England led to a decline of the Indian ice trade.[55]

In the 1890s, the United States imported from Sri Lanka items such as coconut, pearls and precious stones, plumbago, seed and plants, whisky, talc, tea, coffee and copra and exported to the island a variety of items such as salted beef and pork, casks, earthenware, glass and glassware, tinware, kerosene, medicine and citronella. In 1915 kerosene was the most important export from the United States.

In 1926 U.S. imports to Sri Lanka were larger than Australia's and only a little smaller than British India.[56] If the Singer sewing machine and the Ansonia and Seth Thomas clocks were the most famous American imports to Sri Lanka, graphite or plumbago was the most significant export.[57] Sri Lankan graphite was used in the American Civil War, and later for lead pencils. In 1903 the United States was the largest importer of plumbago with Britain as second until 1903, when Germany took second place and an American firm in Sri Lanka was the principal agent for 'Ceylon graphite'.[58] In 1922, 80 per cent of Sri Lankan graphite was imported by America.[59]

For the ordinary people, who cared little for export figures, America was a country of the present embodied in the metallic sewing machines that had conquered every nook and corner of the country and as an imprint on the kerosene containers they cannibalized. For them emulating America made it possible to 'be with the times' without being a colonial subject.

Olcott was convinced that Sri Lanka's Buddhists knew nothing about 'real Buddhism' and this led him to compose *A Buddhist Catechism,* which appeared in both English and Sinhalese on 24 July 1881. He obtained the sanction of Hikkaduwe Sumangala before publishing it. The book became hugely popular in the island. On his third tour, Olcott appears to have developed healing powers which popularized his message well beyond the Sinhalese middle classes. Correspondence between the governor of Ceylon, James Longden, and Colonial Secretary Lord Kimberley mention rumours circulating among Buddhists of the arrival of a messianic figure who will help overthrow British rule. Although Olcott is not mentioned in the reports, reference is made to a King of Righteousness hailing from India and linked to the Buddhist revival, which point towards Olcott.[60]

There was in a sense an imagined America, a land of technically advanced people who were immensely supportive of Buddhism and ready to adopt the ways of the dhamma. This perception came from the publicity given in the local papers to the 1893 World Council of Religions in Chicago[61] and to often exaggerated accounts of the success Anagarika Dharmapala had encountered in convincing Americans of the importance of Buddhist preachings. Readers of the *Maha Bodhi* and *Sinhala Bauddhaya* in Sri Lanka especially were familiar with the personas of the theosophists Olcott and Blavatsky. The letter they had written offering to help the Buddhists of Ceylon had been translated into Sinhala and widely circulated. There were also regular accounts of Buddhism in America where the impression given to the reader was of a country about to be converted to Buddhism through its contacts with Buddhist countries and visiting clerics.[62] Apart from Olcott, other American nationals promoted Buddhism in Sri Lanka: Mary Musaeus Higgins, the German widow of an American officer, was instrumental in founding in 1895 a modern Buddhist school for girls in Colombo; the less well-known Mary de Souza Canavarro converted to Buddhism in a ceremony in New York with Dharmapala officiating and spent three years in Sri Lanka running an orphanage, a school for girls and a Buddhist convent.[63] In short through the repeated accounts of Americans converting to Buddhism and the actual largesse of American philanthropists towards Buddhist schools and orphanages, America acquired in the public eye an aura that no other non-Asian country had at that period.

CONCLUSION

This chapter has shown that nonelite groups were connected to other parts of the world through various ties. In the nineteenth century many felt they belonged to a Buddhist world that extended far beyond the boundaries of their island from Siam to America and included only parts of India in it fold. The capacity to dream of a modern future for Sri Lanka outside colonial models was made possible by the presence of this parallel world. A Buddhist modern imaginary was strangely fashioned by an American connection where Buddhism, materiality and modernity were embodied in an individual – the theosophist Colonel Olcott – who symbolized the islanders' gradual acceptance of practices and machines anchored in the modern world. Among these, the gramophone stood out as a machine that combined a metallic modern exterior with a religious sensibility.

NOTES

1. R.M. Jaffe. 2004. 'Seeking Sakyammuni: Travel and the Reconstruction of Japanese Buddhism', *Journal of Japanese Studies* 30(1), 67.
2. P. Duara. 2001.'The Discourse of Civilization and Pan-Asianism,' *Journal of World History* 12(1), 114
3. S.J. Tambiah. *World Conqueror World Renouncer: A Study of Buddhism and Polity in Thailand against a Historical Background,* Cambridge: Cambridge University Press, 80; M. Peleggi. 2002. *Lords of Things: The Fashioning of the Siamese Monarchy's Modern Image,* Honolulu: University of Hawaii Press, 37.
4. Tambiah, *World Conqueror World Renouncer,* 353.
5. G.D. Bond. 1998. *The Buddhist Revival in Sri Lanka: Religious Tradition, Reinterpretation and Response,* Columbia: University of South Carolina Press; and Malalgoda, *Buddhism in Sinhalese Society.*
6. Tambiah, *World Conqueror World Renouncer,* 217.
7. Prince Dhaninivat. 1965. 'Religious Intercourse between Ceylon and Siam. In the Bangkok Period of Siamese History,' in N.A. Jayawickrama (ed.), *Paranavitana Felicitation Volume on Art and Architecture,* Colombo, 137.
8. Ibid.
9. Ibid., 139.
10. Ibid.
11. S. Collins. 2003. 'What Is Literature in Pali', in S. Pollock (ed.), *Literary Cultures in History: Reconstructions from South Asia,* Berkeley: University of California Press, 649–88.
12. Ven. Phra Anil Sakya. 2008. 'King Mongkut's Buddhist Reforms: The Dhammayut Nikaya and a Pali Script', paper presented at the 10th International Conference on Thai Studies, 9–11 January, Thammasat University, Bangkok, Thailand, http://www.learners.in.th/file/asakya/King%20Mongkut%20and%20Pali%20Script.pdf.
13. Vajiranyanavarorasa, Prince Patriarch. 2003. *History of Wat Bovoranives Vihara,* Bangkok: Karn Sasana Press, 16, cited in Ven. Phra Anil Sakya, 'King Mongkut's Buddhist Reforms'.
14. T. Phanit. 2001. *Kalyannamitr: Religious and Cultural Ties between Sri Lanka and Thailand,* Bangkok: Amarin Printing and Publishing Public Company Limited, 54, cited in Ven. Phra Anil Sakya, 'King Mongkut's Buddhist Reforms'.
15. Malalgoda, *Buddhism in Sinhalese Society,* 165.
16. See de Silva, *A History of Ceylon,* 300–306.
17. Tambiah, *World Conqueror and World Renouncer,* 96.
18. A. Blackburn. 2010. *Locations of Buddhism. Colonialism and Modernity in Sri Lanka,* Chicago and London: University of Chicago Press, 153.
19. Peleggi, *Lords of Things,* 38–39.
20. Blackburn, *Locations of Buddhism,* 143.
21. *Lakmini Pahana,* 28 July 1900.
22. J. Duncan. 1990. *The City as Text: The Politics of Landscape Interpretation in the Kandyan Kingdom,* Cambridge: Cambridge University Press, 113.

23. See H.L. Seneviratne. 1978. *Rituals of the Kandyan State,* Cambridge: Cambridge University Press.
24. Blackburn, *Locations of Buddhism,* 186–96.
25. Peleggi, *Lords of Things,* 39.
26. W. Geiger (trans.). 1950. *The Mahavamsa,* Colombo: Ceylon Government Information Department.
27. J. Davy. 1983[1817]. *An Account of the Interior of Ceylon,* Dehiwela: Tisara Press; A. Bertolacci. 1983[1817]. *A View of the Agricultural, Commercial and Financial Interests of Ceylon,* Dehiwela: Tisara Press.
28. Anagarika [homeless] Dharmapala was the most celebrated preacher and reformer of the period. He was the son of a furniture dealer who attended a Roman Catholic school, then an Anglican school. He worked as a clerk in the Education Department. Following Colonel Olcott's visit to the island in 1880 he became active in the Theosophical Society for almost twenty years. He established the Maha Bodhi Society as the institutional vehicle to restore the Buddhagaya site (where the Buddha was enlightened) and its holy ruins to Buddhist hands. He emerged as a fierce critic of Christian beliefs and a leading agitator for Buddhist revival.
29. The cross-fertilisation of ideas and practices between indigenous Asian constructions of Buddhism were often defined against Christian missionary religious discourses and European understandings of Buddhism. The result was a form of Buddhism which in Sri Lanka has been described as Protestant Buddhism. The nineteenth-century Buddhist revival movement in Sri Lanka is examined in detail in several works including Bond, *Buddhist Revival in Sri Lanka*; R.F. Gombrich and G. Obeysekere. 1988. *Buddhism Transformed: Religious Change in Sri Lanka,* Princeton: Princeton University Press; Malalgoda, *Buddhism in Sinhalese Society.* Anne Blackburn has questioned the characterization of the movement as 'Protestant Buddhism' which tends to portray the shifts in Sri Lankan Buddhism as simply a response to the West and fails to take into account reformist trajectories well under way prior to the nineteenth century. See A.M. Blackburn. 2001. *Buddhist Learning and Textual Practice in Eighteenth Century Lankan Monastic Culture,* Princeton: Princeton University Press.
30. On Buddhagaya see T.G. Thakurta. 2004. *Monuments, Objects, Histories: Institutions of Art in Colonial and Postcolonial India,* New York: Columbia University Press, 268–372.
31. A. Dharmapala. 1965. 'Buddha-gaya: The Holiest Buddhist Shrine', in A. Guruge, *Return to Righteousness. A Collection of Speeches, Essays and Letters of the Anagarika Dharmapala,* Colombo: Ministry of Educational Cultural Affairs, 615–26.
32. Malalgoda, *Buddhism in Sinhalese Society,* 255.
33. M. Wickramasinghe, *Upandasita,* Dehiwela: Tisara Press, 41.
34. *Ceylon National Review* 2(4), July 1907.
35. *Ceylon National Review* 1(2), July 1907.
36. *Ceylon National Review* 1(1), January 1906.
37. R. Bharucha. 2006. *Another Asia. Rabindranath Tagore and Okakura Tenshin,* New Delhi: Oxford University Press.

38. *Ceylon Independent,* 12 October 1922.
39. S.K. Das (ed.). 1996. *The English Writings of Rabindranath Tagore,* vol. 3, *To My Ceylon Audience,* New Delhi: Sahitya Akademi, 760.
40. Ibid., 761.
41. Cited in K.N.O. Dharmadasa. 1992. *The Growth of Sinhalese Nationalism in Sri Lanka,* Ann Arbor: University of Michigan Press, 120.
42. Ibid., 262–86.
43. D. Hellman-Rajanayagam, *The Tamil Tigers: Armed Struggle for Identity,* Stuttgart: Franz Steiner Verlag, 128; K. Kailasapathy. 1984. 'Cultural and Linguistic Consciousness of the Tamil Community,' in Social Scientists Association (SSA), *Ethnicity and Social Change in Sri Lanka,* Colombo: SSA, 107–20.
44. Wickramasinghe, *Sri Lanka in the Modern Age,* 256.
45. Nathan Mss 619, Special Circulation No. 291, Memorandum from Ceylonese Workmen.
46. Sessional Papers III, 1938, Report of a Commission on Immigration to Ceylon, 59–60.
47. *Dinakara Prakashaya,* February 1907.
48. S. Prothero. 1996. *The White Buddhist: The Asian Odyssey of Henry Steel Olcott,* Bloomington and Indianapolis: Indiana University Press.
49. Department of Commerce, British India, by Henry D. Baker, 614.
50. See Malalgoda, *Buddhism in Sinhalese Society,* 58–69.
51. See Blackburn, *Buddhist Learning and Textual Practice,* for a recent critique of concepts such as 'Protestant Buddhism' and Buddhist modernism.
52. Prothero, *The White Buddhist,* 95.
53. D.G. Dickson. 1991. 'The Nineteenth Century Indo-American Ice Trade: An Hyperborean Epic', *Modern Asian Studies* 25(1), 53–89.
54. Ibid., 63.
55. Ibid., 56.
56. *Ferguson's Directory,* 1926, 358–59.
57. C. Pursell. 1995. *The Machine in America. A Social History of Technology,* Baltimore: Johns Hopkins University Press, 184. The American mass-produced clock was made originally out of wood but, subject to warping, was not sold overseas. Once it was made of metal, it became cheap and met no competition.
58. Commerce Reports, U.S. Bureau of Manufactures, Bureau of Foreign and Domestic Commerce, published by Bureau of Foreign and Domestic Commerce, U.S. Department of Commerce, 1912, 1302–303.
59. T.E. Thorpe. 1922. *A Dictionary of Applied Chemistry,* London: Longmans, Green and Co.
60. Ibid., 109–10.
61. In 1893 the city of Chicago hosted the World's Parliament of Religions in the wake of the World's Columbian Exposition. It brought together representatives of Eastern and Western spiritual traditions and opened with Swami Vivekenanda's celebrated speech on Hinduism.
62 *Sarasavi Sanderesa,* 29 August 1905.
63. Tweed, *American Encounter with Buddhism,* 56–57.

Chapter 4

The Gramophone

Soulful Sounds and Sacred Speeches

The gramophone, a black machine with a fantastically shaped horn, brought to life via small black circular disks acoustic effects of the real in the shape of sound waves. Unlike in the written text, there was no symbolic mediation. Time (through the medium of sound) was captured, frozen, stored and released in a near-miraculous fashion for its first users. In colonial Sri Lanka it was not only practices and ideas of listening, performing and music that changed in conjunction with new technologies of recording and playback but religious practices too as the use of gramophone for preaching by lay peoples and monks accelerated the evolution from personalized forms of worship to communal ways of being Buddhist (Figure 11).

In 1877 Thomas Alva Edison succeeded in reproducing sound with a machine he invented and called the phonograph. Others perfected his machine, in particular a Hanover-born American immigrant, Emile Berliner, who devised a way of etching the sound onto a flat disk which reproduced sound better than Edison's cylinder. The turntable that played the disk was named a gramophone through a canny play on sounds, by inverting Edison's 'phonogram'.[1]

The gramophone was the main technological innovation for the reproduction of European and indigenous music in the colony of Ceylon/Sri Lanka. It reached the island in 1900 a few years after its invention, and from 1903 records were available in Sinhala.[2] Gramophones came to be known as 'Morning Glories': their horns were made of glittering brass and came in various colours.[3] They were often constructed with parts imported from Europe and local wood more suitable to the vagaries of a tropical climate.[4]

Figure 11. Gramophone and records. Historical Mansion Museum, Galle Fort (Author's collection)

The situation in Sri Lanka was quite unlike that in Indonesia, where the introduction of the gramophone started with public exhibitions in theatres or clubs or shows where people had to pay to see the marvellous talking machine.[5] There are only a few records of pioneer exhibitors and local promoters. Adolphus W. Andree, a local photographer who moved into the new technology of film projections as early as 1901, is credited with introducing the gramophone to audiences of the Public Hall, a space in the heart of the city which offered until 1898 a diversity of pre-cinematographical spectacles.[6] It was perhaps felt by exhibitors who toured Asia with their talking machines that in this predominantly Theravada Buddhist society where congregational practices or participation in community life were not the norm, the lure of recorded songs would not be powerful enough to attract crowds. Or it could be that the gramophone was no longer a novelty since by 1898 other talking machines such as Edison's phonographs and grapho-phones had been advertised in the local press as accomplishing the same miracles as the gramophone would claim to a few years later: 'These machines will talk and sing in any language'[7] (Figure 12).

Indeed in 1892 an English educator and showman, Douglas Archibald, had exhibited the Edison Improved Phonograph around the world in Australia, New Zealand, Burma, India and Sri Lanka before sailing to Singapore and Java. Archibald was an Oxford graduate, the son of a judge, who after a few years spent in Bengal teaching in Patna College had returned home to work as the principal of a private school at Tunbridge Wells. His

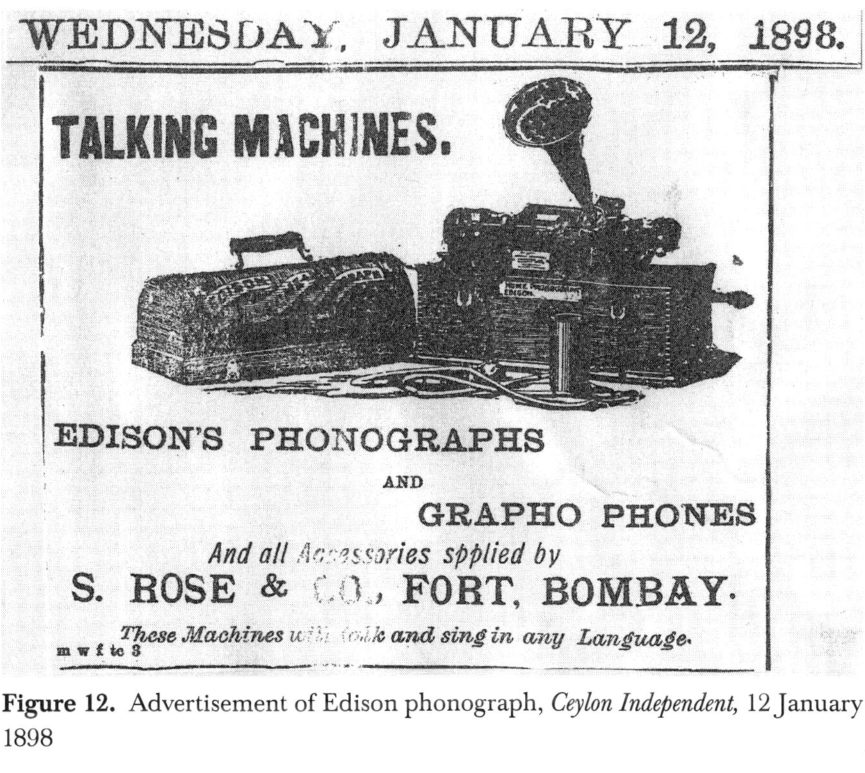

Figure 12. Advertisement of Edison phonograph, *Ceylon Independent,* 12 January 1898

exhibition was advertised in promotional newspaper items before its arrival in Singapore with the title 'Voices from the Grave' and was composed of orations taken in England, America, New Zealand and Australia from 'the men of the time' including the Hon. W.E. Gladstone and the bishop of Colombo. Edison had indeed sent representatives to all parts of the world to immortalize the voices of the famous on wax: apart from Prime Minister Gladstone he had recordings of poets such as Tennyson and Browning and even Bismarck and Emperor Wilhem II.[8] Band records such as of the Salvation Army as well as instrumental music performed in Europe and America would be heard. The only concession to indigenous peoples was the inclusion of Maori recordings.[9] The targeted audience was clearly Europeans and Westernized members of the local bourgeoisies. In Singapore he gave four phonograph exhibitions which were attended by the white ruling class and were reported in the newspapers as having elicited enthusiastic responses on their part.[10]

Two years later in 1900 General Oliver, a Boer prisoner of war in a camp in Sri Lanka, is recorded to have gone to hear a phonograph when out on parole in Colombo and heard the recording of Mr Gladstone's message to Edison. This led to 'mingled feelings in the breasts of its hearers and the exclamation that he was their friend'.[11]

The gramophone was probably imported by affluent persons from the local bourgeoisie who after visiting Europe returned home with new markers of distinction. But the arrival of gramophones on a commercial scale in South Asia is closely linked to the first record pressing factory at Hanover, Germany. Its owner Emile Berliner had invented the flat disk and became the partner of Eldrige Johnson, a brilliant designer of a 'clockspring' motor which put an end to records turned by hand. In 1901 Johnson and Berliner pooled their resources and formed the Victor Talking Machine Company. Discs were initially made out of zinc and recordings done through a system of 'zinc etching', but once recording on wax was invented in 1901 it was possible to copy records more quickly and in larger quantities. They began to supply records and machines to a London-based company established in 1898 called the Gramophone Co. Ltd which had the exclusive access in Britain to Berliner's manufacturing patents. In an agreement of a sort, the world market was shared between these two giant companies.

In 1902 a young American called T.W. Gainsberg representing the Gramophone Company left for India to explore possibilities of gramophone trade and made the first recordings of Indian singers. By spring 1903 the 1,700 discs he had recorded were sent back to Europe to be processed and then shipped back as records to local agents.[12] The Gramophone Company enjoyed a complete monopoly in India using local dealers to personally invest in the record market. By the beginning of the twentieth century the world record market was divided between half a dozen record companies that manufactured equipment, made recordings and were involved in the marketing worldwide.

The only challenge came in the mid-1920s when cheap Japanese machines entered the Indian market. The Victor Talking Machine Company had set up operations in Tokyo and Yokohama to handle the Japan and China market.

There are few sources beyond promotional material from the early history of the gramophone in Sri Lanka. It would have arrived in the island as in other locations as a wonderful, magic talking machine alongside other such machines: typewriters, bicycles, harmoniums, pianos and sewing machines. The spread of gramophones in Sri Lanka was closely linked to the arrival in India of entrepreneurs from Europe representing the major international gramophone companies: Columbia, Pathé-Frères, Odeon and the Gramophone Company.[13] But unlike in India where the Gramophone Company soon dominated the market, in Sri Lanka the market was shared with the Talking Machine Co. of Ceylon – housed at No. 8 Victoria Arcade, Colombo – which administered the distribution and sales for Southern India from its sub-branch[14] (Figure 13). In the late 1920s the Odeon Talking Machine Company was also advertising in Sinhala papers.[15]

The records that were sold in Ceylon in the first decade of the twentieth century were manufactured at the factory at Sealdah in Calcutta. The matrices, shells and galvanoes of the Ceylonese repertoire were shipped from the Deutsch Gramophone record pressing factory as early as in 1907. Some continued to be manufactured in the factory in Hanover and bore the stamp 'Made in Germany'. The Gramophone Company advertisement touched upon the nationalist spirit of the day by claiming that 'Our Indian, Burmese and Ceylonese records are now made at our Calcutta factory using Indian materials by Indian workmen.'[16] Between 1900 and 1910 the Gramophone Company made 44 recordings in Ceylon, a fairly modest amount compared to 4,000 in India, 93 in Java, 97 in Thailand and 121 in Malaya. The abbreviation 'HMV' for 'His Master's Voice' became synonymous with the Gramophone Company from 1924[17] (Figure 14). Ceylon was dealt with in the same manner as other linguistic regions of India, for which special recordings were soon envisaged. By the 1920s recordings in 'Assamese, Bengali, Chattisgarhi, Garkwali, Gujarati, Hindi, Kanarese, Konkani, Kumauni, Malayalam, Marathi, Multani (Lahnda), Pashto, Punjabi, Oriya, Sindhi, Sinhalese, Tamil, Telugu and Urdu' had been made.[18]

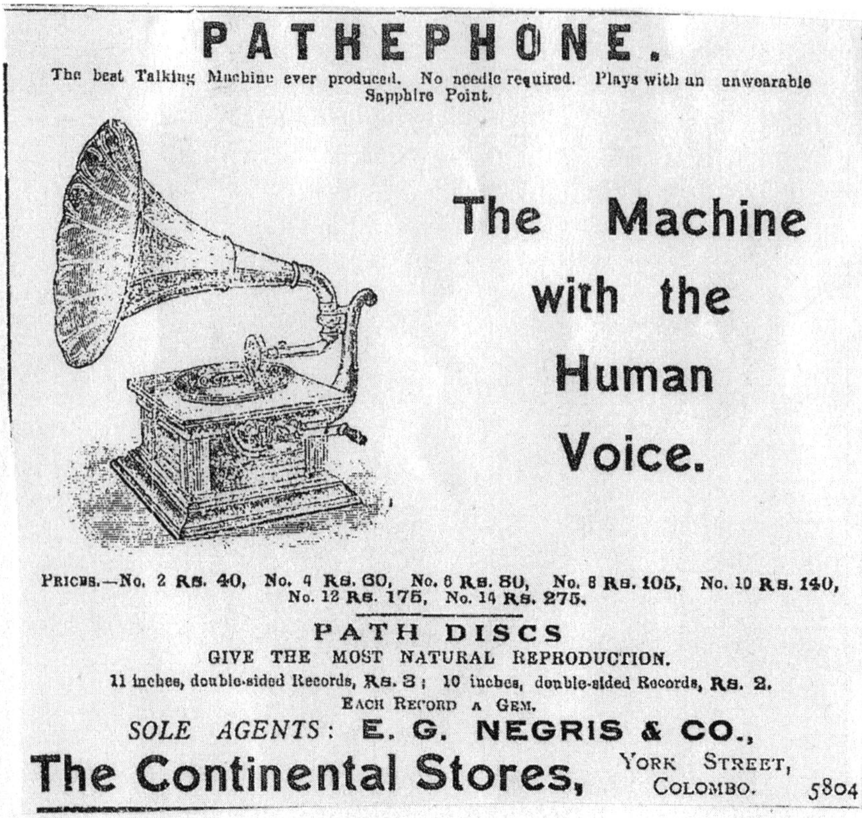

Figure 13. Advertisement of Pathephone, *Times of Ceylon,* 8 March 1912

One cannot completely believe Denham's somewhat exaggerated claim that the gramophone had taken the place of the *rabana* or tambourine. Clearly the gramophone market had extended by the first decade of the twentieth century to the middle classes in cities and villages which included salaried civil servants and newly affluent businessmen. The accessible price of a gramophone testifies to its wide diffusion: at the inception of its production in 1900 the gramophone cost Rs 80; ten years later its price had dropped dramatically as the cheapest machine could cost Rs 10 while an average one varied between Rs 40 to Rs 60 in 1911. Companies such as Talking Machine sold four hundred different sets of records in Sinhalese and Tamil.[19]

H.W. Cave was the main agent for gramophones from 1901 onwards and offered machines on easy payment schemes as well as for hire. A gramophone with a metal trumpet, 200 needles and 6 records could be bought for Rs 100 in cash or with a down payment of Rs 30 followed by six monthly

Figure 14. Gramophone record. Historical Mansion Museum, Galle Fort (Author's collection)

payments of Rs 15. With the gramophone the customer could buy a brass trumpet, a silver-plated trumpet, and teak cases.[20]

There is little information on the records sold for the Sri Lankan market but in the same period a public of Europeans and Europeanised Indians in South India was listening to recordings of 'opera, comic songs, military band music, marches, waltzes, classical and church music'.[21] H.W. Cave boasted a selection of a thousand records, each costing Rs 2 or a dozen for Rs 20. The Odeon Company advertisement mentioned records available in English, Sinhala, Tamil, Hindustani, Arabic and other languages.[22] Catalogues of early recordings between 1908 and 1916 indicate records of an N. Silva, a Niyaman Natarajah in the register of leisure songs and selections from Buddhist texts in Pali by a certain John Perera.[23]

The first Sinhala records were stage songs that belonged to the repertoire of the *Nurthi* theatre. The advent of Nurthi, a form that developed with north Indian influence, particularly the Parsi theatre, brought to the stage a more modernistic blend that was rapidly domesticated to cater to local tastes. Visvanath Lowji, a composer from Bombay, collaborated with John de Silva, a playwright, to produce some of the most popular tunes. These songs were then recorded and their popularity added to that of the theatre.

Playwrights such as C. Don Bastian, the first Nurthi writer, as well as John De Silva and Charles Dias infused a sense of patriotism through their creations that tapped into historical and popular epics.[24]

By 1880 a number of temporary sheds thatched with zinc sheets had sprung up all over Colombo city for the purpose of staging plays to entertain the growing population of Colombo. Although these temporary sheds were given names such as Pavillion Theatre, Public Hall, and Saraswathie Hall, the Tower Hall was the first true theatre to be built in Sri Lanka. It was constructed by an entrepreneur from Maradana known as G.D. Hendrick Seneviratne. Since the clock tower opposite was built to represent the Tower of London, the theatre took the name of Tower Hall Theatre. It was ceremoniously inaugurated on 6 December 1911 by Anagarika Dharmapala and the following day the play *Pandhukabaya* by Charles Dias was staged with Sir Henry McCallum, the governor general, as the chief guest.[25]

The arrival of recording agents and recording machines led to a completely new experience of sound and music among peoples of Sri Lanka. Sound was no longer an ephemeral phenomenon but an object that could be analysed, read and judged and used for multiple purposes from the commercial to the experimental. Notions of what constituted the real and the illusory had to be redefined when confronted with this new kind of real.[26]

The relationship to music also changed. For those who belonged to affluent groups it meant for the first time listening to music or other types of recordings in the home, no longer as a public performance. The first buyers and users were members of the colonial bourgeoisie seeking visible accoutrements to showcase their distinction and wealth. It was an essentially urbanized and multiethnic group whose taste would have varied according to language, religion and degree of Westernization.[27] The regularity of gramophone and record advertisements in local newspapers during the early twentieth century testifies to the limited spread of the machine among individuals for personal use.

The gramophone did not become a household object as the sewing machine did in the twentieth century but was adopted in conjunction with other media for communal purposes. It became a social and political machine that reached out not to the average music lover in his home but to the ordinary people in the form of popular theatres and performance. The *bana* (preachings) of Buddhist priests could now be heard in remote interior villages and people assembled around a common gramophone to listen to plays of a religious, historical or satirical nature. The plays of John de Silva, especially the *Sinhala Parabhawa Natakaya* (*The Degeneration of the Great Sinhalese: A Drama*); translations of epic poems such as the Ramayana; and selections from *Hamlet, Othello* and *Romeo and Juliet* were in demand.[28] After the establishment of Radio Ceylon more people were reached but until the 1940s the radio mainly catered to the Western anglicised market. This left room for the itinerant gramophone operator to perform before a vernacular-speaking audience during the 1920s and 1930s.

The gramophone was used by Anagarika Dharmapala together with a magic lantern to reach out to Sinhalese peoples in rural areas:

> On the 29th of July the Anagarika left Colombo on a preaching tour … He travels in a cart drawn by a pair of bulls, which is useful in manifold ways. He arrives at a certain village in the morning, and if there is a temple in the village he sends out bills announcing the lecture, which usually begins at 9 P.M. He carries with him a magic lantern and a gramophone. The former he uses to exhibit views of the sacred places in India, Burma, Ceylon and Japan. He expounds the Doctrine of Buddha, talks about his travels in Europe, America, India, Japan and Burma and ends by an appeal which stirs the hearts of the audience for greater activity. At midnight the programme ends and he goes to sleep in the cart at one o'clock in the morning. He charges nothing for his lectures, pays all his expenses form the inheritance which he has received from his late lamented father, Mudilyar Hewavitarana, and distributes tracts supplied gratis by the Maha-Bodhi Society. Hundreds of women, men and children come to hear him night after night and they go away pleased.[29]

Beyond the content of the programme Dharmapala's journeys show the openness of people to new technologies that had broken the monopoly of writing for the diffusion of knowledge. It was a new experience of time where 'real time' made of the contingent, chaotic and singular was stored and processed.

A decade later Rev. H.J. Saranankara, who was the incumbent monk at the Isurumuniya Temple in Anuradhapura, made use of the gramophone for his preachings in a modernized temple that foreign observer G.E. Mitton found offensive to the eye:

> A hideous brick structure, used as a preaching hall, is completed by protruding iron girders, and furnished with a gramophone; this stands not far from the rock-cut recumbent statue of the Buddha, in weird contrast which does not in any way seem to jar on the devotees.[30]

As the sewing machine had entered the home of the local people without creating ripples, so the gramophone was unproblematically used as an instrument of propagation of Buddhism by lay preachers and bhikkus. It was only in certain elite circles that it posed problems, more for esthetical than for political or cultural reasons. Art critic Ananda Coomaraswamy was, for instance, a virulent opponent, viewing the gramophone as a sad substitute for the human voice and instruments. He saw the same relation between mechanism and art as between gramophone and music and described the sound of the gramophone as 'refinement of torture'.[31]

But in colonial Sri Lanka, the gramophone was promoted as a technological marvel that had the ability to mechanically reproduce musical and spoken sounds and which liberated and abstracted sound from the specific time and space of its live performance. For a few households the gramophone brought the world inside the home, and European music acquired a familiarity for the Sinhalese. For most others the gramophone became the appendage of a resolutely modern mode of being Buddhist.

NOTES

1. G. Jones. 1985. 'The Gramophone Company: An Anglo-American Multinational, 1898–1931', *Business History Review* 59(1), 76–100.
2. Advertisements for gramophones suggest that these machines were being sold in 1900; see *Ceylon Independent,* 23 July 1900; S. Broughton, M. Ellingham and R. Trillo. 2000. *World Music: The Rough Guide,* vol. 2, London: Rough Guides, 231, date the arrival of the gramophone in Sri Lanka to a year later in 1901.
3. G.N. Joshi. 1988. 'A Concise History of the Phonograph Industry in India', *Popular Music* 7(2), *The South Asia/West Crossover,* 148.
4. T.S. Beng. 1996/1997. 'The 78 RPM Record Industry in Malaya prior to World War II', *Asian Music* 28(1), 11–41.
5. S. Suryadi. 2006. 'The Talking Machine Comes to the Dutch East Indies. The Arrival of Western Media Technology in South East Asia', *Bijdragen tot de Taal-, Land- en Volkenkunde (BKI)* 162(2/3), 270.
6. Tampoe-Hautin, 'Cinéma, Colonialisme et Identité', 85.
7. *Ceylon Independent,* 12 January 1898, 2.
8. F.A. Kittler. 1999. *Gramophone, Film, Typewriter,* Stanford: Stanford University Press, 78.
9. *Strait Times,* 1 May 1892, 5.
10. For a detailed account of the Singapore exhibitions see Suryadi, 'The Talking Machine', 274–76.
11. *Straits Times,* 9 November 1900, 3.
12. P. Gronow. 1981. 'The Record Industry Comes to the Orient', *Ethnomusicology* 25(2), 251.
13. S.P. Hughes. 2002. '"The Music Boom" in Tamil South India: Gramophone, Radio and the Making of Mass Culture', *Historical Journal of Film, Radio and Television* 22(4), 445–73.
14. M.S. Kinnear. 1994. *The Gramophone Company's First Indian Recordings 1899–1908,* Bombay: Popular Prakashan, 52.
15. *Sinhala Bauddhaya,* 31 October 1927.
16. Ibid., 30.

17. P. Gronow, 'The Record Industry', 255.
18. Ibid., 257.
19. Denham, *Ceylon at the Census,* 173.
20. *Ceylon Independent,* 22 April 1901.
21. Hughes, '"The Music Boom" in Tamil South India', 446.
22. *Sinhala Bauddhaya,* 31 October 1927.
23. Kinnear, *The Gramophone Company's First Indian Recordings,* 166, 174.
24. N. de Mel. 2001. *Women and the Nation's Narrative. Gender and Nationalism in Twentieth Century Sri Lanka,* Colombo: Social Scientists Association, 65; Broughton, Ellingham and Trillo, *World Music,* 231.
25. De Mel, *Women and the Nation's Narrative,* 66.
26. See C.A. Lin. 2012. '"The Modern Magic Carpet": Wireless Radio in Interwar Colonial Singapore', *Modern Asian Studies* 46(1), 190. The author shows similar 'cognitive shifts in understanding the world in terms of time, space, science and magic' that came about with the spread of the wireless radio in Singapore as with the gramophone in Sri Lanka.
27. See K. Jayawardena. 2000. *From Nobodies to Somebodies, The Rise of the Colonial Bourgeoisie in Sri Lanka,* Colombo: Social Scientists' Association and Sanjiva Books.
28. Denham, *Ceylon at the Census,* 173.
29. Cited in M.R. Frost. in press. 'Empires of Belief: Print, Politics and Religion in the Indian Ocean World, 1860–1920'. The same tour and use of a magic lantern to show international Buddhist shrines is reported in *Sinhala Bauddhaya,* 15 September 1906.
30. G.E. Mitton. 1917. *The Lost Cities of Ceylon,* New York: FA Stokes Co., 120–21.
31. A. Coomaraswamy. 1981 (1909). 'Gramophones and Why Not', in *Essays in National Idealism,* New Delhi: Munshiram Manoharlal Publishers, 210–11.

Chapter 5

An Asian Modern

Japan

With the introduction of Buddhism into Japan in the 7th century of the Christian era, Japan became Aryanized.

– An Appeal to Japanese Buddhists by A. Dharmapala, *The Young East,* Nov. 1927, 3(6), 192

When writing about the East Asian modern, Prasenjit Duara sought to highlight the idea of the modern as a set of temporal practices and discourses instituted by modernizers embedded in Sino-Japanese interactions. He posited the modern as a hegemonic project among other temporal practices, rather than a preconstituted period or given condition,[1] reminding us that modernizers, nationalists and anticolonialists are not always interchangeable categories. This chapter is less about charting a physical presence of Japan in Sri Lanka or about measuring links or actual circulation between these two countries within the framework of a new transnational moment than about exploring the place Japan occupied both as a trope and as an imaginary in the everyday entry of Sri Lanka into the modern. Understanding Sri Lanka's modern means first of all moving away from a temporal focus which signals the Colebrooke-Cameron Reforms of 1833 as the crucial turning point and looking at the more diffuse experience of ordinary people in Sri Lanka who lived modernity as a shattering but gradual transformation of their material world. What is often overlooked is that in people's perception of the new, of the changing times in which they lived, Japan acted as the antithesis of Britain and a potent source of moral authority. As an Asian and seemingly noncolonial rising power it played a salient role in providing an alternative template for modernizers and people eager to ride the waves of modern times.

By the early twentieth century Japan had acquired a material and spiritual presence in Sri Lanka. It was present spatially: the Colombo headquarters of the main Buddhist association of the country, the Maha Bodhi Society,[2] housed, apart from a free reading room and library, an industrial museum of Japanese goods. Japan was also present in the guise of its people, lay and religious, who began to visit Sri Lanka in great numbers. The *Sarasavi Sanderasa* mentions visits by Japanese people such as the tour of the island by a businessman to investigate agriculture.[3] In 1905 the visit to the island of Prince Arisugawa Takehito and his wife on their return from a European tour created much excitement among local Buddhists. But beyond individuals, these feelings of being connected to Japan were rooted in deeper relations that had gained momentum in the late nineteenth century and were related to the emergence of a 'tightly linked global Buddhist culture'[4] initially embracing Theravada Buddhist countries but later attempting to include Japan as well.

There was, however, a hiatus between Japanese Buddhisms of the Zen, Nichiren and Shingon sort and the practice of Buddhism in Sri Lanka and Southeast Asia.[5] The Sri Lankan monastic community had quite early realized that there was no real chance that the Japanese royalty or Buddhist clerical order would help unite Sri Lankan Buddhists through an imported ordination. Siam instead represented this part of the dream. Japan's aura stemmed less from a sense of a shared Eastern spiritual greatness than from its proven ability as the only Asiatic country in the late nineteenth and early twentieth centuries to have the power to challenge and disturb the imperial powers of the day. It represented the future. By the mid-nineteenth century Japan was a controller and exemplar of modernity. There were two areas where Japan's salience was particularly evident through the romanticisation, exoticisation and admiration of an alternative model of modernity: first Japan's ability to harness up-to-date Western-style rationality, industrialization and planning especially in war, and second its ability to preserve the imagined 'Eastern strengths' of Buddhist spirituality and morality.

THE OUTSIDE WORLD

Japan was not the only country that was present in people's imaginary. Advertisements, newspapers, foreign objects in shops were daily signs that there was a world outside the boundaries of the island. Literacy in the vernacular languages was an important factor that facilitated changes in worldviews although illiterate peoples too were able to consume images of goods that might have come to them by accident – as they still do – in shards and old newspapers used for packaging. Writing in 1927 an appeal to Japanese Buddhists, A. Dharmapala highlighted that technology ensured that distances were easily bridged and that Buddhists could easily cross oceans:

> Japan, China, Tibet, Mongolia, Korea, Siam, Burma, Ceylon, Arakan, Chittagong are Buddhist countries, and now that steam navigation and aeroplanes have made communication easy it is time for the Buddhists to work in mutual sympathy.[6]

Advertisements for foreign goods in the fledgling press were avidly read or looked at. A foreign man in a tuxedo smoking cigarettes would inspire a feeling of distance or envy while a Hindu goddess-like feminine figure on a calendar supplement holding a cake of soap was a familiar and friendly sight. Pictures were sometimes cut out and pasted on the walls of village boutiques. People were then more tempted to read news accounts relating to countries from where these products originated. One cannot imagine that new objects such as the gramophone and the sewing machine would have entered the homes of the people of Lanka if the social world of their users had not been slowly altered by the press of the day. The terrain for the acceptance of the foreign object in their home was prepared by a gradual awareness of the rest of the world.

Among the literate classes of the Sinhalese the awareness of the outside world increased from reading the foreign news section in the local newspapers. Other countries in the British Empire, especially South Africa, India and Burma as well as countries that were not connected to Sri Lanka through any obvious ties, figured prominently in local papers such as the *Lakmini Pahana*. In 1900, a Sinhalese reader could follow all the details of the war in South Africa that pitted Britain against the Boers. He would be familiar with the geographical spaces across the ocean through a constant reading of names such as Transvaal or acquainted with the makers of 'history' such as Kruger or Salisbury. He would also hear about the drought in India and railway construction in Russia. Another event that was well covered in those years was the Boxer Rebellion in China, known in the press as the Chinese War. On the whole, much of world news was related to military developments that involved Britain in one or another way. There was also some interest in trivia: the number of women in the postal service or the wealth of the Greek King.[7] The *Ceylon Observer* contained the latest telegraphic news by the Indo-European line, Singapore and Australian lines as well as from India. It was the first 'Indian journal on Reuters list' and had correspondents in different parts of the world.[8]

JAPAN: AMBIVALENCE TOWARDS WAR, IMPERIALISM

Japan was described in the local press in a different light at different times according to the closeness of its involvement in events that were central to world politics. The general tone employed by Sinhalese writers to write about Japan was, however, unapologetically and uncritically admirative. From the late nineteenth century Japan was represented without any ambiguity as the single Asian military power that was able to use the tools of the West, rationality, planning and industrialization, to overcome its late start and was successful in the path followed. In 1894–5 Japan, with an army equipped by and modelled on the Western powers, had indeed decisively won a war against the archaic forces of China and obtained a comfortable war immunity. The war was reported in Sri Lanka as having been provoked by a dispute over the control of Korea, a vassal state of China, and came to symbolize in the words of a Sinhalese journalist the 'degeneration and enfeeblement' of the Qing dynasty, a fact regularly stressed to contrast a surging Japan with a declining China. It was therefore no surprise that the spread of Japanese power or 'adhipatikama' over Northeast Asia was not interpreted as imperialism, expansionism or colonialism and the installation of a puppet regime in Korea was justified quite earnestly in these terms: 'The Korean emperor handed over the rule over his state peacefully to the Japanese Emperor.'[9] Japanese expansion beyond its national borders was explained as something beyond criticism, unstoppable and inevitable to Sinhalese readers.[10]

Japan's victory over Russia in 1905 made it even more the beacon for Asia and had a profound psychological impact among colonial subjects in Asia. The idea that Japan had a role to play in Asia, which would be to bring Asian people who had no nation-states or sense of collective belonging into the modern era, began to take hold within Japan itself as well as across Asia. As the British viceroy Lord Curzon painfully admitted, 'The reverberations of that victory have gone like a thunderclap through the whispering galleries of the East.'[11] The ascendance of Japan was the proof that a non-European power armed with modern technology could defeat a European power. This was a first rupture in the myth of invincibility of the West and the beginning of a new mind-set where Japan served as the model. A revolution erupted in Iran that put into power a constitutional government, and a few years later the Ottoman Empire was challenged by the Young Turks encouraged by Japan's success. Throughout Muslim Southeast Asia Japan emerged after the war as the 'light of Asia' suddenly materializing as a saviour from Dutch colonialism.[12] The Japanese victory had echoes among the Sinhala elite in a similar fashion. Furthermore the years 1904–5 were crucial years for the mobilization of Sinhalese Buddhists around potent symbols such as liquor, which they presented as a Western import that was contrary to the tenets of Buddhism.[13] More than an attempt to change popular habits, this temperance movement – which at its peak had six hundred local associations with perhaps two hundred thousand members – was for an emerging middle class a way of asserting their status and leadership while promoting a type of cultural identity. These associations or *samagams* supported by the Buddhist clergy were involved in promoting a variety of causes, for instance collecting funds to insure villagers against sickness.[14]

In 1905 Buddhist lay organizations in Sri Lanka collected funds to send to a Japanese Buddhist cleric to be disbursed to the ministry of war in Tokyo as a contribution to Japanese soldiers and sailors wounded in action. Through the text of the letters from Japan by grateful recipients which the newspapers reproduced seeped a clear feeling of solidarity.[15]

Apart from being powerful, the emperor was also shown to be capable of *karuna* (kindness) – a typically Buddhist quality. Had he not pardoned and sent home two French spies initially condemned to eight and ten years of incarceration?[16] At the Treaty of Portsmouth Japan received the southern half of the Island of Sakhalin from Russia and a monetary indemnity. This was less than what the Japanese public had been led to expect, since Japan's initial negotiating position had demanded all of Sakhalin. The Sinhalese press, however, saw in Japan's new position a sign of greatness and *karunava* as the emperor was believed to have agreed to the terms in order to avoid further casualties.[17] Sinhalese journalists were critical of the reporting by the conservative *Times of London* which clearly painted a bleak and false picture (*boruprasiddaya*) of Japan's involvement in Manchuria in order to boost British commercial ambitions to the detriment of Japan.[18] In this tussle Sinhalese readers were on the side of the Asian power.

In the years that followed the Japanese victory over Russia there was constant interest in and bewilderment at the growth of the Japanese naval industry, and the emergence of Japan as a contender to European naval powers was often hailed in exaggerated terms. An editorial predicted for example that by 1910 Japan would be the most powerful naval power worldwide.[19] Japan was seen as bringing pride to all 'Asians', an overarching identity which was increasingly appearing in the local press.[20]

Efforts were made by lay Buddhists in Sri Lanka to mobilize Sinhalese people around the 1905 visit of the Japanese prince and princess to the island upon their return trip to Japan from Europe. Prince Arisugawa

Takehito, although described in the Sinhala press as the heir to the Japanese throne, belonged to a cadet branch of the Japanese imperial family and was a celebrated career officer in the Imperial Japanese Navy. Prince Takehito was sent as a youth into the Buddhist priesthood, and assigned to serve at the *monzeki* temple of Myōhō-in in Kyoto. After the Meiji Restoration, he was recalled to secular life. The prince and his wife went to Europe in 1905 to represent Emperor Meiji at the wedding of German_Crown Prince Wilhelm. He visited Great Britain again on his way back to Japan. During that visit, King Edward VII granted Prince Arisugawa the Knight Grand Cross of the Most Honourable Order of the Bath. The Sinhala press compared the treatment and reception given to Prince Arisugawa by Europe with the lack of interest bestowed to him when he had stopped at Sri Lanka on his outward journey to Europe and visited the Kelaniya temple. An editorial pressed Sinhalese Buddhists to give him a warmer reception on his return journey.[21] Another letter highlighted the Buddhist credentials of the visitors and detailed the temples he was expected to visit. The standing of the prince as a great individual in Asia exemplified an increasingly regional sense of belonging among a section of the Sinhalese Buddhists.[22]

In the late nineteenth century Japan had come to be known through the steady stream of Japanese travellers to Sri Lanka, among whom the two clerics Shaku Kozen and Soen were the most famous. Shaku Kozen had travelled to Sri Lanka in 1886 to study Buddhist precepts and customs and spent seven years in South Asia. Soen travelled to Sri Lanka a year later to 'complete his Zen training, to study Sanskrit and Pali and to survey the state of Buddhism in Sri Lanka'.[23] Both studied under the learned Theravada monk Pannasekhara, a close associate of Hikkaduve Sumangala who had already forged many contacts with American theosophists as well as clerics from other Buddhist countries such as Burma and Thailand. Soen lived mainly in the southern port city of Galle. When he was ordained as a *samanera* (novice monk) there was, according to his own account, much celebration and festivities among the people who considered this an auspicious event. His diary describes a crowd of a thousand people 'who celebrated the event with fireworks and Western style Buddhist hymns'.[24] During his stay in Sri Lanka, Soen completed one of the earliest books on South Asian Buddhism, called *Seinan no Bukkyo* (The Buddhism of the Southwest), in which there were resonances of the thought of lay preacher Anagarika Dharmapala and theosophist Olcott's reform Buddhism, Western Orientalist scholarship and Sri Lankan monastic life.[25]

Kozen studied at Vidyodaya Pirivena, a new monastic training college in Colombo where Sumangala was the principal, and in 1890 was the first recorded Japanese to receive the full monk's Theravada ordination, upasampada. He appears to have been involved with leading monks who opposed Christian missionary activities in the country and in 1890 travelled to Madras as a Japanese representative at the Fifteenth Annual Convention of the Theosophical Society. Both Kozen and Soen attempted 'to save Buddhism in Asia through a renewed focus on Sakyamuni and the creation of a coalition uniting all Asian Buddhists in their effort to repel colonialism and Christianity in Asia'.[26]

While in the late nineteenth century leaders of Buddhist monastic orders had written to Japanese Buddhists to obtain patronage for the Siyam and Amarapura *nikaya* (groups of fraternities), in the decades that followed ties with Japan rested less and less on religious fraternity. At the turn of the century Japan was sought out as an Asian model of a rising militaristic state. In that sense Anagarika Dharmapala's interest in Nichirenism (a philosophy based on the thought and emulation of the life of a thirteenth-century monk called Nichiren) is instructive though it does not illustrate a general trend among Sri Lankans. He visited Japan in 1893, 1889 (a four-month tour), 1902 and 1913. Due to the Japanese government's intense surveillance of Dharmapala during his 1913 visit to Japan there is a near complete record of his activities. In 1902 he met with Tanaka Chigaku (1861–1939) the founder of the lay Buddhist Nichirenism. Chigaku like Dharmapala was in the process of elaborating a form of modern Buddhism that was compatible with a modern national identity. The relationship between Dharmapala and Chigaku is interesting in the light of the rereading of the letters, a man of multiple faces, 'a noble and infinitely compassionate lion king in the manner of the Buddha or a fierce practitioner of the Buddhism of the Lotus Sutra', 'an ultranationalist, fascist and or militarist'.[27] His contacts with Chigaku point to a certain attraction for a kind of thought that would blossom into a fascistic movement in post–Second World War Japan. Chigaku's philosophy was based around the values and actions of Nichiren whom he describes in his *Shumon no ishin* (Restoration of the Sect) as 'the Supreme Commander of the World-Unifying Armed Forces'. The text appears to contain definite elements of aggression and militancy.[28] Chigaku's meeting with Dharmapala in Kamkuara is related in hagiographical accounts of his life. They spoke in translation, Dharmapala speaking in English while their conversation was recorded by a disciple of Chigaku. The conversation centred on Nichiren's prediction that the Buddha Dharma of Japan would take over the leading role from India and illuminate the world. In the same year Dharmapala wrote a pamphlet where he proclaimed the superiority of the Sinhalese – descendants of the Aryans – over the British where interestingly he did not condemn the logic of imperialism, nationalism or racism. In that sense the society of the future envisioned by Dharmapala would emulate the example of the conquering Aryans who had in his writings overrun the Dravidian peoples of South India.[29] The colonial administration in Britain was weary of Dharmapala. In connection to a previously planned visit of Dharmapala to Japan in 1910 which eventually did not take place, the governor of Ceylon had warned Ambassador MacDonald that Dharmapala was planning to 'stir up the Japanese in connection with the 2500 Anniversary of Buddha's birth in 1911'.[30] This did not deter Dharmapala. In 1913 he met various Japanese and foreign individuals, among whom was an Indian teacher of Urdu in Tokyo who was well known for his anti-British views. With his Japanese friends and colleagues the conversation appears to have hovered around the need to forge better trade ties between Japan and India. He also spoke at temples where his message was unequivocally that Buddhism must be spread to the world and supplant Christianity. On a visit to the Kiriyu Textile Trade Association he commented that 'since Indian religion was full of evil practices which were obstacles to change, Japan should send Buddhist priests to India to teach the "correct path" of Buddhist tradition.'[31] Dharmapala's interest in Japan was not unique, as the Sinhala press constantly referred to Japan as a rising Buddhist Asian country, but his conflation of Japanese Buddhism with Aryanism was uniquely bizarre and rarely commented upon.[32]

ETHICAL MODEL: TRADITIONAL WOMEN

Another trope that ran through the Sinhala press of the early twentieth century was the need to emulate Japan in its work ethics and habits. A series of articles entitled 'The Strange Habits of the Japanese' praised the diligence and fearlessness of Japanese police officers as compared to their Sri Lankan counterparts.[33] More space was devoted to describe the mores of the Japanese woman and her behaviour as wife and mother. An article that related the advice given by a Japanese mother to her daughter before her wedding reinscribed the values that the Sinhalese intelligentsia was expecting of the ideal Sinhalese woman. Among these were to be obedient to the husband, never to be jealous as this would lead the husband to lose his love for his wife, never point out mistakes made by the husband, never talk in excess, wake up early, never sleep in the afternoon, spend carefully on the home, not wear flashy clothes and never speak of your husband's wealth or your own wealth before his family.[34] Other articles described marriage customs of the Japanese.[35] Dharmapala on his last visit to Japan in 1912 expressed admiration for the 'gentle, honest character of Japanese women and how the Japanese had been able to maintain their family tradition among themselves for two thousand years'.[36] This image was of course quite selective as Japan in the next decade would be the theatre of a mass culture constructed through the production of cultural institutions, consumers and cultural practices. The Japan that Dharmapala and other members of the literati raved about in the first decade of the twentieth century would be the site of a 'highly commodified consumer culture selling contradictory images of class, gender, cultural traditions and leisure' that coexisted with an 'ethnocentric, essentialist and productivist ideology and apparatus premised on ultimate allegiance to the emperor'.[37] The consumer-subject in Japan was fashioned through both a material culture of housing, clothing, newspapers, books, magazines, movies, records and spectacles and by state ideology and policy. In this modern Japan the state was in close control of the media, radio, cinema and to a lesser extent newspapers, which it censored often quite thoroughly. The complexities of the consumer subject in Japan escaped readers in Sri Lanka who saw the surface image of a technologically advanced country that preserved age-old traditions of the land and continued to honour their emperor. Japanese thinkers' perception of civilization had evolved considerably since the beginning of the Meiji era when there was an urge to reject Asia and adopt everything that came from the West. Okakura Tenshin, the leading bilingual and bicultural thinker of the period, rediscovered Asian civilization during a trip to Europe and began to advocate the special character of Asia as one embodying peace and beauty, 'a broad expanse of love for the Ultimate and the Universal'.[38]

In the space of thirty years Japanese modernity moved away from notions of harmony and syncretism of East and West. Indeed after the Russo-Japanese war it became commonplace among Japanese intellectuals to portray Japan as the leader of an Asian federation because it could harmonise the best of Asian civilization with that of (Western) civilization.[39] Japanese intellectuals of the 1920s to 1930s reflected on the contrary how Japan could be capitalist but not Western, Japanese but not traditional.[40] What was clearly emerging was an idea of Japanese exceptionalism where difference vis-à-vis both Europe and the Japanese pre-Meiji past were stressed.

DEVELOPMENTAL MODEL: INDUSTRIES, SCHOOLS

Sinhalese writers marvelled at the rapid spread of newspapers in Japan since the first publication appeared in 1852. The four thousand newspapers that were published and read in Japan in 1907 indicated the high level of development (*divunuva*) among the Japanese.[41] Their high literacy rate clearly needed to be emulated. There were also frequent accounts of the electrification of Tokyo and admiration for the technical skill that allowed Japanese to install underground electrical cables.[42]

While Japanese students visited Sri Lanka to study Pali at the Vidyodaya Piriveṇa, Sinhalese students were sent to Japan to study Japanese technical industries, financed by Colombo's lay Buddhist associations. In 1912 the Hewavitharana Industrial Centre was founded by Anagarika Dharmapala and Walisinha Harischandra, a leader of the Temperance movement, as the first industrial training school in the country. The school was modelled on the industrial schools Dharmapala had visited in the United States, England, Italy and Denmark. He personally financed the training of U.B. Dolahapillai in textile manufacture at the Higher Technological School of Tokyo.[43] Dolahapillai subsequently became the principal of that institution. One of the main grudges against the British administration was its reluctance to provide the local people with education and training in the sciences and technology. Dharmapala who had visited England four times (1893, 1897, 1904 and 1925–26), and the United States five times (1893, 1896, 1897, 1902–4, 1913–14) was a firm believer in the virtues of science. Following the dichotomy between East and West inscribed by Hegel and others, he wrote for instance:

> Europe is progressive. Her religion is kept in the background ... used for one day in the week, and for six days her people are following the dictates of modern science. Sanitation, aesthetic arts, electricity, etc. are what made the Europeans and American people great. Asia is full of opium eaters, ganja smokers, degenerating sensualists, superstitious, and religious fanatics – Gods and priests keep the people in ignorance.[44]

While Sinhala Buddhist nativists of the more ardent sort were virulently opposed to all things Westernized that were held responsible for the alleged decline of their customs,[45] Dharmapala supported bhikkus learning English, industrial education and attending manual training schools. Science, education and technology would be emulated and habits modernized but at the same time cultural authenticity would be protected. The idea was for the Sinhalese to stand up for themselves as financially scrupulous, clean, courteous, pure, indigenized, industrious and enterprising beings. His message was a fusion of modern technology and economic methods with traditional Buddhist values. The new age was not conceived as the antithesis of tradition but a rediscovery of the true essence of nature and its reintegration in national life.[46] It was seen as a temporal trajectory to freedom that did not entail a complete rejection of the past but a syncretic reinvention of past values in accordance to the times. At the Hewavitharana Weaving School while modern methods were being tested, homespun thread using the chakra (spinning wheel) was also introduced at the school.[47]

According to Dharmapala, nature's domination of Asian and especially Sinhalese people's way of life and thinking was the main obstacle to progress. In his view, however, unlike in the political thought of a contemporary political theorist such as Maruyama Masao, nature and the past needed to be transcended only partially. Dharmapala's position vis-à-vis Europe and Britain in particular exemplified the paradox of the colonized who yearns for a progressive state in the future yet could not possibly choose its colonial master as a model. Japan was showing the path in the views expressed by Dharmapala and others in the Sinhala press to an *abhinava* (modern) future where a selection of Sinhalese values and customs would be preserved.[48]

Japan had quite early seen the opportunities in Sri Lanka. It established a new consulship in Colombo in September 1878 held for a number of years by Lieutenant Colonel Charles Edward Hood Symons.[49] Local entrepreneurs followed suit. A Ceylon Trade Company was formed in the early twentieth century for the purpose of opening up trade with Japan in Ceylon products. The managing director was John Kotelawala, an owner of mines and plantations and the largest producer of thoriante in Ceylon. In 1907 he was planning a visit to Japan allegedly to 'study commercial institutions'.[50]

Sri Lanka was in fact responding to a well-orchestrated strategy by Japan to project itself on the national and world stage as the leader of Asia by virtue of its might as well as the special brand of Buddhist modernity it embodied. In the 1920s an English-language journal called *Young East* published by Sakurai Gicho could boast contributions from 'England, Ceylon, India, Burma, Mongolia, Manchuria, Taiwan, Korea, Hawaii, and the Philippines'.[51] The purpose of the journal was clearly stated as fostering 'better international understanding and peace, friendly cooperation with Asiatic peoples'. Anagarika Dharmapala and Rabindranath Tagore, the Indian advocate of Asianism and close friend of Okakura Tenshin, wrote in the journal.[52] In the same vein the celebration of the Lumbini Festival in Tokyo to commemorate the birth of the Buddha (*hanamatsuri*) was a display of a Japanese desire to reach out to its Asian neighbours.

Issues of *Young East* in the late 1920s evoke the strong ties between Buddhist literati in Sri Lanka and Japan. The journal had agents in London, the Hague, California, Honolulu and Colombo.[53] Since 1927 a regular column appeared in the journal called 'News from Ceylon' authored by J. Vijayatunga, the joint editor of the *Island Review* and agent in Colombo for *Young East*. He deplored that unlike the Burmese, Japanese Buddhists did not visit 'old Buddhist ruins' in Sri Lanka and asked Japanese people to help in the construction of a pilgrim shelter at Anuradhapura. In the past, he reminded his readers, 'Ceylonese have in their small way always sympathised with Japan in times of distress.'[54] Japan was seen by Sinhalese Buddhists as an affluent Buddhist country, hence the appeal to help the Maha Bodhi Society by contributing £5000 to erect a Buddhist preaching hall in London[55] and to build a Buddhist university and a *vihara* (monastery) at Sarnath. This last appeal was translated into Japanese and published in the *Chugai Nippo*, a daily paper published in Kyoto.[56] Many of the articles of *Young East* expounded Japan's technological advances such as a projected trans-Pacific flight by Japanese aviators that would overshadow Lindbergh's trans-Atlantic flight.[57]

CONCLUSION

In colonial Sri Lanka, there was no single way the outside world was conceived by the subjects of the empire over the long nineteenth century. India and Siam, Japan and America were some of the multiple spaces that continued to exist through religious rituals or consumption, sometimes even co-existing, at other times supplanting the frame of the colonial state. The extent, features and sharpness of the image of the outside world differed considerably from individual to individual, and the paucity of data to measure these variations constitute an immense hurdle for the social historian. The British Empire would have weighed most obviously upon lives, intervening in the daily routines of the people and stifling their dream worlds. There would have been a certain amount of practical improvising from a repertoire of 'dispositions' or acquired schemes of perception, thought and action.[58] These imaginaries of an Asian modern modelled on Japan and a modern Buddhism in tune with everyday technologies embodied in the figure of Olcott enabled the market to be produced in the small island of Sri Lanka and colonized consumers to gradually imbibe a modern sensibility.

NOTES

1. P. Duara. 2003. *Sovereignty and Authenticity: Manchukuo and the East Asian Modern*, Boulder: Rowman and Littlefield, 6.
2. The Maha Bodhi society was founded in Sri Lanka in 1891 by Anagarika Dharmapala; one of its original goals was the restoration of the Mahabodhi temple at Buddhagaya (Bihar state, India), the site of the Buddha's enlightenment, which at that time was in the hands of a Hindu landowner.
3. Blackburn, *Locations of Buddhism*, 119.
4. Jaffe, 'Seeking Sakyammuni,' 67.
5. Blackburn, *Locations of Buddhism*, 164.
6. A. Dharmapala. 1927. 'An Appeal to Japanese Buddhists', *Young East*, 3(6), 194.
7. *Lakmini Pahana*, 28 July 1900.

8. 'Catalogue of newspapers, periodicals, books and maps', compiled by A.M. Ferguson and J. Ferguson in *Ferguson's Directory,* 1895, Colombo: Ceylon Observer Press, 4–5.
9. *Dinakara Prakashaya,* 21 January 1907.
10. Ibid.
11. Cited in B. Edstrom. 2002. *Turning Points in Japanese History,* Richmond: Japan Library, 13.
12. M. Laffan. 2006. 'Tokyo as a Shared Mecca of Modernity: War Echoes in the Colonial Malay World', in R. Kowner (ed.), *The Impact of the Russo-Japanese War,* London and New York: Routledge, 222.
13. J.D. Rogers. 1989. 'Cultural Nationalism and Social Reform: The 1904 Temperance Movement in Sri Lanka', *Indian Economic and Social History Review* 26, 319–41.
14. G. Rowell. 2009. 'Ceylon's Kristallnacht: A Reassessment of the Pogrom of 1915', *Modern Asian Studies* 43(3), 623.
15. *Sarasavi Sanderesa,* 11 July 1905.
16. Ibid., 21 July 1905.
17. Ibid., 1 September 1905.
18. *Sinhala Baudhdhaya,* 28 July 1901.
19. *Dinakara Prakashaya,* 22 January 1907.
20. Ibid., 10 June 1907.
21. *Sarasavi Sanderasa,* 18 July 1905.
22. Ibid., 4 August 1905.
23. Jaffe, 'Seeking Sakyammuni', 80.
24. Ibid., 8.
25. Ibid., 81–83.
26. Ibid., 93.
27. G.S. Iguchi. 2006. 'Nichirenism as Modernism: Imperialism, Fascism, and Buddhism in Modern Japan', Ph.D. thesis, University of California, San Diego, 67.
28. Ibid., 73.
29. G.K. Goodman. 1993. 'Dharmapala in Japan, 1913', *Japan Forum* 5(2), 195–202.
30. Ibid., 196.
31. Ibid., 199.
32. Dharmapala, *An Appeal to Japanese Buddhists.*
33. *Sarasavi Sanderasa,* 11 and 18 July 1905.
34. *Dinakara Prakasaya,* 4 May 1907.
35. *Sarasavi Sanderasa,* 18 July 1905.
36. Goodman, 'Dharmapala in Japan,' 200.
37. M. Silverberg. 1991. 'Constructing a New Cultural History of Prewar Japan', *Boundary* 18(3), 62.
38. Okakura Tenshin cited in R. Bharucha. 2006. *Another Asia. Rabindranath Tagore and Okakura Tenshin,* New Delhi: Oxford University Press, 16.
39. Duara, 'The Discourse of Civilization and Pan-Asianism,' 110.
40. Ibid., 87.

41. *Sinhala Baudhdhaya,* 7 July 1906.
42. Ibid., 16 March 1907.
43. N. Wickramasinghe. 2003. *Dressing the Colonized Body,* New Delhi; Orient Longman, 63–64; *Dinamina,* 7 February 1918.
44. Cited in R.F. Gombrich. 1988. *Theravada Buddhism. A Social History from Ancient Benares to Modern Colombo,* London and New York: Routledge and Kegan Paul, 193.
45. M. Roberts. 1997b. 'For Humanity. For the Sinhalese. Dharmapala as Crusading *Bosat'*, *Journal of Asian Studies* 56(4), 1008.
46. B.G. Gokhale. 1973. 'Anagarika Dharmapala: Toward Modernity through Tradition in Ceylon', in B.L. Smith (ed.), *Tradition and Change in Theravada Buddhism. Essays on Ceylon and Thailand in the 19th and 20th centuries,* Leiden: E.J. Brill, 39.
47. Wickramasinghe, *Dressing the Colonized Body,* 65.
48. *Abhinava* means etymologically the 'very new.' See conclusion for further discussion of this concept.
49. A. Wright (ed.). 1907. *Twentieth Century Impressions of Ceylon,* London: Lloyds Publishing, 334.
50. Ibid., 604.
51. J. Snodgrass. 2009. 'Performing Buddhist Modernity: The Lumbini Festival, Tokyo 1925', *Journal of Religious History* 33(2), 140.
52. Ibid., 142.
53. *Young East,* September 1927, 3(4).
54. *Young East,* August 1927, 3(2), and 'News from Adyar', letter to the editor by J. Vijayatuga, June 1927, 95.
55. Dharmapala, *An Appeal to Japanese Buddhists,* 195.
56. *Young East,* December 1927, 3(7), 252.
57. Ibid., 250.
58. P. Bourdieu. 1977. *Outline of a Theory of Practice.* Cambridge and New York: Cambridge University Press.

Chapter 6

Trams, Cars, Bicycles

Modern Machines in the City

Any contrivance for saving human labor has
a great attraction to Sinhalese Buddhists.
– John Ferguson, *Ceylon in 1903,* 58

The experience of the everyday in the early decades of the twentieth century as it was lived in the great metropolitan centres like Tokyo/Yokohama, Shanghai, Calcutta and Rio de Janeiro included relations that stretched far beyond the borders and experience of a singular locale, reaching a new kind of unboundedness, in which space was increasingly torn away from place by 'fostering relations between "absent" others'.[1]

In the smaller capital of Colombo in the Crown colony of Ceylon/Sri Lanka, similar changes in feelings of belonging and territoriality were perceptible. In the city more than in any other location on the island, colonial power felt its first cracks under the combined weight of peoples' desire for respect of their cultural practices circumscribed by new laws on time and space and aspirations for goods that came from distant places, lands which they knew only as strange names or shaded areas on a school map. While rural lives had been slowly changing since the mid-nineteenth century with the growth of a commercialized economy and the taming of nature through road and railway networks, cities became magnets for villagers in search of new opportunities.[2] Their dreams of riches were rarely satisfied as poverty and squalor were the norm for the indigenous and migrant underclasses, working in city factories and the ever-growing port, who were often the victims of stringent colonial laws designed to police the lives of the poor and vagrants. But these new city folk were also in their everyday lives confronting forces at the same time more insidious and invasive than the extractive demands of an aging empire.

Ordinary men met new challenges by the simple act of crossing a road in the Pettah where they could be crushed by a tramway, or knocked down by a motor car driven by a member of the ostentatiously rich indigenous elite or by a careless user of a bicycle. Thus beyond a consciousness of unsatisfied material needs, their social being was being transformed in an imperceptible manner: without them even realizing it, their senses were becoming more alert and acute, their stroll faster, and ears tuned to the whizzing sounds of mechanical wheeled machines. They had to learn new rules of conduct in order to survive in a changing everyday space.

The wealthier city man could now listen to recordings of songs from nationalist plays by John de Silva in his Cinnamon Gardens living room on his own gramophone and have his suits sewn by a local tailoring shop on an American Singer sewing machine. The colonial city provided an arena where colonized peoples' feelings of 'being with the times' through new consumption patterns and new practices of mobility were entangled with yearnings for nation and community. Through or in spite of the intrusion of foreign objects that were often produced in the colonial metropole, a nation congruent with a bounded island-state was growing as the hegemonic imaginary of larger communities.

For the less privileged, practical foreign objects such as umbrellas were appropriated as new elements of style and distinction, while more complex foreign machines were used and through their use transformed into instruments of protest against colonial rulers or class enemies from within: thus the tramway became the mode of transport par excellence of a politically vibrant working class in the city of Colombo, especially at times of crisis.

Machines were ambivalent and endowed with different meanings according to their users and the context in which they were used. They were not entirely new before the late nineteenth century but before this period of industrialization functioned at the margins, in the secluded spaces of the workplace or factory. The relation between man and mechanical machine in Sri Lanka had started with the use of instruments that either replaced or complemented the work of men. While in the early nineteenth century coffee plantations called for supportive machinery in city factories, in the late nineteenth century in the wake of the tea industry most machines were related to the needs to expand transport facilities in the island through the development of roads, railways and port facilities.[3] But machines manned by local people were there long before the plantation economy. Printing machines were the first industrial machines to enter the island. They were brought by the Dutch in the early eighteenth century and used by them to propagate their Christian faith through pamphlets distributed among the literate peoples of the island. Thus at the outset machines had a sacred connection acting as intercessors between the divine and the people.

In 1707 wooden blocks were used by the Dutch for printing. After initial experiments carried out by Gabriel Schade, a press was established in the southern town of Galle by the Dutch. The first document published through the Dutch press in Sri Lanka was a notification named *plakkaat* on 5 April 1737 and the first book on 6 September 1737 in the Sinhala language, a Christian prayer book consisting of forty-six pages. During the Dutch period, all administrative orders were printed in this press. Local people conversant in the vernacular languages were trained on the job in printing and quite early became skilled workers.[4]

In 1796 when the Dutch were routed, the Galle press was dismantled by the British and reestablished in Colombo. Its first publication there was the *Government Gazette* issued on 15 March 1802.[5] New machines of 'the latest pattern' were introduced and the office was described as equipped on 'thoroughly modern lines'.[6] The first Sinhala Buddhist press was not established until much later – in July 1862 – and was known as the Lankopakara Press. The establishment of this press was related to the Buddhist revival movement that gained momentum in the second half of the nineteenth century. Ven. Bulathgama Dharmalankara Sri Sumanatissa MahaThera, the pioneer of the establishment of the Buddhist press, received financial assistance from the king of Siam in establishing this press.[7] Little is known about the workers who manned the print industry, except their numbers, 807 printers and compositors in 1903.[8]

When Sri Lanka became part of the British Empire its material culture underwent a drastic but selective transformation. New products that entered the market were immediately consumed while some took root in the living space of sections of the Sri Lankan population. This was the case with the umbrella, which became an ubiquitous object and appeared luminous and proud in many studio photographs of the day, but also the gramophone, the bicycle and the motorcar. These new objects and artefacts surrounded people, transformed their bodies and possibly redefined their dream world. Objects consumed became part of a culture in the making where they played an important part in mediating social and spatial relationships. Consumption generated an active mode of relations, not only with other goods but also with the domestic collectivity and foreign lands to which the domestic collectively notionally 'belonged'.[1]

Some machines more than others changed people's conception of time, space and the real. In the late nineteenth century the telegraph and telephone, carrying messages at speeds never before encountered, created a new sense of immediacy. Other machines dissolved distances between places: space shrank because of the speed of the bicycles, motor cars and tramcars that appeared on city streets at the turn of the century. The gramophone recording, a 'medium of the disembodied voice',[9] brought a new conception of the real as a background unable to be grasped by human senses alone, but requiring the help of technology.[10] Machines had been present from the eighteenth century in the lives of the few people who worked with them and at the periphery of the lives of others. But in the twentieth century machines acted not only upon the few who owned and used them but also on the rest who were constantly consuming them in images[11] and confronting them through sensorial encounters on the streets of the city.

THE CITY

As Gyan Prakash forcefully states, it is on the stage of the modern city that all great dramas of history have been played out. Colombo is indeed central to the elaboration of a sense of being modern in the colony of Sri Lanka, not so much for a 'breathless intensity'[12] that might have characterized it – it was indeed a far cry from Tokyo or Shanghai – but more in terms of the scale of the transformations that took place in the city during the nineteenth century.

The city of Colombo emerged out of three colonial encounters, the Portuguese, the Dutch and the British. The Portuguese established a trading post in Colombo and built the fort which was taken over by the Dutch when they made Colombo the capital of the maritime provinces under the control of the Dutch East India Company. In 1815 Colombo became the capital of the new British Crown colony of Ceylon. It gradually acquired the features of a modern zoned city where industry, commerce, administration and residence occupied different spaces.

In the early twentieth century Colombo would have been in international terms comparable to a provincial town in Europe, but from 1870 – following the opening of the Suez Canal – it became an international port. Like other port cities in the late nineteenth and early twentieth centuries Colombo helped shape the activity of the people in new ways. The interactions produced novel sets of relationships in a new type of urban environment among the peoples of the region, between the coast and the hinterland and between Europeans and indigenous peoples.[13]

A massive demographic change followed. People migrated from the countryside to the city looking for employment and greater economic opportunities, and in so doing were confronted with new, worldly 'cultural' offerings. The expansion of communication networks facilitated a rural-to-urban migration. From 1901 to 1911 the rate of population increase in Colombo was more than double that of the islands as a whole.[14] The growth of the population was accompanied by a range of new institutions that structured urban life. Colonial-era urbanization produced urban forms, infrastructures, functions and ideas that were entirely novel in Sri Lanka. New types of buildings appeared in the form of factories, hospitals, prisons, asylums, clubs and race courses, parks, botanical gardens, zoos, hotels, courthouses, museums, universities, cinema halls and so forth.

Streets were embellished to new standards with new materials and given new names. Urban governance was institutionalised in the form of a municipality and new regimes of record keeping and taxation, which incorporated new forms of classifying people, property and occupation, were put in place. Similar developments were taking place in other colonial cities where municipal councils that began to run local affairs set out to transform the life of city folk by establishing gas and electricity lighting, piped water and sewage systems.[15]

The city was spatially evolving, incorporating indigenous and recent migrant areas such as Wellawatte that until then had lain outside the boundaries of the city. With the expansion of the port, working-class tenements were springing up in the new dockland areas of Kochchikade and Gintupitiya.[16]

An important feature of the capital city was its diversity. Between the years 1891 and 1921, the Sinhalese inhabitants made up less than half of the population, sharing the urban space with Tamils, Europeans, Muslims, Burghers and Malays. Turner, a colonial administrator, has described the changes that took place in the cities quite predictably in the language of progress and development:

> Of the towns of Ceylon, the most important and progressive is the capital Colombo. It is the main business centre of the island, the seat of the government and its principal officials and the headquarters of the chief mercantile firms. It is consequently the most westernized of all the towns and possesses most of the refinements of modern civilisation, up to date hotels, electric lights, fans and tramways an excellent water supply, an up to date system of water borne drainage, an extensive emporia of goods of all kinds.[17]

Colombo was 'the center for symbolic capital – the site where new commoditized trappings of prestige were displayed both by the British colonial elites and the indigenous elite who absorbed them'.[18] Here the money economy engulfed everyday existence. All the characteristics of a modern city such as insurance companies, hotels, clubs, newspapers and urban entertainment centred on the money economy.

The conspicuous and public consumption of gramophones, fancy clothing, automobiles and expensive toiletries challenged white ownership of high-fashion items. The urban-centred bourgeoisie strived to assume the characteristic 'look' of white society and focused on a small number of highly symbolic, visible, public and relatively affordable commodities. Their aspirations were defined by an assemblage of 'modern' objects.[19]

But changes were also taking place among less-privileged groups through their adoption of new technologies and adaptability to new needs. A Westernization of the self accompanied an 'indigenisation of the spatial structures'.[20] For, just as the capital city, Colombo, was changing and growing into a more metropolitan space, it was also changing into a local space; it was indigenising, a phenomenon which happened in parallel and was often overshadowed by its new visibility as a cosmopolitan port city. The process of indigenising from the 1860s onwards of a city that was a 'foreign implant', first a white male Christian of the Portuguese separated from the 'native city', pushed away the poorer classes to the outskirts in an area known as the Pettah. During the later British period, elite Sri Lankans, who were benefiting from the growth of a plantation economy, began to appropriate European symbols, structures and spaces, carving new landscapes onto the colonial city. New entrepreneurs such as H. Don Carolis & Sons (founded in 1860) or S.L. Naina Marikkar (1888) moved into the Fort and Pettah from the south of the country, opening business premises entirely run by locals. The colonial city was further indigenised by the gradual penetration of Buddhist temples, schools and religious institutions. Older temples in and around Colombo in Kelaniya and Kotte were invigorated while new temples such as the Jayasekaramaya and Dipaduttaramaya were created outside the colonial centre in places like Dematagoda, Kotahena or Maradana. Monastic educational institutions also encircled the colonial city: Parama Dhamma Cetiya Pirivena at Ratmalana in 1845, Vidyodaya Pirivena in Maligakanda in 1873, and Vidyalankara Pirivena at Peliyagoda in 1875 formed a loop around the Christian centre of the country.[21]

MACHINES IN A CITY UNDER SIEGE: READING VEHICLES THROUGH THE 1915 RIOTS

Tramways, cars and bicycles changed the cityscape by allowing its people to move freely and collectively at a speed never before experienced. They appear immobile next to their owners in photographs of the period but in a few colonial texts such as the account of the 1915 riots by P. Ramanathan, one of the Unofficial Members of the Legislative Council, these new machines are shown on the move, in the thick of the action.[22]

In 1915 violence broke out between Sinhalese and Muslims, starting in Kandy opposite a mosque and spreading to other parts of the island. Sinhala crowds attacked the property and the persons of a particular group of Muslims – known as Coast Moors or Indian Moors to denote that they were recent migrants from the Malabar coast of India – killing 25, wounding 189 and raping 4.[23] The origin of the violence lay partly in a dispute between Sinhalese and Muslims over the right of the former to take their processions in front of mosques without ceasing to play their music. The government alleged that the riots had been engineered by leaders of the Temperance movement, a Buddhist movement started a decade earlier that had rallied members of the local elite around anticolonial policies. Among the many readings of what sparked these riots, religious, economic and political factors in the capital city, the role of the Colombo working class, in particular the skilled workers employed in the Railway Department, and more generally the importance of social disorganisation caused by urbanisation have been highlighted.[24]

From the late nineteenth century the city was indeed changing at a pace its residents could not always comprehend (Figure 15). New patterns of social interaction between men, women, communities and machines led to new forms of violence and vandalism. When trams were introduced in Colombo in January 1899, police officers had to travel along with the passengers to

Figure 15. Photograph of Colombo City, Tram (ca. 1910). Author's collection

protect the new machines against stone throwers. Changes in the landscape of the city and the arrival of new forms of transport were only gradually accepted by its residents who were often recent migrants from India or from villages around the Colombo municipality. There were reports of boys placing stones on the tracks in the hope of derailing the trams, and until slower vehicles such as bullock carts and rickshaws got used to their pace, there were a number of street accidents in the city.[25] Such incidents were common in other parts of the empire. In Singapore rickshaw pullers fearing the competition of tramways resorted to similar methods of resistance.[26] In 1908, thirty-eight accidents were reported due to passengers attempting to board or descend from cars in motion, and twelve people were knocked down by tramcars. In one case a gentleman lost control of his bicycle, ran into the back of a standing car and 'sustained slight injuries'.[27] In the early twentieth century, the system of electric tramways ran over two long and populous routes in Colombo, each of about three and a quarter miles and converging on the Colombo Fort. By 1903 people appeared to have shed their apprehensions since over twenty-five thousand passengers per day were travelling on the ten to twelve cars that ran from 6 A.M. to 10 P.M.[28] A year later there were thirty-two trams running at five-minute intervals during rush hours.[29] They carried the working population of the city, skilled and unskilled, who manned the economy. How they felt about their journeys on a machine that speedily transported them to work on another industrial machine in the factory is not recorded. What is known is that workers in the railways still appeared in the early twentieth century to be unaccustomed to the discipline of industrial life, the rule of the clock and timetables, the insistence of punctuality and regular output. They complained against the practice of fines for absence from work as an unjust practice. One pattern worker protested: 'If I am absent (from work) I am the loser. I lose Rs 3 a day.'[30] The work discipline of capitalism was yet to be internalized by Colombo industrial workers.[31]

In the colonial period, the city hummed to the tune of the plantation. In city factories the plantation produce was processed and packed by workers who manned machinery. Others were wage earners in engineering and industrial workshops geared towards the maintenance of transport and repair of machinery that served the plantation sector.[32] There were also privately owned steam-run mills and factories in Colombo geared directly towards the needs of the plantation sector. Prior to 1880 these included thirty-seven large coffee mills with around twenty thousand workers – both men and women – employed in peeling, winnowing, grinding and sizing coffee. There were also several timber mills, factories for the processing of coconut products and a large number of stores where graphite was sorted and packed for shipment. With the transition to tea in the 1880s factories were started in Colombo for the sorting and packing of the leaves, and after the turn of the century, there were mills for the processing of rubber products. There were also several large engineering workshops begun in the nineteenth century for servicing and repairing machinery and a large textile mill in Colombo which mainly produced rough cloth. All these workshops, mills and factories employed large numbers of skilled and unskilled men and women.

In Colombo the labour force, amounting to about 75,000 persons in 1911, was divided between skilled and unskilled labour. Skilled workers were working with heavy machinery as Ferguson commented in the early twentieth century:

> Both Sinhalese and Tamils are good artisans, witness the role of workmen in the government Public Works and Railway Factories of Colombo and the Colombo Iron Works, where ocean-going steamers are repaired, as well as a great variety of machinery is turned out, such as steam engines, water motors and tea, coffee and oil preparing machines.[33]

In 1911 there were nine railway locomotive workshops that employed 2,800 workers – mechanics, blacksmiths, carpenters, fitters and boilermakers who assembled engines and did heavy repairs. The Colombo Ironworks where the plantation machinery was repaired had familiarized native workers with machines. British engineers supervised the 1,000 local workmen.

The city workers were the main actors and spectators of the violence that broke out in 1915. Ponnambalam Ramanathan's *Riots and Martial Law in Ceylon, 1915* can in fact be read as a narrative of the tramcar and motor car's new visibility and multiple uses during riots and collective violence, as the intrusion of wheeled, mechanized machines in a nineteenth-century repertoire of communal violence. In his speech in Council, Ramanathan identifies the car, rather than land, property or title as central to his class belonging: 'We, who are feeding fat on our wealth, who roll along in motor cars and fine carriages, can have no conception of the grinding nature of the life which the people whom we have to deal with are labouring under.'[34]

The ability to move fast from Maradana to Borella of groups involved in rioting, whom he disparagingly refers to as 'the party of rowdies', was facilitated by the tramcars. Trams and bicycles were the mode of transport of the working class of the capital.

Inspector W.E. de Silva describes the scene:

> When the tramcar passed my station and stopped at the junction, all the men in it landed, and I went up to them with my force ... it was the men who came in the tramcar that broke open the boutiques and immediately the resident rowdies rushed in and looted the goods ... I heard that another tramcar load of rowdies had got down at the Jail Road Junction about 8P.M.[35]

Motorcars too were used by the indigenous elites by the first decade of the twentieth century. While the first car was imported in 1899, by June 1913 there were over three thousand vehicles in the country. The United Kingdom supplied more cars to Sri Lanka than all other countries combined. Germany came second and France third. The preferred car in Sri Lanka was the four-cylinder, fifteen-horsepower car. The first motor vehicle that appeared on the roads belonged not to an individual but to the General Post Office and was a van utilised for collecting mail. In March 1899 this single motor vehicle in the streets of Colombo succeeded in colliding with the tramcar and was badly damaged. As a pastiche of the colonial state's urge to police public spaces – even though only one car still travelled the streets of Colombo – the Municipal Council took immediate measures to pass a bye-law for the control of motor cars.[36] Cars became a central part of peoples' everyday lives 'whether they used them or not'.[37] They belonged to a new background of the mundane and the quotidian which often they themselves were not aware of, until as in 1915 cars burst into action as supporting actors in the riots.

To quell the violence and to defuse the situation, Superintendent Attygalle and Mr T.W. Roberts, the commissioner of the Court of Requests, manoeuvred deftly around the city in motor cars while motor cars 'full of armed soldiers were flitting about the town in different directions'.[38] Ponnambalam Ramanathan describes how he had to get a car pass to drive around the city once martial law was declared.[39] According to Order III (3) police officers were given the power to commandeer private motor cars with owners subject to arrest if they refused to hand over their cars. What appears to have happened was a misuse of the seized vehicles:

> The cars, thus seized, were to be used by parties of four soldiers or less to scour the country, not only where disorder existed, but also where disorder was likely to occur. The cars were often used for amusement and holiday journeys of even 200 miles, and were returned months afterwards to the owners in a ruined condition without any compensation.[40]

It was clear from Ramanathan's complaint that cars were for the local bourgeoisie a powerful status symbol as well as evidence that they belonged to the same world as the colonizer. Permitting common soldiers, often Punjabis, to despoil the cars was a way of humiliating them. For many city people the sound of cars became synonymous with the arrival of the military and arbitrary arrests of Sinhalese in possession of items deemed suspicious by the police.

But there is also evidence of Sinhalese nationalists promoting attacks on Moors, moving around in cars and distributing rolls of Lion flags.[41] The '1915 riots' were severely suppressed. A number of excesses were committed by the British authorities who came to regard the clashes as part of a conspiracy against them by the Sinhalese. Men associated with the Buddhist temperance movement[42] were arbitrarily imprisoned and at least 63 people were killed by the army and police. English volunteers – tea planters and employees of commercial firms – appear to have flogged and shot people indiscriminately. When the violence ended 412 persons, mainly belonging to the Sinhalese community, were charged. Of these 34 were sentenced to death.[43]

Alongside the motorcar and the tram, the bicycle made an entry onto the stage of communal violence.[44] Men on bicycles went from village to village 'calling out that the Moors were coming' thus creating fear and instigating mobs into attacking the Moors and destroying their property.[45]

At the turn of the century many state institutions such as the Ceylon Police, army, the bank and post office had begun to adopt bicycles to deal with emergencies. Hudson Model C bicycles were supplied to the police force in order to 'bring the men and machines into use in times when telephones are out of order. In case of fire' and in banks and post offices one bicycle was to be kept in each station 'for use in an emergency'.[46] The bicycle was still conceived as an eccentricity although a toll had been immediately put in place for bicycles (together with tricycles and jinrickshaws) when these vehicles left the boundaries of the city of Colombo. Mr G. Walker, a member of the Legislative Council, still described cycling 'as a healthful as well as popular amusement'.[47] A few years later, the bicycle was no longer a leisure vehicle and had spread to a much larger population. James Ferguson noted that men in sarongs, i.e. from non-Westernised social groups, were riding bicycles: 'Bicycles have of late become very common and are freely used even by Sinhalese wearing çomboys or "petticoats".'[48] By 1903 bicycles were being made locally.[49] In 1911 bicycles were used all over the countryside in Ceylon. Denham cited the haughty words of a Kandyan *ratemahatmaya* (chieftain) about the democratization of the bicycle: 'Manual labourers with bare bodies can be seen riding bicycles on village roads.' Indeed the bicycle was quite affordable: cheaper ones ranged in price from Rs 60 to 90 while the better-quality ones went up to Rs 125. Native artisans bought spare parts and made them into functional bicycles.[50]

The bicycle was perfected in 1892 with the invention of the pneumatic tyre but since 1860 smiths and mechanics had been tinkering with it. From 1875 to 1885 the most common machine in use was the high-wheeled penny-farthing, also known as the 'ordinary', a machine that was rather dangerous to ride due to its precarious balance. To deal with issues of balance tri-and quadricycles were built with wheels three or four feet in diameter. Queen Victoria herself began to ride one of these. Although the modern type of bicycle was invented in 1876 it became popular only when the pneumatic tyre was adopted in 1890. A few years later this type of bicycle was visible on roads in Ceylon.[51] In 1897 the first case of a bicycle theft was reported from the police quarters at Maradana. The police storekeeper's bicycle was stolen while he attended a dance. The culprit was a fitter at the government factory.[52]

Foreigners and colonial administrators popularized the bicycle by using it for treks or in their work. In 1897–99 an American traveller and mountaineer Fanny Bullock Workman cycled with her husband for 1,800 miles in Sri Lanka.[53] Leonard Woolf is said to have used a bicycle for all of his travel in Sri Lanka presumably when as a young government agent in Hambantota he went on his visits around the countryside.[54] Schoolteachers also used bicycles to get about in the city, emulating British public school habits.[55]

Machines were interdependent in the nineteenth century. In the Britain of the 1860s and 1870s manufacturers often changed their production in part because the international situation destabilized the industry: this was the case of 'weapon makers, sewing machine manufacturers and agricultural machine producers' who shifted their production to bicycles. In 1869 the Coventry Sewing Machine Company morphed into the Coventry Machinists Co. Ltd and embarked on a production of velocipedes. Interestingly genius technicians such as James Starley too moved from watchmaking to sewing machines to velocipedes. A same development was seen in the United States where Albert A. Pope contracted with the Weed Sewing Machine Company. The first high-wheeled Ordinary bicycles were produced by the Weed company by using its sewing machine manufacturing equipment with only special fixtures and cutting tools added.[56]

Family resemblances between machines were played with in advertisements that often relied on different 'modern allusions', such as sewing machines paired with bicycles in display. 'The two emerged as mass produced goods at the same time, required similar production techniques and were often produced by the same firms. The treadle on the side suggested the wheel of a bicycle or a car.'[57]

Because durables were expensive, consumers needed to derive maximum and multiple utility from a product. This led to the development of numerous other skills, mostly self-taught, for the recycling and repair of goods such as sewing machines, bicycles and radios. In colonial Sri Lanka new trades grew out of new needs. There were thirty umbrella sellers and one bicycle repairer in 1903.[58] Repair shops for bicycles were listed for the first time in 1926 in the Ferguson's trade list.[59] Other new trades had sprung up in the cities: watch repairers, music teachers, motor car hirers.

The social life of machines was long and varied with use, resale, reuse and repair. As Karl Marx astutely remarked, when the appearance of its use value is exhausted products become once more a merely material husk in a reversal of what happened when the object is consumed and sheds its material nature to become a product.[60] What then happens to commodities when they cease to be commodities but continue to retain – at least for a while – their form as objects? Even in death a machine had a life in a symbolic sense. 'Remains and debris' were used.[61] Old machines were sold for cannibalization; toys were built of old machines. But the machine lost its value as sign in a system of value, both monetary and social. It acquired a subversive value as it informed the consumer of the fate of commodities, a fate carefully repressed in advertisements.

CONCLUSION

The consumption of foreign goods crossed class divides. What differed was the nature of the relationship of the consumer with the commodity. While anglicised elites sitting in their bungalows virtually lost themselves in the foreignness of the goods and became part of their world, more episodic and less-privileged consumers transformed their newly acquired possessions into local products.[62] The city spawned new forms of and new arenas for confrontation and communication; gradually indigenized, it became culturally and demographically an 'in between space'.[63] Through their use of machines such as the tram and the bicycle, city folk of all classes were whisked into the modern era. Yet the encounter of the modern in their everyday life would bring the common person together with immediate pleasures and occasional fulfilment of desires, a sense of loss of anchors and discontent.

NOTES

1. H. Harootunian. 2000. *History's Disquiet: Modernity, Cultural Practice and the Question of Everyday Life,* New York: Columbia University Press, 64.
2. For a survey of the social transformations that took place in the nineteenth century see in particular De Silva, *History of Sri Lanka,* 307–463; Wickramasinghe, *Sri Lanka in the Modern Age,* 6–155.
3. See I. Munasinghe. 2002. *The Colonial Economy on Track. Roads and Railways in Sri Lanka (1800–1905),* Colombo: SSA.
4. See T. Kularatne. 1995. 'Introduction of Printing to Sri Lanka (Ceylon). The Dutch Press in Ceylon (1736–1796)', *Libri* 45(2), 65–78.

5. This was followed by newspapers such as the first English newspaper, *Colombo Journal,* printed at this press in 1832 and the *Ceylon Observer* in 1834 which was the first independent newspaper published in Ceylon. The *Lakmini Pahana* newspaper was printed in 1862 at a press owned by Hendrick Perera. However, the first unregistered Sinhala newspaper, *Lanka Lokaya,* was printed on 10 September 1860 at the Lanka Loka Press in Galle.
6. Wright, *Twentieth Century Impressions of Ceylon,* 106.
7. Wickramasinghe, *Sri Lanka in the Modern Age,* 78.
8. Ferguson, *Ceylon in 1903,* lvi.
9. A. Weidman. 2003. 'Guru and Gramophone: Fantasies of Fidelity and Modern Technologies of the Real', *Public Culture* 15(3), 468.
10. Ibid., 462.
11. Cited in M. Featherstone. 2004. 'Automobiles: An Introduction', *Theory, Culture and Society* 21(1), 1–24; R. Barthes. 1972. *Mythologies,* New York: Hill and Wang.
12. G. Prakash and K. M. Cruse (eds). 2008. *The Spaces of the Modern City,* Princeton: Princeton University Press.
13. K. McPherson. 2002. 'Port Cities as Nodal Points of Change: The Indian Ocean, 1890s–1920s', in L.T. Fawaz and C.A. Bayly (eds), *Modernity and Culture: From the Mediterranean to the Indian Ocean,* New York: Columbia University Press, 75–95.
14. B.L. Panditharatne. 1964. 'Trends of Urbanization in Ceylon 1901–1953', *Ceylon Journal of Historical and Social Studies* 7(2), 206.
15. T. Frash. 2012. 'Tracks in the City: Technology, Mobility and Society in Colonial Rangoon and Singapore', *Modern Asian Studies* 46(1), 97.
16. N. Perera. 2002. 'Indigenising the Colonial City: Late 19th-century Colombo and Its Landscape', *Urban Studies* 39(9), 1703–21.
17. L.J.B. Turner. 1927. *Handbook of Commercial and General Information for Ceylon,* Colombo: Government Printer, 4.
18. Roberts, 'For Humanity, for the Sinhalese', 1011.
19. Appadurai has signalled how consumption tends to create classes 'for themselves' and the central role of commodity consumption in identity creation. He adopts a Weberian approach thus complementing Marx's discussion of class when he introduces the notion of estates (*Staende*) as defined by lifestyle sustained by consumption. A. Appadurai (ed.). 1986. *The Social Life of Things. Commodities in Cultural Perspective,* Cambridge: Cambridge University Press.
20. Perera, 'Indigenising the Colonial City', 1718.
21. Ibid., 1703–21 and 1709–14; N. Perera. 2009. 'People's Spaces: Familiarization, Subject Formation and Emergent Spaces in Colombo', *Planning Theory* 8(51), 51–75.
22. P. Ramanathan. 1916. *Riots and Martial Law in Ceylon, 1915,* London: St Martin's Press.
23. M. Roberts. 1994. *Exploring Confrontation. Sri Lanka: Politics, Culture and History,* Chur: Harwood Academic Publishers, 182–212.
24. See R.N. Kearney et al. 1970. 'The 1915 Riots in Ceylon: A Symposium', *Journal of Asian Studies* 29(2), 219–66; A.P. Kannangara. 1984. 'The Riots of 1915 in

Sri Lanka: A Study in the Roots of Communal Violence', *Past and Present* 102, 130–65.
25. A.C. Dep. 1969. *A History of the Ceylon Police II (1866–1913),* Colombo: Times of Ceylon.
26. Frash, 'Tracks in the City', 104.
27. *Straits Times,* 6 July 1901, 3.
28. Ferguson, *Ceylon in 1903,* cxxii.
29. Munasinghe, *The Colonial Economy on Track,* 85.
30. Sessional Paper I, 1913, Railway Commission, evidence of K.L. George Silva and J. Solomon Perera, SP.
31. On the working conditions of labour in the late nineteenth and twentieth century see K. Jayawardena. 1972. *The Rise of the Labour Movement in Ceylon,* Durham: Duke University Press.
32. Ibid., 4–12, gives the following estimates:
    Of the 1.7 million working population, which in 1911 which formed 41 percent of the total population, over a million were described in the Census Report as nonagricultural wage earners … the plantation population of 400,000 immigrants … and 191,000 'industrial workers' … 136,000 traders; 105,000 'general laborers'; 67,000 domestic servants; 37,000 government servants; and 53,000 workers in transport.
33. Ferguson, *Ceylon in 1903,* 58, cited in Jayawardena, *Rise of the Labour Movement,* 6.
34. P. Ramanathan, *Riots and Martial Law in Ceylon,* 195.
35. Ibid., 28.
36. Dep, *A History of the Ceylon Police,* 364–65.
37. M. Sheller. 2007. 'Bodies, Cybercars, and the Mundane Incorporation of Automated Mobilities', *Social and Cultural Geography* 8(2), 175.
38. Ibid., 29.
39. Ibid., 45, 47.
40. Ibid., 75–76.
41. G. Rowell. 2009. 'Ceylon's Kristallnacht: A Reassessment of the Pogrom of 1915', *Modern Asian Studies* 43(3), 643.
42. On the Temperance movement see Bond, *Buddhist Revival in Sri Lanka* ,and J.D. Rogers, 1989. 'Cultural Nationalism and Social Reform: The 1904 Temperance Movement in Sri Lanka', *Indian Economic and Social History Review* 26, 319–41.
43. Wickramasinghe, *Sri Lanka in the Modern Age,* 121.
44. Ramanathan, *Riots and Martial Law in Ceylon,* 17.
45. Cited in Rowell, 'Ceylon's Kristallnacht', 634.
46. *Straits Times,* 7 July 1897, 2; *Straits Times,* 1 April 1896, 2.
47. *Singapore Free Press and Mercantile Advertiser,* 27 February 1896.
48. Ferguson, *Ceylon in 1903,* 102.
49. Ibid., 58.
50. Denham, *Ceylon at the Census,* 174.
51. G.C. Mendis. 1946.*Ceylon under the British,* 2d revised edn, Colombo: Colombo Apothecaries Co., Ltd Educational Publishers.

52. Dep, 'History of the Ceylon Police', 360.
53. K. Olsen. 1994. *Chronology of Women's History,* Westport: Greenwood.
54. R. Poole. 1989. 'Bloomsbury and Bicycles', *English Literary History* 56(4), 955.
55. Master of Trinity College in Kandy (Ramanathan, *Riots and Martial Law in Ceylon,* 256).
56. W.E. Bijker. 2009. 'King of the Road. The Social Construction of the Safety Bicycle', in F. Candlin and R. Guins (eds), *The Object Reader,* London: Routledge, 277.
57. Coffin, 'Credit, Consumption and Images of Women's Desires', 767.
58. Ferguson, *Ceylon in 1903,* lviii.
59. *Ferguson's Directory,* 1926, 821.
60. K. Marx. 1973. *Grundrisse. Foundations of the Critique of Political Economy,* trans. Martin Nicolaus, Harmondsworth: Penguin Books, 91.
61. C. Lévi-Strauss. 1966. *The Savage Mind,* Chicago: Chicago University Press.
62. On the social, relational and active nature of consumption see, Appadurai, *Social Life of Things.*
63. P. Scriver and V. Prakash. 2007. *Colonial Modernities: Building, Dwelling and Architecture in British India and Ceylon,* Abingdon: Routledge.

Chapter 7

A Tailor's Tale and Machines in the Home

It is through quotidian acts performed by men and women that ideas of what it meant to be modern were given shape and form. To capture a fleeting sense of what this might have been, the historian must move her gaze to the scale of the home and the tailoring shop, away from issues of trade and consumption in empires, or connections between states and violence in colonial cities towards the everyday life of men and women enmeshed in prosaic acts of cooking, mending, sewing, eating, drinking, washing and sleeping.

How space and time was ordered differed according to the level of affluence of people, their occupation and their gender. Bourgeois women who, like their counterparts in Victorian Britain, did not venture out of their home to work in the fields, structured their day so as to include a period devoted to domestic chores and family time within the safe confines of the home. But most significantly, this period witnessed a blurring of the boundaries between the separate spaces of home and workplace by the entry of a noisy time-saving machine into this formerly protected space of the home. This created an accelerated time in the household that was rearranged to accommodate this metallic object; the workplace of tailors too would have been affected although it is doubtful that this spawned the types of regimes of punctuality, precision and scheduling that prevailed in industrial labour.

THE TAILORING SHOP

The introduction of the sewing machine led to a number of changes in the gender and ethnic valorisation of the art of sewing. It feminized and gentrified tailoring with the birth of seamstresses in the city but also drew minority communities into the tailoring profession who were more likely to possess moveable income to invest in machines. Furthermore with the conquest of the sewing machine, the tailor too entered a new world of speed and replication.

During Dutch rule over the island, working people such as bakers, butchers or tailors were kept under tight control. Colonial authorities enforced a strict price control of products and more importantly linked the granting of permission to practice trades to religious conformity. Governor van Goens ordered that no one 'shall be admitted to the tailors' guild unless they prove their eligibility by diligent church attendance'.[1] This accelerated the decline of the Hannalis, the caste of Sinhalese tailors described by John Davy as being 'very few' in the early nineteenth century[2] who worked mainly in the courts of the kings. Under new colonial rule without such religious restrictions, tailoring became a more widely caste-, ethnic- and gender-distributed profession. Unlike in Swat where the appearance of sewing machines in the 1890s led to the creation of a new caste of 'tailors' from an array of 'castes in the middle range of the hierarchy' in Sri Lanka the congruence between caste and occupation melted rather than formed a new consolidated caste.[3]

Early census data on tailors allow us to numerically chart the changes that took place in Sri Lanka during the late nineteenth and beginning of twentieth century. The Census of Ceylon of 1871 indicates that there were 3,256 tailors and seamstresses across the entire island. Tailoring was clearly an urban occupation, and interestingly women engaged in this activity as well, unlike in India for instance where it was a predominantly male profession.[4] The 1891 census gives some very interesting information on the gender and ethnic distribution of tailors and seamstresses. In the coastal Negombo district there were 153 male tailors and 520 seamstresses. Of the women, 176 were under the age of fourteen years. No European tailors were listed in 1891. The majority of tailors and seamstresses were Sinhalese (86 males and 338 females); then came the Moors or Muslims (8 males and 89 females); Burghers and Eurasians (33 males and 53 females) and Tamils (26 men and 40 females).[5] From these figures it appears clearly that the profession of sewing and mending clothes was undertaken by both sexes. Did the introduction of the sewing machine in the 1880s and 1890s lead to more men taking up this occupation? The gradual change in the ethnic distribution of tailors and seamstresses may indicate that buying a sewing machine demanded a certain capital which Muslims and Burghers who were engaged in nonagricultural professions were more likely to acquire in the early twentieth century.

The colonial economy in the nineteenth century was not for indigenous entrepreneurs an easy terrain to conquer. The commerce of the city of Colombo was dominated by European and Indian merchants and by local traders belonging to minority groups. The majority of local merchants were small retailers who faced fierce competition from Borah, Memon, Parsi and Chettiar traders from India mostly located in the Pettah, the centre of non-European trade. The paucity of Sri Lankan entrepreneurs in trade was mainly due to their lack of access to credit on reasonable terms. Foreign-owned banking institutions, essentially British-owned banks with headquarters in London or India, practiced a deliberate policy of discrimination. They limited their customers to British and foreign business interests as well as the Nattukottai Chettiars. There was no chance for a common person to obtain credit from a British-owned bank such as the Bank of Ceylon even though they had branches in Kandy and Galle.[6] The lending policy of the banks catered to the needs of the British business and trade. There was an open distinction made between local and foreign clients. Foreign banks had two separate departments for Europeans and non-Europeans. A local customer would never meet the bank manager and would instead be met by a shroff, a local intermediary who was responsible for either guaranteeing or recommending non-Europeans who wanted credit, and who obtained commissions from both the bank and the customer. There was one attempt at launching an indigenous bank between 1917 and 1921 by Jeronis and Haramanis Soysa which collapsed after a few years due to inadequate capital and bad management. But a common person wanting to purchase a sewing machine was not the type of client that this bank would have entertained. Most Sri Lankans relied on loans from Chettiars or Pathan (Afghan) moneylenders. In 1933 there were estimated to be 556 Chettiar firms in the island with head offices in India and interests all over Asia. They were given loans from the foreign banks in Sri Lanka often without security and on the shroff's guarantee but at a rate (known as the Chetty rate) 2 to 3 per cent above the commercial bank rate. Chettiars in turn lent to local people on security considered unsound by the banks and charged rates of interest ranging from 10 to 20 per cent. The Chettiar provided loans for all purposes from agriculture, trade, consumption and dowries to expenditure on weddings.[7] A potential buyer of a sewing machine also had the option of being part of a *seethu* credit group, a form of saving that was common among lower-income people and has survived as a practice until today. Each person of a group of twenty-four would contribute for example 1 rupee per week and the money collected would be given each week to one member of the group.

Ferguson's directories of the early twentieth century provide the historian with some fragmentary information on tailors and their trade. When we compare the tailoring establishments in 1903, 1914–15 and 1925 in Colombo, Galle and Kandy, certain trends can be discerned. First there is clearly an ethnic specialization: tailors are distributed among Sinhalese, Muslims and Burghers, with a clear domination of the latter two groups. Listings of tailoring establishments in Colombo from 1903 to 1926 show a net increase in the number of Muslim tailoring shops with names such as Abdul Rahaman, Idroos and Sheriff, Lalchand and Co., Obema Lebbe Marikkar, Sufi Brothers, Yusoof B.K, and Paiva and Sons that still remain in living peoples' memories. The same trend is visible in Galle and Kandy where there was a relatively large Muslim community.[8] The story of one of these tailors – Mr A.S. Idroos – is one of hard work and perseverance. Idroos started work in and outside the Galle Face Hotel in the early 1880s. Twenty-five years later he employed twenty experienced tailors and supplied residents as well as travellers to Colombo arriving at the harbour. His representatives would board the ships in order to obtain orders from the passengers. He supplied military as well as civil garments and exported ready-made clothes to countries that included India, the Straits and Australia.[9] Another Muslim tailor from Kandy appears in the narrative of the 1915 riots as a victim of the violence. While he survives, his two nephews who come to his rescue are arrested for stabbing some Sinhalese men:

> In this state of high tension, while the crowd was still standing in the street craving for a conference with the Government Agent, someone kicked at the door of Muhammadan tailor, who madly rushed among the people, until he was felled to the ground.[10]

Another discernible trend is that from 1915 onwards larger establishments owned by British interests such as Cargills Ltd, Smith Campbell and Co. Ltd, Miller and Co. Ltd, Grand Central Stores and Modern Drapery Stores moved into the lucrative tailoring business. Some tailoring establishments such as Whiteaway Laidlaw & Co., Drapers and Outfitters, advertised themselves as users of sewing machines – an added proof of quality tailoring in 1918. The era of the street tailor was retreating while larger business groups were now offering services that were once the preserve of the individual tailor.[11]

Furthermore in the 1920s there appeared a new occupational category of dressmakers – of thirty-one listed, fifteen were women holding names such as Madame Aimee or Miss Clara de Silva in response to the embourgeoisement of the middle classes in Sri Lanka.[12] Mrs Clarence, dressmaker in Kollupitiya, Colombo, provides us with some information on the type of clothing generally ordered: men's shirts, with and without collars; white coats; night gowns (ladies); chemises; petticoats; flannel gowns; Oxford shirts; coloured calico skirts; pajamas and trousers.[13] Her clientele clearly included the British residents or the Westernized local residents of the capital. Some tailors were more specialized: Alfred Martin and Co. Ltd, Civil and Military Tailors, sold broadcloth, Venetian and cashmeres as well as Bedford cords for riding breeches and advertised tweed suiting and trousers and materials 'in all textures suitable for wearing in any part of Ceylon and England'.[14]

One of the tailors mentioned in the 1926 *Ferguson's Directory* has left traces of his life and business which by chance I was able to retrieve. The principal document is 'the humble petition of Francis Pieterz of St Monica, Dematagoda, Colombo' dating 19th March 1926 to the Police Magistrate Colombo. He introduces himself as a master tailor who started a business in March 1923 at no 100 Main Street Colombo under the 'name and style of F. Pieterz, gent's tailor.' In September of 1923 he employed a person called Joseph Mariam Britto of Pettah, Colombo, as a 'working partner' and the firm was thereafter registered as Britto, Pieterz and Co. The petitioner claims that 'all the capital and furniture and sewing machines and the stock in trade necessary for the working of this business' was supplied by him. At some point he resolved that he would have to dissolve the 'so-called partnership as he could not agree with the said Britto on matters connected with the business, especially', as he found out, 'that the said Britto was attempting to make himself the sole owner of the establishment'. Following the departure of Britto to India on 22 February Pieterz took the opportunity 'upon the advice of a lawyer' to assert his claim as sole proprietor of the business. He locked the doors of the shop and placed a watchman to guard it. At midnight of the same day fifteen men belonging to the party of Britto arrived on the spot, threatened the watchman and 'forcibly' placed two locks of their own on the doors. After he made a complaint to the Pettah police station Pieterz had those locks broken and replaced the watchman. The next day once again the doors had been relocked! Pieterz then asked for police protection against Britto and his gang. The petition also includes an inventory of the clothes that were being made in the shop: among them were a tweed full suit, a satin dress, a blazer coat and many other items.[15]

The tailor was an ubiquitous part of the everyday life of the city folk. E.F.C. Ludowyk's memoir provides an insight into the personalized style of the tailor and his role in the community: the shoemaker like the tailor came to his home in Galle to measure and fit the clothes. The tailor who cut his clothes later blossomed into a maker of hoods for motor cars. The trousers he provided were, it seems, ill cut and frayed his thighs.[16]

By 1935 tailors had formed a corporation called the Ceylon Tailors Federation. They were heard petitioning the government for the imposition of a quota on sewn goods imported from Japan and complained that imports from Japan had led to a situation where tailors in Sri Lanka were unemployed and seen begging in the streets.[17] The street tailor had come of age and had increasingly to compete with home sewing by middle-class women who until then had relied on specialist tradesmen for sewing clothes and other home items.

WOMEN AND HOME

In the home the machine followed the rhythms of family life, blended into it, merged with other activities in a polysynchronic way. It did not constitute a separate domain, instead becoming part of the everyday life of the Sinhala bourgeois family. The location of the machine in a visible place in the house, the sitting room or dining room table, led to its integration with other objects, some foreign, others local.

Its central place in the bourgeois home indicated the consensus around a machine that accelerated time and transformed the pace of living. During the early twentieth century, the home of yesterday was clearly discarded for a dwelling more in tune with changing times. However, when Sinhalese city folk in the early twentieth century returned for family celebrations or religious festivals to their ancestral home in the gama they re-entered a home space that appeared in their eyes bucolic and essentially different from their bourgeois homes of Colombo. Lost in their nostalgia for things past, they closed their eyes to the fact that in this perceived authentic space of the village house, the outside world had already encroached, denting the pristine world they yearned for. The ambivalent attitude to home by the emerging Sinhalese educated classes/literati epitomizes their acceptance of the modern as an inevitable yet not totally ethical path to progress. Home in the village and the city was fashioned as a miniature nation in the making, a terrain that was traversed by many makers, owners, workers and visitors; a terrain that was also constantly transformed by new objects and machines whose ubiquitous presence instilled new ways of being and behaving among the people.

Some changes were more visible to the eye. Houses were now more solid and weather proof. More tiled houses were being built at the turn of the nineteenth century as many local town boards made it a prerequisite. Over the heads of many Sinhalese people lay tiles brought from overseas, often from Mangalore in British India. Tiled houses were conspicuous along the southern coast road to Galle and were for a colonial administrator such as E.B. Denham, writing in 1911, a 'marked sign of prosperity' that explained why imports of bricks and tiles had increased by 66 per cent since 1901.[18]

Writing in the late eighteenth century, Robert Knox was perplexed by the simplicity of the village houses in the Kandyan kingdom. This was quite a contrast to the brick and tiled house of the early twentieth century:

> Their *Houses* are small, low, thatched Cottages, built with sticks, daubed with clay, the walls made very smooth. For they are not permitted to build their houses above one story high, neither may they cover with tiles, nor whiten their walls with lime, but there is a *Clay* which is as white, and that they use sometimes.[19]

Denham and other colonial voices of the early twentieth century were probably overly eager to see change. Other witnesses gladly recorded the ubiquity of traditional structures. A typical Sinhalese rural house was still described by Ananda Coomaraswamy in 1907 as a simple framed one-storeyed timber and mud walled building with a thatched roof. It contained a square courtyard open to the sky, surrounded by an internal verandah which was used for all the activities of living and working. Of this the 'poorest house … had but one room, few more than two or three'.[20]

The essential character of the Sinhalese rural house underlined by Coomaraswamy was its openness, which reflected the lack of hierarchical ordering in its conception. He highlighted the absence of a purified zone, of segregation of visitors from the life of the family and attempt to segregate or screen the women from visiting or resident men who are outside the immediate family circle. The ordinary Sinhalese home reflected in his view the Buddhist rejection of structuring of social and family life. Coomaraswamy's romantic vision of the Oriental Buddhist rural house was, of course, just as partial as Denham's vision of a proliferation of brick houses. For in the home described by Coomaraswamy as an open but empty shell of Buddhist virtue, furniture and new objects were by the early twentieth century already visible: alongside baskets, wooden mortars, graters (*hirimane*) and flat stones to grind spices were clocks and mirrors. These new objects contributed to redefining social relations within communities in the same way as the stool (*bankuwa*) did in the past. Furniture was indeed involved in prescribing acceptable behaviour. The stool without a back in Sinhalese homes was from the time of Knox's narration in the eighteenth century a subtle means of establishing and consolidating caste hierarchies through modes of sitting in a higher or lower position according to status: 'They sit upon a mat on the ground, and eat. But he, whom they do honour and respect, sits on a stool and his victuals on another before him,'[21] while richer people used 'banks of clay to sit on; which they often daub over with soft *Cow-dung,* to keep them smooth and clean.'[22]

While the houses and lifestyles of the Sinhalese aristocracy have been examined with some detail, the middle and lower classes have not generated similar interest.[23] Of the house interiors of the Burgher community in the Pettah in the nineteenth century some descriptions remain: 'The furniture was generally of ebony or calamander, sometimes elaborately carved. The dining room generally had a long table to seat the large families of those times. On a massive side-board would be laid the family's silver or crystal and porcelain.'[24]

Although figures tell us that a century and a few decades later the Singer sewing machine entered the village home, we have few accounts of the way it was received. It was the first domestic machine that Sinhalese people from all walks of life encountered, bought and used. Yet it was not the first foreign object in village and city homes: house inventories of the early twentieth century give lists of a variety of products from other countries, from German silver trays and spoons and China matting on the floor to Japanese pictures painted on glass.[25] It was often an eclectic ensemble of objects but through the entry of foreign objects familiarity with the outer world was conveyed and status gained in a new manner. One of the few detailed accounts of the furniture in an 'ordinary villager's house' is given in Denham's report of 1911. With the sense of detail of an apothecary he described the furniture in the house of a villager in the Colombo *Mudaliyar*'s division.[26] The furniture was mainly functional but of good quality, for instance, a satinwood almairah and jakwood bed was mentioned. The pictures on the walls in other simple households were also generally of a religious nature: saints or Virgin and Child or birth and renunciation of Prince Siddhartha. Pictures of kings and queens of Europe too were popular and available even in shops in interior villages. These images linked colonised subjects across the subcontinent, but they were far from being a one-dimensional community of servants of the raj: in the house of a *Vidana Arachchi,* Japanese pictures hung on the walls.

With Western clothes sewn by women or tailors using sewing machines, Western-style hygiene was also entering the home; one saw increasingly dressing tables in bedrooms, combs and hair powder boxes. The custom had been to have the toilet and bathroom separated from the rest of the house.

A painting of three Sinhalese women and a child dressed in pastel-coloured, beautifully draped sarees, one of them sewing while the others pensively surround the woman sitting at a sewing machine, illustrates the way in which women blend into the décor made of flowering plants (Figure 16). The home is portrayed as a female and feminine place.

The drape of the sarees suggests gentleness and domesticity as in paintings of the Dutch masters which portrayed women engaged in domestic ac-

Figure 16. Oil painting. Courtesy Mr Hemaka Amarasuriya, former chairman of Singer in Sri Lanka

tivities such as sewing, reading or holding flowers. The painting suggests a conflation between animate woman and inanimate room which can be read as visual depiction of women's ideal role in a culture in flux where parts of Sinhalese village cultural habitus merge with foreign technology. There was a clear overlay between women's bodies and the interior space of the home similar to the conflation that was so visible in bourgeois Europe and North America.[27]

The sewing machine, a wheeled object made of steel, might first appear to disturb the peaceful order of sexes. But steel could be made supple and gentle by positioning it in an otherwise feminine environment. Just as the body was decorated according to criteria of morality and fashion, the machine in the home was often subject to beautifying by its makers as well as by its users. Just as there were rules of what they could wear and not wear, there were rules on what to use in the various rooms of the house. Items of furniture were dressed with decorative accessories. Pianos as well as sewing machines were covered with dust ruffles that resembled the frills on the long skirts or saris that they wore. Objects were draped like women's bodies. These correspondences remained for as long as the Sinhalese bourgeois woman – unlike women from the Burgher community who had much earlier taken up employment as music teachers, seamstresses, caterers and governesses – shied away from the labour force.[28]

WOMEN AND NATION

The woman was not only the embodiment of the home in Sri Lanka, the extension of her corporeal and spiritual self, but also in these anticolonial times the embodiment of the nation in the making. It was not wealth and status that was shown but markers of authenticity.

The body was a key site of the colonial encounter as recent works in the field of colonial studies have suggested. Policies on the body in the Javanese colonial situation have been shown to have spawned 'a set of behaviors, a template for living, a care of the self, an ideal of domesticity'.[29] But in many of these studies the focus is the colonial encounter and genealogies of the intimate in the domestic space of the coloniser rather than of the colonised. Although this signals a paradigm shift in colonial studies there is still a need to narrate the transformation in the world views, habits and material cultures of the colonised, and to describe what James Duncan calls their 'embodied practices' through a reading of the margins of colonial documents.[30] We know for instance that before the advent of 'colonial soap', people in Sri Lanka, a land generally endowed with natural lakes, rivers, waterfalls and hydraulic tanks, used to wash their bodies and clothes frequently with natural products such as sandalwood. 'No soap is used for washing clothes, dipping garments in water and striking them against a flat stone' was the most common method as described in 1807 by Reverend James Cordiner.[31]

Colonial documents are silent on the reactions of the natives to new products and on what types of concerns were voiced, although the native body was an imagined space that generated pervasive concern in official, settler, missionary and planter discourses and practices, epitomised in the British civil servant E.B. Denham's detailed account of the material culture of the natives in 1911.[32]

In the colonial state, the colonised body was transformed gently as well as coerced and disciplined into becoming a docile body. Just as in Southeast Asia where the body of the native was described as different – Ann Stoler describes how Javanese nursemaids were instructed to hold their charges away from their bodies so that the infants would not 'smell of their sweat' – in Sri Lanka native bodies were considered lacking hygiene and discipline.[33] On the plantations, workers resisted attempts to transform them into abstract, docile bodies by rejecting the highly routinised plantation regime through the few weapons of the weak – desertion, thefts, minimising work – they had at their disposal. But in a situation of unequal power they had to comply overtly.

Through the contact with cosmetics the body of the native man and woman became both a desiring body and a healthier body more adapted to labour. This feature was important since the goals of the colonisers were essentially economically motivated. In the villages and cities hygiene was sold as a consumer product, while in the plantations a combination of Western hygiene and control transformed the Tamil labourer from a 'weak, stupid, ill-fed, badly clad person' through being 'well housed, well cared for, well fed, and employed at regular and sufficient work' into 'a strong, intelligent, lusty labourer'[34].

A letter to the editor of the *Sinhala Jatiya* castigated this new trend in women which was 'to waste money unnecessarily to beautify themselves, following the latest fashions and using strange things like perfume'.[35] Society's equilibrium that was between the *dharmistha* (righteous) and un-dharmistha was clearly acquiring the traits of a consumption society where the equilibrium was between consumption and its denunciation.[36] This critique of wastage made a value judgement based on the distinction between necessities and luxuries. What was feared indeed was the gradual imposition of a consumer culture as had happened in Europe. Modern consumption would produce a passive, subordinated population which would no longer be able to realize its 'real needs'. The consumer was now presented with a choice of soaps, each adapted for a particular situation. An advertisement of the Chiswick soap company mentions a variety of soaps, including imperial and red poppy, odourless soaps, snowflake potash soap, saddle soap, saddle paste and chiswick compound.[37] Later in the twentieth century in Africa, institutional forms of communication more advanced than in Sri Lanka in the early years of the century were used to spread the gospel of cleanliness and other colonial forms of propaganda – demonstration and cinema vans, radio, African newspapers, women's clubs, health lectures, mission schools, beauty contests and fashion shows.[38] The spread of soaps and powders in rural Sri Lanka as well as more direct 'lessons of hygiene' in Africa were part of the general attempt to promote 'civilised' manners and discipline in the comportment of the self and the practice of everyday life in different colonial situations. Thus with the acquisition of new hygienic habits and the entry of new products into the homes of the natives throughout the empire, a process of homogenisation was taking place.

MACHINES AND THE NATION

If novels reflect to a certain extent people's perception, the petite bourgeoisie did not consider 'sewing' a very respectable profession. This is apparent for instance in Piyadasa Sirisena's *Maha Wiyawula* (The Great Confusion) published in 1938 where the poor but virtuous female character is compelled to live in the slums of Slave Island and sew clothes.

There was, however, a need for this new technology on the part of women. The times had clearly changed. In Martin Wickramasinghe's short story entitled *Narak wu pitibaduna* (A Spoilt Pot of Dough) a miserly Sinhala merchant sighs about the fact that young women want scissors and a sewing machine while in 'our time' women cut their clothes with the 'mannaya', the large knife used in the kitchen to cut vegetables or fish.[39]

But there was no real opposition to the sewing machine on the part of the Sinhala literati of the day. Indeed the sewing machine contributed to strengthen and disseminate the familiar tropes of nineteenth-century domesticity founded on the contrast between the public and the private, industry and home, male and female. The colonial construction of domesticity and its engagement with native ideas of the role of women in the family provided many of the 'prior meanings' that shaped the consumption of sewing machines by middle-class women. In this new household, domestic tasks – sewing was one of them – were increasingly seen as the sole and inherent province of women.

Until other time-saving machines such as the washing machine or leisure goods such as the television and video player, the sewing machine was the favoured item which composed the movable goods of the dowry of a middle-class bride. Although there is no data about it, it is a known fact as many older people would testify that they were given a machine by their family on marriage or that the family machine was handed down to a daughter leaving the home.

The work of Partha Chatterjee on the creation of a 'new woman' in Bengal has shown that the nationalist project was not so much a dismissal of modernity as an attempt to 'make modernity consistent with the nationalist project'.[40] Chatterjee has furthermore argued that it is through the fixing of her 'essential femininity' in terms of culturally visible "spiritual" qualities that were manifest through her dress, habits, social demeanour and religious behaviour, that the colonized bourgeois Bengali woman could traverse the public sphere. His categorization of bourgeois womanhood as 'spiritual' as opposed to the 'material' qualities embodied in man has been sharply critiqued by feminist scholars writing on Sri Lanka although not for the reasons I would adduce. Malathi de Alwis has analysed the new woman in colonized Sri Lanka using the concept of 'respectability'. Her work has shown how 'the careless and restless bodies, and inattentive and obstinate minds of native girls were disciplined and moulded in missionary schools via a 'gospel of gentility' that sought to produce 'respectable' ladies who were both pious and industrious, restrained and gentle. Both Chatterjee and de Alwis, by focusing on bourgeois women in Bengal and Sri Lanka, have failed to underscore working-class women's encounter with machines that embody the material world. The working-class home became a site of production thus challenging any interpretation through a clear material/spiritual template and questioning the virtue of 'nationalism' as a driver of change.

The skill of sewing was part of the qualities that needed to be acquired. For poorer women it would procure employment opportunities; for bourgeois women it was a marker of domesticity. It embodied the Christian virtues of piety, industry and docility. It was linked in many ways to the missionary project of transforming heathen bodies into respectable ones.[41] The Singer shop in Colombo conducted sewing classes especially for women at a sewing school in Wellawatte and promoted sewing in three girls' schools. 'The girls', said the principal of one of the schools, 'have spent their time very profitably.'[42]

The Sinhala literati promoted a lifestyle of simplicity and modesty, thus constructing a new kind of 'moral economy' for women. The perception of respectability was mobilized by Sinhala Buddhist nationalists to ridicule Sinhala women who were perceived to be too Christian and modern. Certain activities were coded as unrespectable: this included going to movies and parties, playing the piano, tennis and cards, pursuing athletics, drinking alcohol, smoking, riding horses and bicycles, driving cars and so on. Interestingly the sewing machine does not appear in these lists, as it belonged to the world of labour rather than leisure. Indigenous and Christian notions of morality worked together to produce the idea of respectability around the sewing machine. Unlike the bicycle about which there was an implicit discourse suggesting that it had a sexual effect of stimulating women, the image of automated femininity at a sewing machine did not appear threatening to the Sinhalese man or carry sexual associations.

CONCLUSION

The interaction between the sewing machine and its users in colonial Sri Lanka testifies to the multiplicity of notions of time that coexisted under what scholars speciously refer to as colonial modernity. In everyday life the march to modern time-competence, from untimed to timed cultures governed by E.P. Thompson's triptych of clocks, class and capitalism of a task-oriented peasant society, was simply not taking place everywhere or in an undifferentiated manner.[43] An alternative account is rather about 'the degree and type of interaction and mutual construction among several coexisting time-senses'.[44] But there were among labouring classes new elements of everyday temporal structuring, around trading and domestic activities – including sewing – that came with the arrival of time-saving machines such as the sewing machine. Tailors' work, however, remained tied to the demands of clients for particular tasks for which they had the freedom of assigning the time needed. The practice of mechanical reproduction did not modify the tailor's control of his life but offered him means of saving time and possibly a more efficient way of managing his timetable.

The machine in the factory refashioned people's relation to work, creating new forms of alienation and, as the next chapter will show, new gods to address the new plights of the workers. The machine transformed people's relation to the home, which was now conquered by domestic instruments that intruded into the everyday life of bourgeois and ordinary folk. The machine helped stitch the nation for the literati of the day as they either accepted it as a bearer of moral virtues conforming to authenticity or critiqued it as a threat to the nation they were attempting to model. The colonized self-defined themselves and were defined by others through their relation to a modern world of machines.

NOTES

1. Cited in Jayawardena, *From Nobodies to Somebodies,* 5.
2. B. Ryan. 1953. *Caste in Modern Ceylon. The Sinhalese System in Transition,* New Brunswick: Rutgers University Press, 113–14.

3. F. Barth. 1960. 'The System of Stratification in Swat. North Pakistan', in E.R. Leach (ed.), *Aspects of Caste in South India, Ceylon and North West Pakistan,* London: Cambridge University Press, 137.
4. Census of Ceylon 1871, Table VI, 97; Census of Ceylon 1871, Table VII, 97–98, 187; David Arnold has examined the image of the *darzi* as it appears in narratives and iconography of colonial life in India before the advent of the sewing machine as an example of the inertia and stagnation of India. They were predominantly Muslim although not exclusively. Arnold, 'Global Goods and Local Usages', 407–29 and 411–14.
5. Census of Ceylon 1891 Table no LXV, 374–75.
6. The Bank of Ceylon opened in 1841 and later merged with the Oriental Bank to form the Oriental Bank Corporation in 1851.
7. Jayawardena, *From Nobodies to Somebodies,* 135–39.
8. *Ferguson's Directory,* 1903, 773; *Ferguson's Directory,* 1914–15, 931, 940, 947; *Ferguson's Directory,* 1926, 843.
9. Wright, *Twentieth Century Impressions of Ceylon,* 489.
10. Ramanathan, *Riots and Martial Law in Ceylon,* 55.
11. *Ferguson's Directory,* 1903, 773; *Ferguson's Directory,* 1914–15, 931, 940, 947; *Ferguson's Directory,* 1925, 764.
12. List of tailors in *Ferguson's Directory,* 1926, 843.
13. *Ferguson's Ceylon Handbook and Directories,* 1925, 27.
14. *Ferguson's Directory,* 1880, advertisement, xi.
15. Petition in the private collection of the family of Francis Pieterz.
16. E.F.C. Ludowyk. 1989. *Those Long Afternoons: Childhood in Colonial Ceylon,* Colombo: Lake House Bookshop, 75.
17. *Straits Times,* 14 December 1935, 19.
18. Denham, *Ceylon at the Census,* 159.
19. R. Knox. 1681. *A Historical Relation of Ceylon,* 87, http://www.gutenberg.org/files/14346/14346-h/14346-h.htm#d0e11060.
20. See R. Lewcock, B. Sansoni, Laki and C. Anjalendran. 1998. *The Architecture of an Island. The Living Legacy of Sri Lanka,* Colombo: Barefoot Ltd; Coomaraswamy, *Medieval Sinhalese Art,* cited in ibid., 20.
21. Knox, *Historical Relation of Ceylon,* 87.
22. Ibid., 87.
23. See Y. Gooneratne. 1986. *Relative Merits. A Personal Memoir of the Bandaranaike Family of Sri Lanka,* London: C.Hurst Publ.; A. Pieris. 2007. 'The Trouser under the Cloth. Personal Space in Colonial-Modern Ceylon', in P. Scriver and V. Prakash (eds), *Colonial Modernities: Building, Dwelling and Architecture in British India and Ceylon,* London: Routledge, 119–218.
24. D. Brohier. 1994. *Dr Alice de Boer and Some Pioneer Women Doctors in Sri Lanka,* Colombo SSA, 23.
25. Denham, *Ceylon at the Census,* 166.
26. The *mudaliyar* was the chief headman and the administrator of a *korale* in British times.

27. B. Gordon. 1996. 'Woman's Domestic Body. The Conceptual Conflation of Women and Interiors in the Industrial Age', *Wintherthur Portfolio* 31(4), *Gendered Spaces and Aesthetics,* 281–301.
28. Brohier, *Dr Alice de Boer,* 3–14.
29. Stoler, *Carnal Knowledge and Imperial Power,* 1.
30. J. Duncan. 2002. 'Embodying Colonialism? Domination and Resistance in Nineteenth Century Ceylonese coffee Plantations', *Journal of Historical Geography* 28(3) 317–36.
31. J. Cordiner. 1807. *A Description of Ceylon,* London: London: Longman, Hurst, Rees and Orme, 118.
32. Denham, *Ceylon at the Census of 1911.*
33. Stoler, *Carnal Knowledge and Imperial Power,* 6.
34. J.S. Duncan, 2007. *In the Shadows of the Tropics: Climate, Race and Biopower in Nineteenth Century Ceylon,* Aldershot: Ashgate, 88.
35. *Sinhala Jatiya,* 1 February 1923.
36. J. Baudrillard. 1996. *La Société de Consommation,* Paris: Gallimard, 79.
37. *Ferguson's Directory,* 1895, 870b.
38. T. Burke. 1996b. 'Sunlight Soap Has Changed My Life: Hygiene, Commodification, and the Body in Colonial Zimbabwe,' in H. Hendrickson (ed.), *Clothing and Difference: Embodied Identities in Colonial and Post-Colonial Africa,* Durham and London: Duke University Press, 189–212.
39. M. Wickramasinghe. 1924. 'Narak Wu piti baduna', in *Gehaniyak,* Dehiwela: Tisara Prakasakayo.
40. P. Chatterjee. 1993. *The Nation and Its Fragments,* New Delhi: Oxford University Press.
41. M. de Alwis. 1997. 'The Production and Embodiment of Respectability: Gendered Demeanours in Colonial Ceylon', in M. Roberts (ed.), *Collective Identities Revisited,* vol. 1, Colombo: Marga Instittute, 178–79.
42. *The Red S Review,* Wellawatte Sewing School, 31 August and 30 September 1935.
43. E.P. Thompson. 1967. 'Time, Work-Discipline and Industrial Capitalism', *Past and Present* 38, 56–97.
44. P. Glennie and N. Thrift. 1996. 'Reworking E.P. Thompson's "Time, Work-Discipline and Industrial Capitalism"', *Time and Society* 5(3), 292.

Chapter 8

Working like Machines

> When they [coolies] work they are almost like machines.
> – *Labour Commission Report*, 1908, 533

While Marx recognized a history of human labour that lay concealed in every human artefact, Walter Benjamin distinguished multiple histories wedded as a whole, a history of production, but also of circulation and consumption and use. Objects, he argued famously, stored the unconscious of the collective. But some objects were more than mediators or embodiments of our sense of ourselves and our sense of others. In the colonial world, prey to a great transformation, some objects, in particular the machines that manned the booming capitalist economy, appeared to many as strange and powerful things worthy of fearful worship. Machines became more than objects that moved people or made things, they acquired a quality that linked them to their users in a nonfunctional way. They became gods of a sort, alien technological gods, and signified a terrible loss of control on the part of humans.

We do not know the names of the subordinated men and women in rural and urban Sri Lanka who, as the long nineteenth century unfolded, were able to grasp a new kind of freedom by navigating with dexterity through the sclerosed institutions of the colonial state. But colonial censuses and reports tell us that a fair number left their villages to answer the call for labour in the cities where they fell prey to the lure of goods, and that a few others were determined enough to tame the written word and discover new worlds of meaning. What this moment of history offered them, a moment that unlike famous battles is not commemorated by states or citizens, was a freedom to write a new life script for themselves and fashion singular and different futures outside the daily humiliation of their subjected beings. These choices weighed also against all the predetermined habits and patterns of behaviour that had lightly punctuated their quotidian life-cycles from birth to death.

The Punchi Menikas and Hinihammis of jungle villages and the 'coolies' on tea plantations[1] were left out and remain so even today. In fact most people in the colony simply ignored these possibilities or, reading them as unreachable, retreated back into those practices of self-deception that are so characteristic of subject peoples who fear the sweet loss of servitude.

Yet these were abhinava times for those who took the leap, where in the space of a decade they would see the landscape of their land mutating into something they would never had conceived even in their dreams. There were no strict rules according to which they had to behave and they lived their lives in a working space full of new demands, new objects and machines that performed faster, work that humans had before that executed for generations but at a tranquil and slower pace. Their lives were not, however, performed from a blank sheet of experience or through building something entirely new from nothingness. In these new practices appeared the ghosts of other times, reproduced and refashioned but nevertheless present.

After a period of stupor and bewilderment when they were seen, child-like, collecting the traces in the mud left by car tires or standing in expectation on the side of the road waiting for a vehicle to whizz by, came the period of experimentation. They soon got accustomed to using these machines, trams, cars and bicycles that took them from one place to another faster than their own legs or bullock carts; they bought sewing machines that worked faster than the needle and thread of the past and used them in the comfort of their homes, but sometimes they let other machines draw them to the city or plantation factory where their sweat was exchanged for monetary gain.

But what was happening inside these people, how this age of the machine affected them, tormented, exhilarated them and transformed their common sense[2] is not accounted for, except in the record of a few practices that give the historian who holds her lens very close to the ground a clue but no hard evidence about the texture of people's everyday life.

LABOUR AND THE HETEROGENEOUS TIMES OF THE SELF

On Norton Bridge in the hill country of Sri Lanka not far from the Maskeliya Reservoir a few factories are nestled among lush, green tea plantations traversed by thin, winding roads. Descendants of Indian immigrants from South India who came to the island in the late nineteenth century as 'free' workers, technically on monthly contracts, continue to provide the labour force, women as pluckers and men in the factories and other capacities. The circumstances in which these men and women settled in these areas, so different from the village India they left behind, and lead self-contained lives as a cog in the capitalist estate economy has been described and dissected.[3] Their numbers, caste membership – they were generally not Brahmins – and the conditions in which they toiled and resisted rules imposed by the plantation system have been elaborated. Clearly they were not 'free', as planters tried to control them by legislation, indebtedness and force. Views differ on the part played by the Sinhala labour force in the plantation sector: did the Sinhala peasantry refuse to work on plantations as common knowledge assumes or were they willingly left aside and made landless by the British who expropriated their lands? It is more likely that as in other plantation systems local labour was simply not sought as Tamil labour cohorts were in good supply and willing to submit to the stringent work conditions.[4]

Perceptions are often more important than reality, and Tamil plantation workers were for long perceived as being responsible for the plight of the dispossessed Sinhala peasantry whose land was taken over by planters in the nineteenth century through laws such as the Wasteland Ordinance of 1840. Resentment vis-à-vis the workers who were benefiting from the new economy seeped deep. Even government documents identified Indian plantation workers as culprits: 'The peasant's main occupation is agriculture, but his holding is too small to permit him to earn his livelihood from its produce. He is ready to take subsidiary employment, agricultural or otherwise, but the avenue of employment on the plantations is blocked by Indian labour.'[5]

The cognitive map of the men who first experienced terrible machines and fought against nature, cast as victims, culprits or simply labour, is not deemed worthy of memory. Even among social historians the inner worlds of the plantation workers, their rituals, how they lived and related to the new environment in which they were for many years compelled to remain for lack of choice or will has elicited little interest as though their lives had no sense outside labour relations.[6] Not surprisingly, the map of communities in the Report of the Census of Ceylon of 1911 represents all other communities in their 'imagined' national dress standing firmly in regions of the map, facing the gaze of the reader. Only the Indian Tamil – this was the colonial term for him – is represented as a worker, bent and toiling, evading the reader's eye[7] (see Map 2).

The present, however, speaks to us about a past inhabited by fear and spectres. In several tea factories today, factory workers worship at shrines to Rodhaimuni, a 'small deity', in the words of local people. Estate workers were and are generally Hindus, worshippers of Siva, Vishnu, Murugan, Vinayagar, Ganesh, Kathiresan, yet they also worship newer guardian deities

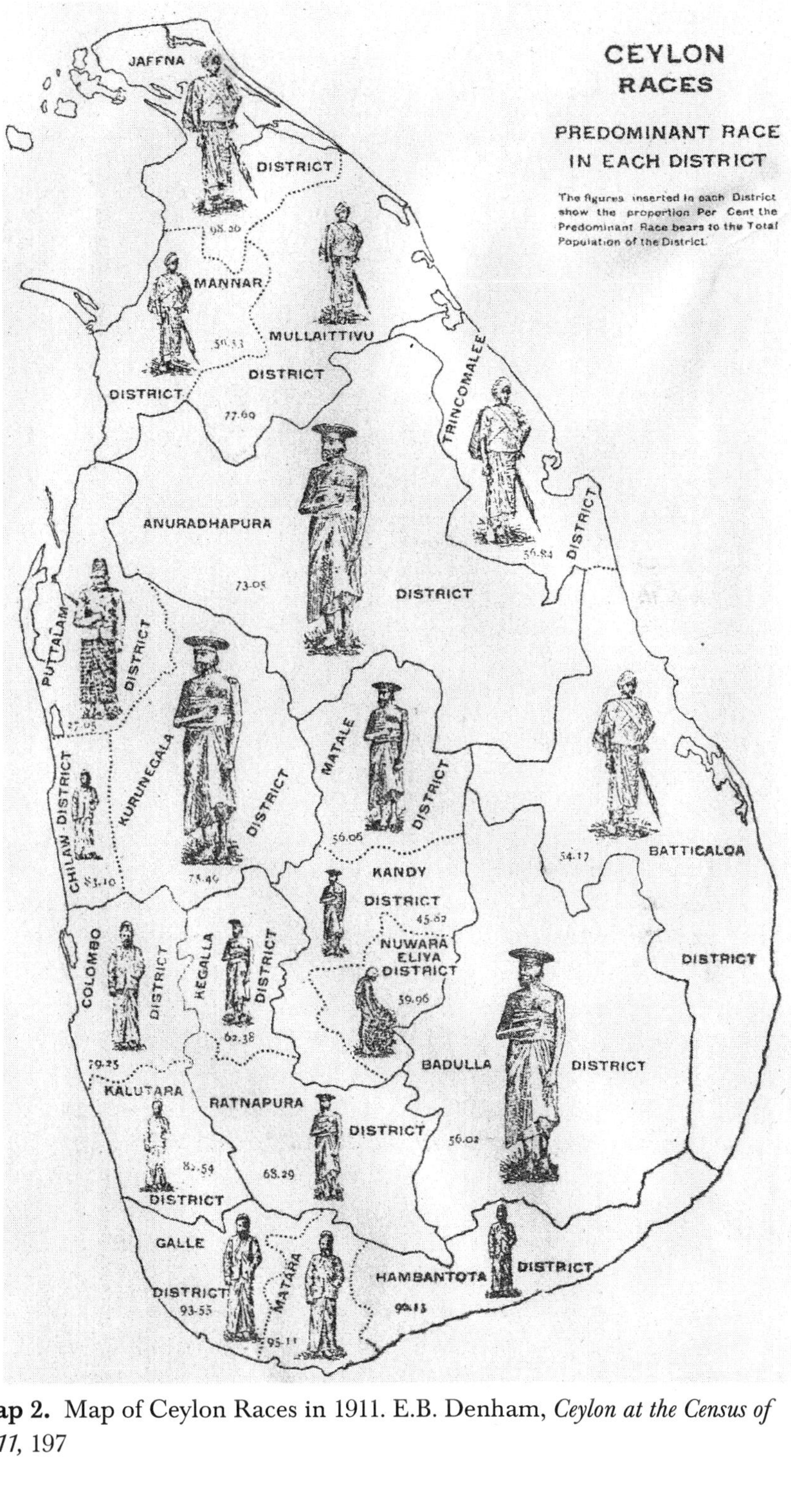

Map 2. Map of Ceylon Races in 1911. E.B. Denham, *Ceylon at the Census of 1911*, 197

who embody the particular situation in which they found themselves as immigrant workers transplanted to fields and tea factories far away from home. These non-Sanskritic, meat-eating deities include, apart from Rodhaimuni – the factory deity – other less well defined deities such as Muniandym Karuppan, Madesamy and Mrudaiveeran.

These shrines were probably created at the beginning of the plantation era in the late nineteenth century when workers arrived from India to the wooded hill country at the centre of the island after a long trek through snake-infested jungle where they were at the mercy of predators. And as there were no temples in their untamed environment, they set up forest shrines to protect them from unforeseen dangers and to give them the courage and strength to face the unknown.

In Hatton, 'rotha' or 'rodhais' is endowed with many meanings. For some workers, it refers to the "roller." The names Rodhaimuni and Kambimuni seem to be linked to the wheels of the machines in the tea factories and the cables used in earlier days to send tea leaves that had been plucked. Rodhaimuni is also known by other names such as Ella muni and Mahamuni, the meanings of which are not clear.

Stories reveal that Rodhaimuni was brought to Sri Lanka by the god Krishna on Krishna's own shoulders. The sea was crossed by placing stones and Krishna came by jumping from stone to stone, a story that is reminiscent of the story of King Ram, an incarnation of god Krishna who built a bridge across the Palk Straits with the help of the monkey king Hanuman. In the estate shrines, there are no statues of Rodhaimuni and the deity is normally symbolized by a lingam-shaped stone placed under a big tree. On a side of the stone, various iron objects are also placed (iron clearly symbolizes factories and work sites). At the entrance to the tea plantation in Norton Bridge one can see a *thrishulaya* (trident), an iron rod and an iron bar placed next to the stone symbolizing Rodhaimuni. Normally, cigars, meat (e.g., liver of a goat) and arrack are offered to him. This *pooja* (worship) offered once a year is a social event where mutton is cooked and shared among the community with arrack – the alcoholic drink distilled from the coconut – within the holy place itself. Blood of a goat is applied on machines in the factory and on other instruments used. If the pooja is not offered, there are stories of the machines at the factory working by themselves at midnight. Other people seem to describe Rodhaimuni as the god for cursing and for *huniyam* or black magic. Rodhaimuni smokes, eats and drinks just as the poor workers do and acts as the god for huniyam and cursing, offering perhaps for the estate workers an outlet when other forms of protest are impossible or too circumscribed by the unions and the management.[8]

There are other small deities associated with machines and tools: Kavatasami is the deification of *kavattu,* the tea-cutting or pruning knife. When the labourers are finished cutting, they will worship him, though the deity is just a cut tree, not a structure or idol like Rodhaimuni. Kalundasami is worshipped by pluckers.[9] Interestingly these rituals are restricted to males except for women who have passed menopause.[10]

Thus capitalist production and a factory system transplanted to the highlands of Sri Lanka led to the creation of deities who would look after the workers and their handling of machinery (Figure 17). Shrines were located next to the factory to satisfy the spiritual needs of the workforce. In Calgary, another estate in the hill country, the shrine to Rodhaimuni contained a stone image and the god's weapon and symbol (Vairavar). The management probably encouraged these beliefs as they allowed workers to accept the inevitability of work-related accidents – perceived as the Rodhaimuni wanting blood – and coming to terms with these by performing animal sacrifices such as killing a kid goat rather than demanding better work conditions.[11]

Accidents rarely made news but appeared now and then in the midst of other more important accounts as in the proceedings of the Labour Com-

Figure 17. Tea factory. Undated. www.historyofceylontea.com/photo-album.html

mission of 1908. There the chairman of the commission mentioned the case of a man who 'got his hand cut off in the factory and preferred to become a vagrant' although the estate was prepared to support him.[12] Another planter listed the pay of coolie workers where men received 33 cents a day and women 25 cents, while 'factory hands get more', probably due to the dangers inherent to handling machines.[13]

Machines, roads, bridges and railways have claimed the lives of their makers many times in the annals of history. Tales of blood and dismembered workers in the memories of plantation workers and factory workers are not unique to a colonial setting of power relations but are connected to anxieties about technological innovation. Sacrificial offerings were made in the late 1920s at the Tjolomadoe sugar mill in Central Java and blessed by the Netherlands East Indies governor general A.C.D. de Graeff. The belief among workers was that a ghost needed to be appeased with animal sacrifices and if not, a machinist might be drawn into the cogs and 'the sugar for a while runs red.'[14] In the Bolivian city of Oruro, miners conduct rites to a spirit known as uncle, Tio, who may turn malevolent if not provided with offerings. Icons are made to represent him:

> His body is sculptured from mineral. The hands, face and legs are made from clay. Often, bright pieces of metal or light bulbs from the miners' helmets form his eyes. The teeth may be of glass or of crystal sharpened like nails, and the mouth gapes, awaiting offerings of coca and cigarettes. The hand stretches out for liquor. In the Siglo XX mine the icon has an enormous erect penis.[15]

On tea plantations in Assam too there are stories dating from the onset of factories about machines that demanded the sacrifice of virgins and English sahibs who caught a woman by a rope and sacrificed her to the machine by decapitation once a year 'when machines were being overhauled in winter or during the first days of harvest'.[16] The Biswa Karma Puja is a ritual held every October to conjure the spirits of the machine. Mantras are sung by a Nepali priest in a shed close to the generator room, incense and food offered to a statue of a deity 'a burly, blue, and long haired male figure brandishing spanners and wrenches'.[17] Workers then follow the priest holding a clay pot of smoking incense who anoints the machines which have been stopped for the occasion with vermillion powder, moving from machine to machine. Other machines such as bicycles and motorized vehicles too were anointed.

FROM ROLLERS TO RODHAIMUNI

While the history of man's encounter with machines was never recorded, machines themselves have a history entrenched in the technological advances and the labour-saving technologies devised by capital. It was on tea factories built by British planters in the late nineteenth century that the people of Sri Lanka first encountered industrial machines and factory-style discipline.[18] There machine, labour power and capital cost were factored into a new equation where efficiency was the decisive determinant.

In the 1880s and 1890s more land had come under tea cultivation than any period thereafter. The tremendous increase in crop production placed a great burden on the processing facilities, which were struggling to cope with the high intakes of green leaf.[19] It was clearly evident that the largely manual manufacturing process that was being used until then was inadequate, and that an efficient, mechanised process was necessary. The first Tea House or factory was built in Sri Lanka in 1873 by James Taylor, bolstered by the success of his initial experimentation with converting green leaf into black tea. It was of wattle and daub and had hessian lofts in which to wither the leaf. He invented a tea leaf roller, which was powered by a 20-ft. water wheel, as he realized that manual rolling was not only inefficient, but also expensive. This was perhaps the moment of the birth of Rodhaimuni, but no records exist on this matter.

The demand for mechanisation created by burgeoning tea production was a golden opportunity for enterprising inventors and engineers. In a relatively short time clever machines that mimicked manual operations, albeit at much higher speed and efficiency, were invented and became mandatory in a tea factory. Thus a new ancillary industry, for producing tea-processing machinery, was born. The first successful tea-rolling machine was invented by the Walker brothers in 1880, and manufactured by their firm, John Walker & Co. In 1884, John Walker helped build the first central tea factory in Fairyland estate that belonged to J.A. Rossiter who developed tea estates in the foothills of Mount Pedro. Walker was also commissioned to build for a cost of 35,000 rupees a factory for the Carolina plantation in the Watawala area that became a model that was emulated by many other planters. It measured 30 meters long and 13 meters high and had three floors. Power was by steam generated by firewood. The design stood the test of time and was little changed over the next half century. John Brown was another resourceful British inventor and entrepreneur whose Triple Action Roller eclipsed the Walker Economic Roller. This new ancillary engineering industry, however, was concentrated in the hands of British firms and helped further consolidate British influence in its colonial outpost. Technology developed in the 1880s with the manufacture of the first "Sirocco" tea dryer by Samuel C. Davidson in 1877, and the manufacture of the first tea-rolling machine adapted from the steam engine by the engineer John Walker in 1880 set the conditions that would be required to make commercial tea production a reality.[20] This was consolidated in 1884 with the construction of the Central Tea Factory on Fairyland Estate (Pedro) in Nuwara Eliya. As tea production in Sri Lanka progressed, new factories were constructed introducing innovative methods of mechanization brought in from England. In the Mariawatte tea estate factory – which was in the early nineteenth century the site of the first coffee estate – only 3 to 5 per cent of the labour was necessary to man the machines.[21]

While the mechanisation process has been documented and can be dated, nothing remains of the men who worked the machines except a few photographs in company archives (Figure 18). Erased from history, they left only shrines to be passed on to their descendants. Their encounter with machines was mediated through new rituals that incorporated the iron tools from other lands into their own imaginary made of protective and sometimes vengeful gods. Their relation to objects is the only clue left to understanding their entanglement with the capitalist economy at an everyday level.

Among Muslims one can find similar beliefs. Closer to us, about fifty years ago when the jungle around Akairapattu in the Eastern Province was cleared for the Gal Oya irrigation scheme, marvellous things happened. Legend has it that the earth-moving equipment froze up and a previously

Figure 18. Worker in tea factory. Undated. www.historyof ceylontea.com/ photo-album.html

unknown saint called Sikander emerged in a dream to explain that he had been buried in the forest for centuries. A mosque was then built in the 1950s with a saint's tomb to appease him.[22] Work could go on.

Religious rituals and customs easily enter the domain of the modern and soften its sharp angles. Writing about India, Chakrabarty asserted that 'labor, the activity of producing, is seldom a completely secular activity.'[23] In the times of gods where work rituals often invoke divine or superhuman presence, humans were not the only meaningful agents. Subaltern historians have narrated the presence of the supernatural in the history of labour. The machines embedded in the modern world, produced in modern factories to feed the modern needs of a consumer, belong to the world of gods through these common rituals. It is not a vestige of the past, a nostalgia or a continuity from previous times or as E.P. Thompson famously said a practice 'haunted by the legend of better days';[24] it is rather firmly grounded in the present, transformed by it and transforming it at the same time. Gyan Pandey too has shown in his work on the Julahas, a community of weavers in North India, how for them work and worship were two inseparable activities. This was epitomized in the fact that they called themselves 'weavers of light' and that in the process of weaving different prayers were recited.[25]

On the day of Vishvakarma puja in the jute mills of Calcutta in the 1930s, machinery was worshipped. Tools and other emblems were placed on an altar, incense burnt, a goat decapitated. Instrument worship or Ayudha Pooja (literally meaning 'worship of the weapons') is a festival observed in different forms and traditions. It is a public holiday in India. Some people bless the tools by which they make a living, by cleaning them, showing respect. For instance a tailor might decorate his sewing machine, and a driver his vehicle. Shopkeepers and merchants observe Ayudha Pooja by decorating their shops, the cash register etc. in honour of Lakshmi, the goddess of prosperity and wealth. In Uttar Pradesh farmers worship their tractors. Any piece of machinery including washing machines, televisions, kitchen grinders, vehicles, machines in factories, computers are honoured on this day which is a holiday for many institutions, including factories and scientific laboratories.[26] In some communities the Ayudha Pooja festival is observed in honour of the goddess Durga. The legend has it that after the goddess destroyed the demons, the devotees thanked the weaponry for protecting them, and the tradition of weapon worship began. The pooja consists of anointing things with sandalwood and other pastes, adorning them with flowers or breaking coconuts and offering camphor flame.

The Lacandon Mayans of Chiapas in southern Mexico offer food and incense to the spirit of material objects such as sewing machines that were introduced to the community by a team of anthropologists. Their religion is a form of syncretic Catholicism which incorporates remnants of pre-Columbian beliefs, rites and world views. The same ritual was performed for ceramic stoves, for water tanks and for other objects and technologies that were alien to local culture. Through symbolic action – they were ritually fed and blessed with candles, incense, songs and prayers – they became part of the human community and of the social order.[27]

Turning our historian's gaze to man and machine sheds light on the inadequacy of notions such as modernity to describe the condition of colonized peoples in the early twentieth century. Modern they were, when they worked the machine in the tea factory, but they were suffused with a fear for it and a respect that belonged to another time. The same duality can be seen in the way a machine of the future, the sewing machine, entered the bourgeois home and absorbed the self of the woman, stripped her of her freedom and chained her to a mythic past of domesticity and feminine values. But at the same time one senses from the rare pictures of the period depicting these machines and their users a gentle integration of the machine into the experience of everyday practice. Rather than duality of experience which Partha Chatterjee has famously suggested in his notions of inner and outer domains, you had here another process at play. What was being constructed was an identity informed less by bricolage than by a form of cultural 'code switching'. It was not a question of borrowing or moving back and forth between local practices and Western ones, but welding aspects of both within a same practice.[28]

NOTES

1. L. Woolf. 1974. *Village in the Jungle,* Colombo: Hansa Publishers.
2. I find the Gramscian concept of common sense useful to think with as a mode of transcending culture as predetermining the social worlds of the subjugated. See Q. Hoare and G.N. Smith (ed. and trans). 1996. *Selections from the Prison Notebooks of Antonio Gramsci,* Hyderabad: Orient Longman.
3. See the copious body of writings on the Sri Lankan plantations, including historical summaries: L. Jayawardena. 1972. 'The Supply of Sinhalese Labour to Ceylon Plantations (1830–1930). A Study of Imperial Policy in Peasant Society', Ph.D. dissertation, Cambridge: Cambridge University; D. Moldrich. 1989. *Bitter Berry Bondage. The Nineteenth Century Coffee Workers of Sri Lanka,* Kandy, Sri Lanka: Co-ordinating Secretariat for Plantation Areas; M. Roberts. 1970. 'The Impact of the Waste-Lands Legislation and the Growth of Plantation on the Techniques of Paddy Cultivation in British Ceylon: A Critique', *Modern Ceylon Studies* 1, 157–98; V. Samaraweera. 1981. 'Masters and Servants in Sri Lankan Plantations: Labour Laws and Labour Control in an Emergent Export Economy', *Indian Economic and Social History Review* 18(2), 123–58; I.H. Vanden-

Driesen. 1982. *Indian Plantation Labour in Sri Lanka: Aspects of the History of Immigration in the 19th century,* Nedlands: I.H. VandenDriesen Centre for South and Southeast Asian Studies, University of Western Australia; political economic accounts: A. Bandarage. 1983. *Colonialism in Sri Lanka: The Political Economy of the Kandyan Highlands 1833–1886,* Berlin: Mouton Publishers; R. Kurian. 1989. *State, Capital and Labour in the Plantation Industry in Sri Lanka 1834–1984,* Amsterdam: Amsterdam University Press; E. Meyer. 1992. 'From Land-grabbing to Land-hunger: Highland Appropriation in the Plantation Areas of Sri Lanka during the British Period', *Modern Asian Studies* 26, 321–61; D.R. Snodgrass. 1966. *Ceylon. An Export Economy in Transition,* Homewood: R.D. Irwin; and anthropological studies: V. Daniel. 1993. 'Tea Talk: Violent Measure in the Discursive Practices of Sri Lanka's Estate Tamils', *Comparative Studies in Society and History* 35, 566–600; O. Hollup. 1994. *Bonded Labour, Caste and Cultural Identity among Tamil Plantation Workers in Sri Lanka,* Colombo: Charles Subasinghe and Sons; W. Wesumperuma. 1986. *Indian Immigrant Plantation Workers in Sri Lanka: A Historical Perspective 1880–1910,* Kelaniya: Vidyalankara Press; P. Peebles. 2001. *Plantation Tamils of Ceylon,* London: Leicester University Press; V. Kanapathipillai. 2009. *Citizenship and Statelessness in Sri Lanka. The Case of the Tamil Estate Workers,* London: Anthem Press.

4. See Peebles, *Plantation Tamils of Ceylon,* 30.
5. Kandyan Peasantry Commission Report, 1951, Colombo: Government Publications Bureau, 5.
6. V. Daniel, however, has written about them and pointed to the way estate workers rejected the precision and disciplinary impulses of the plantation economy by substituting the approximations of the agricultural world of their past.
7. Denham, *Ceylon at the Census of 1911,* 197.
8. I am grateful to Dileepa Vitharana, Open University, Nawala, Sri Lanka, for sharing these insights with me.
9. This information was provided by D. Bass in a private communication.
10. A. Phillips. 2005. 'The Kinship, Marriage and Gender Experiences of Tamil Women in Sri Lanka's Tea Plantations,' *Contributions to Indian Sociology* 39(1), 117.
11. See Hollup, *Bonded Labour,* 280–82.
12. Labour Commission Report, 1908, 521.
13. Ibid., 123.
14. J. Pemberton. 2009.'The Ghost in the Machine', in R.C. Morris (ed.), *Photographies East. The Camera and Its Histories in East and Southeast Asia,* Durham: Duke University Press.
15. M.T. Taussig. 1980. *The Devil and Commodity Fetishism in South America,* Chapel Hill: University of North Carolina Press, 143.
16. P. Chatterjee. 2001. *Time for Tea,* Durham: Duke University Press, 230.
17. Ibid., 231.
18. See M.K. Bamber. 1967. 'The Tea Industry', in A. Wright (ed.), *Twentieth Century Impressions of Ceylon,* London: Lloyds Publishing Co., 249–52; D.M. Forrest. 1967. *A Hundred Years of Ceylon Tea 1867–1967,* London: Chatto and Windus.

19. See for example Snodgrass, *Ceylon an Export Economy in Transition;* Bandarage, *Colonialism in Sri Lanka.*
20. A number of tea firms have produced their own histories of the tea industry, see for example M. Fernando. 2000. *The Story of Ceylon Tea,* Colombo: Mlesna, and for written accounts and photographic archives on tea in Sri Lanka see "The History of Ceylon Tea." http://www.historyofceylontea.com/. Accessed 24 November 2012.
21. B. Pfaffenberger. 1993. 'The Factory as Artefact,' in P. Lemonnier (ed.), *Technological Choices: Transformations in Material Cultures since the Neolithic,* London: Routledge, 338–71.
22. B. Klem. 2011. 'Islam, Politics and Violence in Eastern Sri Lanka', *Journal of Asian Studies* 70(3), 741.
23. D. Chakrabarty. 1997. 'The Time of History and the Times of Gods', in L. Lowe and D. Lloyd (eds), *The Politics of Culture in the Shadow of Capital,* Durham: Duke University Press, 35.
24. Cited in D. Chakrabarty. 2001. *Provincializing Europe: Postcolonial Thought and Historical Difference,* Princeton: Princeton University Press, 79.
25. Ibid., 43–44.
26. S. Sarukkai. 2003. 'Praying to Machines,' *Leonardo Electronic Almanac* 11(8), http://leoalmanac.org/journal/Vol_11/lea_v11_n08.txt.
27. D. Boremanse. 2000. 'Sewing Machines and Q'echi Maya Worldview', *Anthropology Today* 16(1), 11–18.
28. J.J. Gumperz. 1982. *Discourse Strategies,* Cambridge: Cambridge University Press, uses the concept of code switching to describe the juxtaposition within the same speech exchange of passages of speech belonging to different grammatical systems or subsystems.

Conclusion

Metallic Modern

Une machine Singer dans un foyer nègre
Arabe, indien, malais, chinois, annamite
Ou dans n'importe quelle maison
Sans boussole du tiers monde
C'était le dieu lare qui raccommodait
Les mauvais jours de notre enfance.
– René Depestre*

As the global system became more intrusive, an influx of goods from the British Empire, America and Japan virtually flooded a small colony such as Sri Lanka. The colonized became consumers, not only of products from the empire but from outside. It is through the gradual fashioning of a market society by an array of actors such as multinational companies, tradesmen, shopkeepers, advertisers, writers and readers and the consequent spread of consumption and desires for more and more goods that the modern, as I have argued in this book, emerged as an everyday notion in colonial Sri Lanka. Over the years, while reading pieces of evidence from different archives which I often felt were insufficient or too tentative, the importance of seeking the contours of a 'modern' in the life of ordinary people struck me as a crucial key into the politics of the present.

The words that are used today in Sinhala to describe the idea of modern, *nutana* and *navina,* both words from the Sanskrit, came to common parlance after the 1930s. Martin Wickramasinghe, the iconic Sri Lankan novelist of the twentieth century, author of a seminal work entitled *Gamperaliya* (The Changing Village), used the terms in his editorial columns in the two Sinhalese daily newspapers, *Dinamina* and *Silumina* in the 1920s and

1930s and also in his other critical works. But in the late nineteenth century these words were not common. Most Sinhalese writers used the term abhinava or nava to denote the period, which literally means 'new'. Some writers used the term *varthamana* (the present, the now) to describe their time. For example John de Silva's play *Sinhala Parabhavaya Natakaya* (1902), a satire on the upper classes, uses the term *varthamanakalika,* literally the 'present times', in the introduction to the play.[1] If an essential part of being modern is thinking you are modern, then modernity, I suggested in this book, was understood as an aspiration to be with the times.[2] The term we use today (*nuthanathvaya*) to translate 'modernity' was not used in the early twentieth century. Being with the times, it seemed, was practiced by ordinary people through acts of consumption – such as buying a sewing machine or a bicycle – that spawned changes in their everyday life.

The difficulty in finding reliable sources that help the historian in her task of understanding the processes involved in the fashioning of imaginaries explains partly the scant interest in the consumer as a social group displayed in scholarship on colonial Sri Lanka. The consumer, like 'class', 'citizen' or 'nation', must not of course be taken as a natural or universal category but rather the product of historical identity formations in which actors – through available traditions – make sense of the relationship between material culture and collective identity.[3]

To uncover this elusive consumer it was necessary to try out particular writing and research strategies. This book, for instance, adopts various frames of reference other than the national, what I called 'scales' in my introductory chapter. This strategy helped to show that the trajectory of the sewing machine, produced by an American multinational corporation as 'one of the first standardized and mass-marketed complex consumer goods to spread around the world' cut across the political boundaries of empire. This book has looked at some of the global and regional webs of inspiration, imaginaries and materialities and local experiences in the city and labour arenas that shaped the historical experience of peoples across the empire who lived through the nineteenth and twentieth centuries.

As I mentioned, this book is not about the impact of the sewing machine on society. Indeed, a single object cannot, in my view, be orphaned from the spatial and temporal context in which it exists nor can a single commodity generally be usefully isolated as the driver of putative social change: 'In the world of goods', Harvey Molotch cogently argues, 'as in worlds of any sort, each element is just one interdependent fragment of a larger whole.'[4] The creation of a market imaginary was spawned by many parallel dynamics which only a multiscopic historical gaze can attempt to capture. This book is thus as much about existing interconnected moments that fostered the creation of market imaginaries as about experimenting with a historical approach that straddles many spatialities.

The study of consumption of commodities over time and in different locations has produced a number of works of quality to which this book has referred.[5] In the case of South Asia, interestingly, it is not only the absence of data that explains the rarity of studies on colonial consumption. One of the reasons the historiography of South Asia has overlooked the role of the market on people's imaginary is related to an ideologically grounded refusal to see the colonized/disempowered as purely 'consumers of modernity'[6] and its eagerness to see them moving in 'uncontaminated autonomous cultures' that create 'a reservoir of anticolonialism'.[7] This has been the case in both the nationalist historiography of the twentieth century as in the critique of the nationalist writings that dominated the field in the last three decades.[8] The rise of the consumer in India and Sri Lanka under colonial rule has evoked little interest compared to the flurry of excellent studies on consumerism in East Asia. In the few studies that deal with India it is more often the campaign to promote *khadi* (homespun cotton cloth) and the consequent turn to indigenous craft and consumption practices that is stressed rather than the adoption of foreign goods by the people.[9] The reason was of course that the scale of changes in countries such as China and Japan was in no way comparable to those in the Indian subcontinent. But certain trends were common, for example the growth of urban cultures where new forms such as department stores mushroomed, creating around them new cultural practices. Colombo did not have architectural monuments such as the Shanghai department stores Sincere and Sun Sun, but Cargills offered the bourgeois clientele of Colombo a similar experience. As the leading commercial presence in many parts of the rapidly developing world, Singer stores represented modernity and progress to consumers and were a model of vanguardism, electric lighting and cash registers providing the neophyte a lesson in modernity.[10]

While it is important to steer clear of an overly romanticized view of consumption as resistance and with de Certeau recognize the relative powerlessness of the consumer, the example of the reception of the sewing machine in Sri Lanka brings further evidence that in their everyday lives consumers manage, make do and often (quite literally) take liberties. 'Everyday life invents itself by poaching in countless ways on the property of others.'[11] Thus the consumption of the sewing machine is best studied as a form of production, a poiesis whose meaning is often hidden and needs to be revealed. This book has not tried to read in the representation of the machine by the literati, advertisers and sellers what it meant to its users. But it has suggested that uncovering the uses or the ways of operating of the consumers of the machines throws light on how they reappropriate the space organized by techniques of social and cultural production of the colonial state. De Certeau describes these procedures as ruses, as 'clandestine forms taken by the dispersed, tactical and makeshift creativity of groups or individuals already caught in the nets of "discipline"'.[12]

If one pushes the argument further one could suggest that Western consumer forms, even if they came to Sri Lanka through the emulation of an Asian country, Japan, turned out to be a more successful Western influence than the less eagerly sought, for example, political democracy. Certainly among the majority of Sinhala people who were excluded from the arena of formal politics until 1931 when universal suffrage was granted, democracy was a hazy concept. If anything freedom from colonial rule was something they could comprehend, but this yearning was not couched in any explicitly articulated notions of sovereignty, citizenship or rights. Consumer goods on the other hand were easily appropriated. But consumerism as it was practiced in the Western metropoles was never duplicated.

An often-formulated question is whether these third-world 'fées' or fairies mentioned in the poem of René Depestre were empowered by access to consumer goods such as the sewing machine and services associated with new forms of consumption. The argument made is that 'commodity forms and market-driven networks of communication and sociability can yield a voice to subjects, specifically women who have been disempowered by economic inequality, exclusion from democratic processes, and social and cultural discrimination.'[13] Gender studies have either focused on the battle for political representation that eventually led women in Sri Lanka to gain the vote before any other nation in Asia or else the Janus effect of nationalism on women, at the same time emancipator and creating new chains. The nature and spread of commodity forms in the colonial local has never been looked at except in relation to the nationalist adoption or rejection of certain goods. We do not know – because we have never searched – how many shops there were in villages, what they sold and what was bought. Today as the archive is more and more depleted we have no alternative than to extrapolate from the meagre details pruned in novels, advertisements, photographs and people's memories.

In Sri Lanka it seems that if there had been emancipatory spaces of the early twentieth century they were soon reappropriated by national and transnational patriarchal power, thus leading to new forms of degradation such as the *jukikeli* (or *juki* girl) of the twenty-first century employed in assembly lines by the transnational garment industry.[14]

Thus goods and technology appear to empower and disempower according to circumstances. In colonial Sri Lanka, it is just as difficult to argue that consumerism was encouraged by the state as a way of keeping the natives content, hence depoliticized, as it is difficult to prove that through acts of consumption consumers reappropriated spaces organized by techniques of sociocultural production generated by the colonial state. Nor was there any apparent intentionality on the part of advertisers and foreign companies to civilize through the spread of consumption patterns.

The market seemed to have a logic of its own separate from political considerations. But increasingly subjectivities, identities and solidarities were created by commodities. Goods came to represent and even constitute people, groups and institutions. Class, gender and nation were constituted through the acquisition and use of goods. Thus in the early twentieth century a family's social identity was beginning to be constituted through the goods contained in the home rather than purely through caste and landed wealth. Taste conferred social distinction.

New class differentiations, gender and national consciousness were, however, manifest not only through consumption patterns but through the use made of goods, as in the case of the sewing machine that acquired different meanings in the urban bourgeois home and in the working-class or village home. Marker of authenticity, respectability and thrift in the former, it became a marker of status and upward mobility in the latter.

How did ordinary people navigate their colonial condition and make sense of it? This book is an attempt at integrating into a single historical narrative the histories of peoples who rarely appear in the text: the peasant in his/her village, the tailor or seamstress in his/her shop, the shopkeeper in his/her city store, the worker in his plantation factory. Their idea of the modern, I suggest, emanates from their relation to a changing material world. It was material and self-indulgent and looked inward and outward all at once since it aimed at adapting – within the confines of an imagined authentic culture – manners and habits in the home and the everyday life through new practices and new modes of consumption.

In these modern times, when most machines were made of steel and iron, none more than the sewing machine epitomized this 'metallic modern', multidimensional sense of being that inhabited the peoples of Sri Lanka under colonialism.

NOTES

* A Singer machine in a negro home
Arab, Indian, Malay, Chinese, Annamite
or in any third world house
without a compass
was the god of the home
who would mend

the bad days of our youth
(author's translation)

1. I owe these insights to Sandagomi Coperahewa, Department of Sinhalese, University of Colombo, Sri Lanka.
2. C. Bayly. 2004. *The Birth of the Modern World 1780–1914,* Malden, MA: Blackwell, 10–12.
3. F. Trentmann. 2006. 'The Evolution of the Consumer. Meanings, Identities, and Political Synapses before the Age of Affluence', in S. Garon and P.L. Maclachlan (eds), *The Ambivalent Consumer: Questioning Consumption in East Asia and the West,* Ithaca and London: Cornell University Press, 42.
4. H. Molotch. 2005. *Where Stuff Comes From,* New York and London: Routledge, 1.
5. On the colonial/consumption nexus see especially, T. Burke and J. Comaroff. 1985. *Body of Power, Spirit of Resistance: The Culture and History of a South African People,* Chicago: Chicago University Press, and R. Mrazek. 2002. *Engineers of Happy Land. Technology and Nationalism in a Colony,* Princeton: Princeton University Press. The literature on gendered aspects of technology offers interesting insights but has not ventured into colonial situations. See for example the work on R. Oldenziel. 1999. *Making Technology Masculine: Women, Men, and the Machine in America, 1880–1945,* Amsterdam: Amsterdam University Press.
6. Chatterjee, *The Nation and Its Fragments,* 5.
7. Harootunian, *History's Disquiet,* 49.
8. I have made this point more forcefully in N. Wickramasinghe. 2011.'Colonial Governmentality: Critical Notes from a Perspective of South Asian Studies', *Comparative, Zeitschrift fur Globalgeschichte und VergleichendeGeselleschatsforschung* 21(1), 32–40.
9. Two recent examples are: L.N. Trivedi. 2007. *Clothing Gandhi's Nation: Homespun and Modern India,* Bloomington: Indiana University Press, and R. Ramagundam. 2008. *Gandhi's Khadi: A History of Contention and Conciliation,* New Delhi: Orient Longman.
10. Godley, 'Selling the Sewing Machine around the World', 296; C. Pursell. 2007. *The Machine in America: A Social History of Technology,* Baltimore: Johns Hopkins University Press.
11. M. de Certeau. 1984. *The Practice of Everyday Life,* Berkeley: University of California Press, xii.
12. Ibid., xiv.
13. V. de Grazia (ed.) with E. Furlough. 1996. *The Sex of Things: Gender and Consumption in Historical Perspective,* Berkeley: University of California Press, 275.
14. As S. Hewamanne, in her excellent *Stitching Identities in a Free Trade Zone* (2007. Baltimore: University of Pennsylvania Press, 250) explains, *Juki* is the brand name of a Japanese industrial sewing machine used in garment factories in the free trade zones of Sri Lanka. The term *jukikeli* used disparagingly to describe women workers is a pun on the Sinhala term *keli* which means both 'pieces' – with reference to pieces of cloth sewn using Juki machines – and 'girl' in Sinhala slang.

Glossary

Abhinava	new, novel
Ahimsa	nonviolence
Amarapura Nikaya	fraternity of non-Goyigama Buddhist monks, so named because its founder received ordination from Burmese monks in Amarapura, a former capital of Burma
Anagarika	homeless
Arya	high status obtainable through the performance of meritorious acts
Aryavarta	north India in Sanskrit texts
Bana	Buddhist sermon
Bankuwa	stool
Bhikkhu	ordained Buddhist monk
Buddhagaya	religious site and place of pilgrimage associated with the Mahabodhi Temple Complex in Gaya district in the Indian state of Bihar, famous for being the place where Gautama Buddha is believed to have reached enlightenment
Buddha sasana	Buddhist teachings and the institutions that sustain them
Bodhisatva	A being dedicated to helping other beings to achieve enlightenment. Also the Buddha in his previous births
Cetiya	caitiya (Sanskrit); objects/relics or memorials used to remember Gautama Buddha
Chakravartin/ cakravarti	world ruler, universal emperor

Chakra	wheel, circle; denotes the 'wheel of becoming' or 'round of existence'; also the spinning wheel
Chetty	merchant community of south Indian origin, mostly found on the western coast of Sri Lanka, near Colombo
Coolie	1. Kuli, aboriginal tribe of Gujarat; 2. generally, unskilled labourer (pejorative)
Dalada Maligawa	Temple of the Sacred Tooth in Kandy
Dansala	hall where food is given free particularly to pilgrims on Poya days
Danaya	alms giving
Devale	shrine dedicated to a deity
Dhamma	Buddha's teachings
Dharmistha	righteous
Durava	Sinhalese caste; generally associated with toddy tapping
Gama	village
Gathas	verses
Goyigama	Sinhalese caste, cultivators
Hela	the supposedly pure Sinhalese language, free from Sanskrit influence
Hirimane	grater
Huniyam	sorcery
Jataka	tales relating to the previous births of Gautama Buddha
Karava	Sinhalese caste, generally associated with fishing
Low-Country	districts in the Western and Southern Provinces, the Chilaw district and the western part of the Puttalam district
Maha Sangha	Great Order of Bhikkus
Mahavamsa	'Great Chronicle' composed in four parts, the first in the sixth century, the second in the thirteenth, the third in the fourteenth and the last in the eighteenth. In the European edition only the first part is called the Mahavamsa. The latter parts form the Culavamsa.

Nayakkars	dynasty whose origins were in South India who ruled the Kandyan Kingdom from 1739 to 1815
Nikaya	group of monasteries under single leadership
Parampara	lineage, succession
Perahera	procession, pageant
Pirith	ritual chanting of Buddhist texts
Pirivena	monastic college for education of monks
Pooja/puja	worship
Poya day	full moon day of the month
Prapthidanaya	ceremony of thanksgiving
Rajakariya	(literally) king's duty; encompassed any service to the king, a lord or a temple in the Kandyan kingdom. In British times also denoted compulsory service to the state
Rajarata	north-central part of the island
Ramanna/ Ramanya nikaya	Buddhist fraternity founded in the nineteenth century by monks having received higher ordination in Burma
Ratemahatmaya	chieftain
Sakra	also known as Indra, deity protector of Buddhism
Samanera	novice monk
Sangha	Buddhist monastic community
Sasana	teaching of the Buddha; community of devotees
Sastra	oracle
Siyamnikaya	fraternity or sect of Buddhist monks dominated by Goyigama caste
Suttas	Buddhist scriptures
Thera	honorific term for Buddhist monk
Tripitaka	sacred canon of Theravada Buddhism written in the Pali language
Trishulaya	trident
Upasampada	higher ordination
Up-Country	Central and North-central Provinces, the provinces of Uva and Sabaragamuwa, the Kurunegala district and part of the Puttalam district, the Sinhalese divisions of the districts of Batticaloa, Trincomalee and Mullaitivu

Vahumpura	Sinhalese caste; generally associated with juggery making
Vaishnavites	believers in the god Vishnu
Vamsa literature	literature about the lineage
Vedda	descendant of the ancient inhabitants of Sri Lanka predating arrival of the Sinhalese
Vesak	second month of the Sinhalese calendar (May–June); day marking the birth, enlightenment and passing away of the Buddha
Vihara	Buddhist monastery

Bibliography

Primary Sources

Newspapers and Magazines

Ceylon Independent
Ceylon National Review
Dinakara Prakashaya
Dinamina
Lakmina
Lakmini Pahana
Sarasavi Sanderesa
Singapore Free Press and Mercantile Advertiser
Singer Free Press and Mercantile Advertiser
Sinhala Baudhdhaya
Sinhala Jatiya
Straits Times
Young East

Archival and Private Collections

Private collection of the family of Francis Pieterz
Nathan Mss 619, Special Circulation No. 291, Memorandum from Ceylonese Workmen
Sri Lanka National Archives (SLNA), 5/63/150/(7)
Wisconsin Historical Society Archives, Singer Papers

Reports and Publications

Census of Ceylon, 1871
Census of Ceylon, 1891
Ceylon Law Reports, 1887–97

Commerce Reports, U.S. Bureau of Manufacturers, Bureau of Foreign and Domestic Commerce, Published by Bureau of Foreign and Domestic Commerce, U.S. Department of Commerce, 1912

Consular Reports, U.S. Bureau of Foreign Commerce, U.S. Department of Commerce and Labor GPO, 1905

Department of Commerce, Special Consular Reports, No. 72, 1915

Department of Commerce, Monthly Consular and Trade Reports, No. 300, 1905

Ferguson's Directory, Colombo: Ceylon Observer Press, 1880, 1895, 1903, 1914–15, 1925, 1926

Ferguson's Ceylon Handbook and Directories, 1925

Kandyan Peasantry Commission Report, Government Publications Bureau: Colombo, 1951

Labour Commission Report, 1908

Public Health Reports (1896–1970), 19(53), (Dec. 1904)

Railway Commission, Sessional Paper I, 1913

Report of the Proceedings at the Presentation of an Address to R.M. Patell, Esquire JP, Agent of India, Burmah and Ceylon, The Singer Manufacturing Company, 1911, (Smithsonian Institute Libraries)

Report of a Commission on Immigration to Ceylon, Sessional Paper III, 1938

Special Consular Reports, U.S. Bureau of Foreign Commerce, U.S. Department of Commerce and Labor, U.S. Bureau of Manufacturers, GPO, 1900

Amicus Annual, 1915

Red S. Review, Wellawatte Sewing and School, 31 August and 30 September 1935

Secondary Sources

Anderson, B. 1991. *Imagined Communities: Reflections on the Origins and Spread of Nationalism,* rev. ed., London: Verso.

Appadurai A. (ed.). 1986. *The Social Life of Things. Commodities in Cultural Perspective,* Cambridge: Cambridge University Press.

Appadurai, A. 1996. *Modernity at Large: Cultural Dimensions of Globalization,* Public Worlds series, vol. 1, Minneapolis: University of Minnesota Press.

Arendt, H. 1958. *The Human Condition,* Chicago and London: University of Chicago Press.

Arnold, D. 2011. 'Global Goods and Local Usages: The Small World of the Indian Sewing Machine, 1875–1952', *Journal of Global History* 6, 407–29.

Arnold, D. and E. de Wald. 2012. 'Everyday Technology in South and Southeast Asia. An Introduction', *Modern Asian Studies* 46(1).

Bamber, M.K. 1907. 'The Tea Industry', in Arnold Wright (ed.), *Twentieth Century Impressions of Ceylon,* London: Lloyds Publishing, 249–52.

Bandarage, A. 1983. *Colonialism in Sri Lanka: The Political Economy of the Kandyan Highlands 1833–1886,* Berlin: Mouton Publishers.

Barth F. 1960. 'The System of Stratification in Swat. North Pakistan', in E.R. Leach (ed.), *Aspects of Caste in South India, Ceylon and North West Pakistan,* London: Cambridge University Press, 113–46.

Barthes, R. 1972. *Mythologies,* New York: Hill and Wang.

Barua, S.B. 1991. *Studies in Tagore and Buddhist Culture,* Calcutta: Sahitiya Samsad.

Baudrillard, J. 1996. *La Société de Consommation,* Paris: Gallimard.

Bayly, C. 2004. *The Birth of the Modern World 1780–1914,* Malden, MA: Blackwell.

Bayly, C.A., S. Beckert, M. Connelly, I. Hofmeyr, W. Kozol and P. Seed. 2006. 'AHR Conversation: On Transnational History', *American Historical Review* 111(5), 1441–64. http://www.historycooperative.org/journals/ahr/111.5/introduction.html.

Benjamin, W. 1979. *Illuminations,* trans. Harry Zohn, New York: Shocken Books.

——. 2002. *The Arcades Project,* Cambridge: Harvard University Press.

Beng T.S. 1996/1997. 'The 78 RPM Record Industry in Malaya prior to World War II', *Asian Music* 28(1), 1–41.

Berger, J. 1972. *Ways of Seeing,* London: BBC and Penguin Books.

Bertolacci, Anthony. 1817/1983. *A View of the Agricultural, Commercial and Financial Interests of Ceylon,* Dehiwela: Tisara Press.

Bharucha, R. 2006. *Another Asia. Rabindranath Tagore and Okakura Tenshin,* New Delhi: Oxford University Press.

Bijker, W.E. 2009. 'King of the Road. The Social Construction of the Safety Bicycle', in F. Candlin and R. Guins (eds), *The Object Reader,* London: Routledge, 263–64.

Bissel, D. 1999. *The First Conglomerate. 145 Years of the Singer Sewing Machine,* Brunswick: Audenreed Press.

Blackburn, A. 2010. *Locations of Buddhism: Colonialism and Modernity in Sri Lanka,* Chicago: University of Chicago Press.

Blackburn, A.M. 2001. *Buddhist Learning and Textual Practice in Eighteenth Century Lankan Monastic Culture,* Princeton: Princeton University Press.

Bond, G.D. 1998, *The Buddhist Revival in Sri Lanka: Religious Tradition, Reinterpretation and Response,* Columbia: University of South Carolina Press.

Bonnier, B. 2003. 'Barthélémy Thimonnier et le machine a coudre, 1793–1857', in Institut des Etudes regionales et des patrimonies (eds), *Creations et solidarities dans la grandevilleouvriere,* Saint Etienne: Université de St Etienne, 155–221.

Boremanse, D. 2000. 'Sewing Machines and Q'echi Maya Worldview', *Anthropology Today* 16(1), 11–18.

Bourdieu, P. 1977. *Outline of a Theory of Practice.* Cambridge and New York: Cambridge University Press.

Brandon, R. 1977. *A Capitalist Romance: Singer and the Sewing Machine,* Philadelphia and New York: J.B. Lippincott.

Brohier, D. 1994. *Dr Alice de Boer and Some Pioneer Women Doctors in Sri Lanka,* Colombo: SSA.

Bronner, Y. 2010. *Extreme Poetry. The South Asian Movement of Simultaneous Narration,* New York: Columbia University Press.

Broughton, S., M. Ellingham and R. Trillo. 2000. *World Music: The Rough Guide,* vol. 2, *Latin and North America, Caribbean, India, Asia and Pacific,* London: Rough Guides.

Burke, T. 1996a. *Lifebuoy Men, Lux Women. Commodification, Consumption and Cleanliness in Modern Zimbabwe,* Durham and London: Duke University Press.

——. 1996b. 'Sunlight Soap Has Changed My Life: Hygiene, Commodification, and the Body in Colonial Zimbabwe', in H. Hendrickson (ed.), *Clothing and Difference: Embodied Identities in Colonial and Post-Colonial Africa,* Durham and London: Duke University Press, 189–212.

Burke, T. and J. Comaroff. 1985. *Body of Power, Spirit of Resistance: The Culture and History of a South African People,* Chicago: Chicago University Press.

Burton, A. (ed.). 2003. *After the Imperial Turn: Thinking with and through the Nation,* Durham and London: Duke University Press.

Carstensen, F.V. 1984. *American Enterprise in Foreign Markets. Singer and International Harvester in Imperial Russia,* Chapel Hill and London: University of North Carolina Press.

Chakrabarty, D. 1997. 'The Time of History and the Times of Gods', in L. Lowe and D. Lloyd (eds), *The Politics of Culture in the Shadow of Capital,* Durham: Duke University Press, 34–60.

——. 2001. *Provincializing Europe: Postcolonial Thought and Historical Difference,* Princeton: Princeton University Press.

Chatterjee, P. 1993. *The Nation and Its Fragments,* New Delhi: Oxford University Press.

——. 2001. *Time for Tea,* Durham: Duke University Press.

——. 2004a. 'The Nation in Heterogeneous Time', in *The Politics of the Governed. Reflections on Popular Politics in Most of the World,* New Delhi: Permanent Black.

——. 2004b. *The Politics of the Governed: Reflections on Popular Politics in Most of the World,* New Delhi: Permanent Black.

Coffin, J.G. 1994. 'Credit, Consumption and Images of Women's Desires: Selling the Sewing Machine in Late Nineteenth Century France', *French Historical Studies* 18(3), 749–783.

Collins, S. 2003.'What Is Literature in Pali', in Sheldon Pollock (ed.), *Literary Cultures in History: Reconstructions from South Asia,* Berkeley: University of California Press, 649–88.

Coomaraswamy, A. 1981[1909].'Gramophones and Why Not', in *Essays in National Idealism,* New Delhi: Munshiram Manoharlal Publishers, 210–11.

Cooper, F. 2005. *Colonialism in Question: Theory, Knowledge, History,* Berkeley: University of California Press.

Cooper, F. and L.A. Stoler (eds). 1997. *Tensions of Empire: Colonial Cultures in a Bourgeois World,* Berkeley and London, University of California Press.

Cordiner, J. 1807. *A Description of Ceylon,* vol. 1. London: Longman, Hurst, Rees and Orme.

Cote, J. 2009. 'Strangers in the House: Dutch Historiography and Anglophone Trespassers', *Review of Indonesian and Malaysian Affairs* 43(1), 75–94.

Daniel, V. 1993. 'Tea Talk: Violent Measures in the Discursive Practices of Sri Lanka's Estate Tamils', *Comparative Studies in Society and History* 35, 566–600.

Darwin, J. 1997. 'Imperialism and the Victorians: The Dynamics of Territorial Expansion', *English Historical Review* 112(545), 614–42.

Das, S.K. (ed.). 1996. *The English Writings of Rabindranath Tagore,* vol. 3., *To My Ceylon Audience,* New Delhi: Sahitya Akademi, 760–66.

Davies, R. 1969. '"Peacefully Working to Conquer the World": The Singer Manufacturing Company in Foreign Markets, 1854–1889', *Business History Review* 43(3), 299–346.

——. 1976. *Peacefully Working to Conquer the World,* New York: Arno Press.

Davy, J. 1969[1821]. *An Account of the Interior of Ceylon,* Dehiwela: Tisara Press.

De Alwis, M. 1997. 'The Production and Embodiment of Respectability: Gendered Demeanours in Colonial Ceylon', in M. Roberts (ed.), *Collective Identities Revisited,* vol. 1, Colombo: Marga Instittute, 105–44.

De Certeau, M. 1984. *The Practice of Everyday Life,* Berkeley: University of California Press.

De Grazia, V. 2005. *Irresistible Empire: America's Advance through Twentieth Century Europe,* Cambridge: Harvard University Press.

De Grazia, V. with E. Furlough. 1996. *The Sex of Things: Gender and Consumption in Historical Perspective,* Berkeley: University of California Press.

De Mel, N. 2001. *Women and the Nation's Narrative: Gender and Nationalism in Twentieth Century Sri Lanka,* Colombo: SSA.

Denham, E.B. 1912. *Ceylon at the Census of 1911,* Colombo: HC. Cottle, Government Printer.

Dep, A.C. 1969. *A History of the Ceylon Police II (1866–1913),* Colombo: Times of Ceylon.

De Silva, K.M. (ed.). 1973. *History of Ceylon,* vol. 3, Peradeniya: University of Ceylon.

Dharmadasa, K.N.O. 1992. *The Growth of Sinhalese Nationalism in Sri Lanka,* Ann Arbor: University of Michigan Press.

Dharmapala, A. 1927. 'An Appeal to Japanese Buddhists', *Young East* 3(6), 194.

——. 1965, 'Buddha-gaya: The Holiest Buddhist Shrine', in A. Guruge, *Return to Righteousness. A Collection of Speeches, Essays and Letters of the Anagarika Dharmapala,* Colombo: Ministry of Educational Cultural Affairs, 615–26.

Dickson, D.G. 1991. 'The Nineteenth Century Indo-American Ice Trade: An Hyperborean Epic', *Modern Asian Studies* 25(1) 53–89.

Domosh, M. 2004. 'Selling Civilization: Towards a Cultural Analysis of American's Economic Empire in the Late Nineteenth and Early Twentieth Centuries', *Transactions Institute of British Geographers* 29(4), 453–67.

——. 2006. *American Companies in an Age of Empire,* New York and London: Routledge.

Duara, P. 2001. 'The Discourse of Civilization and Pan-Asianism', *Journal of World History* 12(1), 99–130.

——. 2003. *Sovereignty and Authenticity: Manchukuo and the East Asian Modern,* Boulder: Rowman and Littlefield.

Duncan, J. 1990. *The City as Text: The Politics of Landscape Interpretation in the Kandyan Kingdom,* Cambridge: Cambridge University Press.

——. 2002. 'Embodying Colonialism? Domination and Resistance in Nineteenth Century Ceylonese Coffee Plantations', *Journal of Historical Geography* 28(3), 317–36.

——. 2007. *In the Shadows of the Tropics: Climate, Race and Biopower in Nineteenth Century Ceylon,* Aldershot: Ashgate.

Edstrom, B. 2002. *Turning Points in Japanese History,* Richmond: Japan Library.

Eperjesi, J.R. 2005. *The Imperialist Imaginary Visions of Asia and the Pacific in American Culture,* Hanover and London: University Press of New England.

Featherstone, M. 2004. 'Automobiles: An Introduction', *Theory Culture and Society* 21, 1–24.

Ferguson, J. 1903. *Ceylon in 1903,* Colombo: A.M. & J. Ferguson.

Fernando, M. 2000. *The Story of Ceylon Tea,* Colombo: Mlesna.

Fieldhouse, D. 1984. 'Can Humpty-Dumpty Be Put Together Again? Imperial History in the 1980s', *Journal of Imperial and Commonwealth History* 12(2), 10–23.

Fisher-Tine, H. and M. Mann (eds). 2004. *Colonialism as Civilizing Mission. Cultural Ideology in British India,* Wimbledon: Anthem Press.

Fletcher, M.E. 1958. 'The Suez Canal and World Shipping 1869–1914', *Journal of Economic History* 18(4), 556–73.

Forrest, D.M. 1967. *A Hundred Years of Ceylon Tea 1867–1967,* London: Chatto and Windus.

Frash, T. 2012. 'Tracks in the City: Technology, Mobility and Society in Colonial Rangoon and Singapore', *Modern Asian Studies* 46(1), 97–118.

Frost, M.R. in press. 'Empires of Belief: Print, Politics and Religion in the Indian Ocean World, 1860–1920'.

Gallagher, J. and R.E. Robinson. 1953. 'The Imperialism of Free Trade', *Economic History Review,* 2d series, 6 (1), 1–15.

Garland, S. 1917. 'Sewing Circles Round the Globe', *ASIA, Journal of the American Asiatic Association* 17, 37–40.

Geiger, W. (trans.). 1950. *The Mahavamsa,* Colombo: Ceylon Government Information Department.

Glennie, P. and N. Thrift. 1996. 'Reworking E.P. Thompson's "Time, Work-Discipline and Industrial Capitalism"', *Time and Society* 5(3), 275–99.

Godley, A. 2001. 'The Global Diffusion of the Sewing Machine, 1850–1914', *Research in Economic History* 20, 1–45.

——. 2006. 'Selling the Sewing Machine Around the World. Singer's International Marketing Strategies, 1850–1920', *Enterprise and Society* 7(2), 266–67.

Gokhale, B.K. 1973. 'Anagarika Dharmapala: Toward Modernity through Tradition in Ceylon', in B.L. Smith (ed.), *Tradition and Change in Theravada Buddhism. Essays on Ceylon and Thailand in the 19th and 20th centuries,* Leiden: E.J. Brill, 30–39.

Gombrich, R.F. 1988. *Theravada Buddhism. A Social History from Ancient Benares to Modern Colombo,* London and New York: Routledge and Kegan Paul.

Gombrich, R.F. and G. Obeysekere. 1988. *Buddhism Transformed: Religious Change in Sri Lanka,* Princeton: Princeton University Press.

Goodman, G.K. 1993. 'Dharmapala in Japan, 1913', *Japan Forum* 5(2), 195–202.

Gooneratne, Y. 1986. *Relative Merits. A Personal Memoir of the Bandaranaike Family of Sri Lanka,* London: C. Hurst.

Gordon, A. 2006. 'From Singer to Shinpan: Consumer Credit in Modern Japan', in S. Garon and P. Maclachlan (eds), *The Ambivalent Consumer: Questioning Consumption in East Asia and the West,* Ithaca and London: Cornell University Press, 114–62.

——. 2008. 'Selling the American Way: The Singer Sales System in Japan, 1900–1938', *Business History Review* 82, 671–99.

——. 2012. *Fabricating Consumers: The Sewing Machine in Modern Japan,* Berkeley: University of California Press.

Gordon, B. 1996. 'Woman's Domestic Body. The Conceptual Conflation of Women and Interiors in the Industrial Age', *Wintherthur Portfolio,* Gendered Spaces and Aesthetics 31(4), 281–301.

Gosh, D. and D. Kennedy (eds). 2006. *Decentring Empire. Britain, India and the Transcolonial World,* New Delhi: Orient Longman.

Green N.L. 1994. 'Art and Industry. The Language of Modernisation in the Production of Fashion', *French Historical Studies* 18(3), 722–48.

Gregory, J.M. 2006. 'A History of the Sewing Machine to 1880', *Transactions of the Newcomen Society,* 76, 127–29.

Gronow, P. 1981. 'The Record Industry Comes to the Orient', *Ethnomusicology* 25(2), 251–84.

Guha, R. 1997. *Dominance without Hegemony: History and Power in Colonial India,* Cambridge: Harvard University Press.

——. 1999. *Elementary Aspects of Peasant Insurgency in Colonial India,* Durham and London: Duke University Press.

Guha, R. and G. Spivak (eds). 1988. *Selected Subaltern Studies,* New York: Oxford University Press.

Gumperz, J.J. 1982. *Discourse Strategies,* Cambridge: Cambridge University Press.

Hall, C. (ed.). 2000. *Cultures of Empire: Colonizers in Britain and the Empire in the Nineteenth and Twentieth Centuries: A Reader,* Manchester: Manchester University Press.

Harootunian, H. 2000. *History's Disquiet: Modernity, Cultural Practice and the Question of Everyday Life,* New York: Columbia University Press.

Hazareesingh, S. and J. Curry-Machado. 2009. 'Editorial: Commodities, Empires and Global History', *Journal of Global History* 4, 1–5.

Hellman-Rajanayagam, D. 1994. *The Tamil Tigers: Armed Struggle for Identity,* Stuttgart: Franz Steiner Verlag.

Hewamanne, S. 2007. *Stitching Identities in a Free Trade Zone,* Baltimore: University of Pennsylvania Press.

Hinnels, J.R. and A. Williams. 2007. *Parsis in India and the Diaspora,* London: Routledge.

Hoare, Q. and G.N. Smith (ed. and trans.). 1996. *Selections from the Prison Notebooks of Antonio Gramsci,* Hyderabad: Orient Longman.

Hollup, O. 1994. *Bonded Labour, Caste and Cultural Identity among Tamil Plantation Workers in Sri Lanka,* Colombo: Charles Subasinghe and Sons.

Hughes, S.P. 2002. 'The Music Boom' in Tamil South India: Gramophone, Radio and the Making of Mass Culture', *Historical Journal of Film, Radio and Television* 22(4), 445–73.

Iguchi, G.S. 2006. 'Nichirenism as Modernism: Imperialism, Fascism, and Buddhism in Modern Japan', Ph.D. thesis, University of California, San Diego.

Jaffe, R.M. 2004. 'Seeking Sakyammuni: Travel and the Reconstruction of Japanese Buddhism', *Journal of Japanese Studies* 30(1), 65–96.

Jayawardena, K. 1972. *The Rise of the Labour Movement in Ceylon,* Durham: Duke University Press.

——. 2000. *From Nobodies to Somebodies. The Rise of the Colonial Bourgeoisie in Sri Lanka,* Colombo: Social Scientists' Association and Sanjiva Books.

Jayawardena, L. 1972. 'The Supply of Sinhalese Labour to Ceylon Plantations (1830–1930). A Study of Imperial Policy in Peasant Society', Ph.D. thesis, Cambridge University.

Jones, G. 1985. 'The Gramophone Company: An Anglo-American Multinational, 1898–1931', *Business History Review* 59(1), 76–100.

Joshi, G.N. 1988. 'A Concise History of the Phonograph Industry in India', *Popular Music* 7(2), 147–56.

Kailasapathy, K. 1984. 'Cultural and Linguistic Consciousness of the Tamil Community', in Social Scientists Association (SSA) (ed.), *Ethnicity and Social Change in Sri Lanka,* Colombo: SSA, 107–20.

Kanapathipillai, V. 2009. *Citizenship and Statelessness in Sri Lanka. The Case of the Tamil Estate Workers,* London: Anthem Press.

Kannangara, A.P. 1984. 'The Riots of 1915 in Sri Lanka: A Study in the Roots of Communal Violence', *Past and Present* 102, 130–65.

Kaplan A. and D.E. Pease (eds). 1993. *Cultures of United States Imperialism,* Durham and London, Duke University Press.

Katzenstein, P.J. 1998. *Cultural Norms and National Security: Police and Military in Postwar Japan,* Ithaca: Cornell University Press.

Kearney, R.N. et al. 1970. 'The 1915 Riots in Ceylon: A Symposium', *Journal of Asian Studies* 29(2), 219–66.

Kemper, S. 2001. *Buying and Believing: Sri Lankan Advertising and Consumers in a Transnational World,* Chicago: University of Chicago Press.

Kinnear, M.S. 1994. *The Gramophone Company's First Indian Recordings 1899–1908,* Bombay: Popular Prakashan.

Kittler, F.A. 1999. *Gramophone, Film, Typewriter,* Stanford: Stanford University Press.

Klem, B. 2011. 'Islam, Politics and Violence in Eastern Sri Lanka', *Journal of Asian Studies* 70(3), 730–53.

Knox, R. 1681. *A Historical Relation of Ceylon,* http://www.gutenberg.org/files/14346/14346-h/14346-h.htm#d0e11060.

Kularatne, T. 1995. 'Introduction of Printing to Sri Lanka (Ceylon). The Dutch Press in Ceylon (1736–1796)', *Libri* 45(2), 65–78.

Kurian, R. 1989. *State, Capital and Labour in the Plantation Industry in Sri Lanka 1834–1984,* Amsterdam: Amsterdam University Press.

Laffan, M. 2006. 'Tokyo as a Shared Mecca of Modernity: War Echoes in the Colonial Malay World', in R. Kowner (ed.), *The Impact of the Russo-Japanese War,* New York: Routledge Curzon, 219–38.

Lester, A. 2006.'Imperial Circuits and Networks: Geographies of the British Empire', *History Compass* 4/1, 124–41.

Lévi-Strauss, C. 1966. *The Savage Mind,* Chicago: Chicago University Press.

Lewcock, R., B. Sansoni, Laki and C. Anjalendran. 1998. *The Architecture of an Island. The Living Legacy of Sri Lanka,* Colombo: Barefoot Ltd.

Lin, C.A. 2012. '"The Modern Magic Carpet": Wireless Radio in Interwar Colonial Singapore', *Modern Asian Studies* 46, 1, 190.

Ludowyk, E.F.C. 1989. *Those Long Afternoons: Childhood in Colonial Ceylon,* Colombo: Lake House Bookshop.

Magee, G.B. and A.S. Thompson. 2010. *Empire and Globalisation. Networks of People, Goods and Capital in the British World c. 1850–1914,* Cambridge: Cambridge University Press.

Malalgoda, K. 1976. *Buddhism in Sinhalese Society, 1750–1900: A Study of Religious Revival and Change,* Berkeley: University of California Press.

Marx, K. 1973. *Grundrisse. Foundations of the Critique of Political Economy,* trans. M. Nicolaus, Harmondsworth: Penguin Books.

Mbembe, A. 2001. *On the Postcolony,* Berkeley: University of California Press.

McClintock, A. 1995. *Imperial Leather: Race, Gender and Sexuality in the Colonial Context,* London: Routledge.

McGilvray, D. 2008. *Crucible of Conflict: Tamil and Muslim Society on the East Coast of Sri Lanka,* Durham: Duke University Press.

McPherson, K. 2002. 'Port Cities as Nodal Points of Change: The Indian Ocean, 1890s-1920s', in L.T. Fawaz and C.A. Bayly (eds), *Modernity and Culture: From the Mediterranean to the Indian Ocean,* New York: Columbia University Press, 75–95.

Mehaffy, M.M. 1997. 'Advertising Race/Raceing Advertising: The Feminine Consumer (-Nation), 1876–1900', *Signs* 23, 131–74.

Mendis, G.C. 1946. *Ceylon under the British,* 2nd rev. ed., Colombo: Colombo Apothecaries Co., Ltd Educational Publishers.

Metcalf, T. 2007. *Imperial Connections: India in the Indian Ocean Arena 1860–1920,* Berkeley: University of California Press.

Meyer, E. 1992. 'From Land-grabbing to Land-hunger: Highland Appropriation in the Plantation Areas of Sri Lanka during the British Period', *Modern Asian Studies* 26, 321–61.

Mintz, S.W. 1985. *Sweetness and Power: The Place of Sugar in Modern History,* New York: Viking.

Mitton, G.E. 1917. *The Lost Cities of Ceylon,* New York: FA Stokes Co.

Moldrich, D. 1989. *Bitter Berry Bondage. The Nineteenth Century Coffee Workers of Sri Lanka,* Kandy, Sri Lanka: Co-ordinating Secretariat for Plantation Areas.

Molotch, H. 2005. *Where Stuff Comes From,* New York and London: Routledge.

Moon, K. 2005. *Yellowface: Creating the Chinese in American Popular Music and Performance, 1850–1920,* New Brunswick: Rutgers University Press.

Mrazek, R. 2002. *Engineers of Happy Land. Technology and Nationalism in a Colony,* Princeton: Princeton University Press.

Munasinghe, I. 2002. *The Colonial Economy on Track. Roads and Railways in Sri Lanka (1800–1905),* Colombo: Social Scientists Association.

Oldenziel, R. 1999. *Making Technology Masculine: Women, Men, and the Machine in America, 1880–1945,* Amsterdam: Amsterdam University Press.

Olsen, K. 1994. *Chronology of Women's History,* Westport: Greenwood.

Panditharatne, B.L. 1964. 'Trends of Urbanization in Ceylon 1901–1953', *Ceylon Journal of Historical and Social Studies* 7(2), 203–17.

Peebles, P. 1995. *Social Change in Nineteenth Century Ceylon,* New Delhi: Navrang.

——. 2001. *Plantation Tamils of Ceylon,* London: Leicester University Press.

Peleggi, M. 2002. *Lords of Things: The Fashioning of the Siamese Monarchy's Modern Image,* Honolulu: University of Hawaii Press.

Pemberton, J. 2009. 'The Ghost in the Machine', in R.C. Morris (ed.), *Photographies East. The Camera and Its Histories in East and Southeast Asia,* Durham: Duke University Press, 29–56.

Perera, N. 2002. 'Indigenising the Colonial City: Late 19th Century Colombo and Its Landscape', *Urban Studies* 39(9), 1703–21.

——. 2009. 'People's Spaces: Familiarization, Subject Formation and Emergent Spaces in Colombo', *Planning Theory* 51–75.

Pfaffenberger, B. 1993. "The Factory as Artefact', in P. Lemonnier (ed.), *Technological Choices: Transformations in Material Cultures since the Neolithic,* London: Routledge, 338–71.

Phillips, A. 2005. 'The Kinship, Marriage and Gender Experiences of Tamil Women in Sri Lanka's Tea Plantations', *Contributions to Indian Sociology* 39(1), 107–42.

Pieris, A. 2007. 'The Trouser Under the Cloth. Personal Space in Colonial-Modern Ceylon', in P. Scriver and V. Prakash (eds), *Colonial Modernities: Building, Dwelling and Architecture in British India and Ceylon,* London: Routledge, 119–218.

Poole, R. 1989. 'Bloomsbury and Bicycles', *English Literary History* 56(4), 951–66.

Prakash, G. and K.M. Cruse (eds). 2008. *The Spaces of the Modern City,* Princeton: Princeton University Press.

Prince Dhaninivat. 1965. 'Religious Intercourse between Ceylon and Siam. In the Bangkok Period of Siamese History', in N.A. Jayawickrama (ed.), *Paranavitana Felicitation Volume on Art and Architecture,* Colombo: Gunasena & Co., 135–42.

Prothero, S. 1996. *The White Buddhist: The Asian Odyssey of Henry Steel Olcott,* Bloomington and Indianapolis: Indiana University Press.

Pursell, C. 2007. *The Machine in America: A Social History of Technology,* Baltimore: Johns Hopkins University Press.

Rajagopal, A. 2001. 'The Violence of Commodity Aesthetics. Hawkers, Demolition Raids, and a New Regime of Consumption', *Social Text* 19(3), 91–113.

Ramagundam R. 2008. *Gandhi's Khadi: A History of Contention and Conciliation,* New Delhi: Orient Longman.

Ramanathan, P. 1916. *Riots and Martial Law in Ceylon, 1915,* London: St. Martin's Press.

Raychaudhuri, T. 1979. 'Indian Politics as Animal Politics', *Historical Journal* 22(3), 747–63.

Revel, J. 1996. *Jeux d'echelles. La Micro-analyse a l'experience,* Paris: Gallimard Le Seuil.

Riccini, R. 1998. 'History from Things: Notes on the History of Industrial Design', *Design Issues* 14(3), 43–64.

Roberts, M. 1970. 'The Impact of the Waste-Lands Legislation and the Growth of Plantation on the Techniques of Paddy Cultivation in British Ceylon: A Critique', *Modern Ceylon Studies* 1, 157–98.

——. 1994. *Exploring Confrontation. Sri Lanka: Politics, Culture and History,* Chur: Harwood Academic Publishers.

——. 1997a. 'Elite Formation and Elites 1832–1931', in M. Roberts (ed.), *Collective Identities Revisited,* Colombo: Marga Institute, 267–92.

——. 1997b. 'For Humanity. For the Sinhalese. Dharmapala as Crusading *Bosat*', *Journal of Asian Studies* 56(4), 1006–32.

Roces, M. and L.E. Roces (eds). 2007. *The Politics of Dress in Asia and the Americas,* Eastbourne: Sussex Academic Press.

Rogers, J.D. 1989. 'Cultural Nationalism and Social Reform: The 1904 Temperance Movement in Sri Lanka', *Indian Economic and Social History Review* 26, 319–41.

Rowell, G. 2009. 'Ceylon's Kristallnacht: A Reassessment of the Pogrom of 1915', *Modern Asian Studies,* 43(3), 619–48.

Ryan, B. 1953. *Caste in Modern Ceylon. The Sinhalese System in Transition,* New Brunswick: Rutgers University Press.

Said, E. 1979. *Orientalism,* New York: Vintage.

Samaraweera, V. 1981. 'Masters and Servants in Sri Lankan Plantations: Labour Laws and Labour Control in an Emergent Export Economy', *Indian Economic and Social History Review,* 18(2), 123–58.

Sarukkai, S. 2003. 'Praying to Machines', *Leonardo Electronic Almanac* 11(8), leoalmanac.org/journal/Vol_11/lea_v11_n08.txt.

Schinkel, A. 2005. 'Imagination as a Category of History: An Essay concerning Koselleck's Concepts of *Erfahrungsraum* and *Eerwartungshorizont*', *History and Theory* 44, 42–54.

Scott, D. 1995. 'Colonial Governmentality', *Social Text* 43, 191–220.

——. 1999. *Refashioning Futures: Criticism after Postcoloniality,* Princeton: Princeton University.

——. 2004. *Conscripts of Modernity: The Tragedy of Colonial Enlightenment,* Durham and London: Duke University Press.

Scott, P. 'The Location of Early Overseas Multinationals in Britain 1900–1839: Patterns and Determinants', *Regional Studies* 32(6), 489–501.

Scriver, P. and V. Prakash. 2007. *Colonial Modernities: Building, Dwelling and Architecture in British India and Ceylon,* London: Routledge.

Seneviratne, H.L. 1978. *Rituals of the Kandyan State,* Cambridge: Cambridge University Press.

Sheller, M. 2007. 'Bodies, Cybercars, and the Mundane Incorporation of Automated Mobilities', *Social and Cultural Geography* 8(2), 175–97.

Silverberg, M. 1991. 'Constructing a New Cultural History of Prewar Japan', *Boundary* 18(3), 161–89.

Sinha, M. 1995. *Colonial Masculinity: The 'Manly' Englishmen and the 'Effeminate Bengali' in the Late Nineteenth Century,* Manchester: Manchester University Press.

Snodgrass, D.R. 1966. *Ceylon. An Export Economy in Transition,* Homewood: R.D. Irwin.

Snodgrass, J. 2009. 'Performing Buddhist Modernity: The Lumbini Festival, Tokyo 1925', *Journal of Religious History* 33(2), 133–48.

Spencer, J. 2007. *Anthropology, Politics and the State. Democracy and Violence in South Asia,* Cambridge: Cambridge University Press.

Stoler, A. 2002. *Carnal Knowledge and Imperial Power: Race and the Intimate in Colonial Rule,* Berkeley and Los Angeles: University of California Press.

——. 2010. *Along the Archival Grain: Epistemic Anxieties and Colonial Common Sense,* Princeton: Princeton University Press.

Stoler, A.L. (ed.). 2006. *Haunted by Empire: Geographies of Intimacy in North American History,* Durham and London: Duke University Press.

Suryadi, S. 2006. 'The Talking Machine Comes to the Dutch East Indies. The Arrival of Western Media Technology in Southeast Asia', *Bijdragen tot de Taal-, Land- en Volkenkunde (BKI)* 162(2/3), 269–305.

Tambiah, S.J. 1976. *World Conqueror World Renouncer: A Study of Buddhism and Polity in Thailand against a Historical Background,* Cambridge University Press.

Tampoe-Hautin, V. 2009. 'Cinéma, Colonialisme et Identité: naissance et évolution du cinéma au Sri Lanka (1896–1966)', Ph.D. diss., Université de la Réunion, St Denis.

Taussig, M.T. 1980. *The Devil and Commodity Fetishism in South America,* Chapel Hill: University of North Carolina Press.

Taylor, J. 2012. 'The Sewing Machine in Colonial Era Photographs: A Record from Dutch Indonesia', *Modern Asian Studies* 46(1), 71–95.

Thakurta, T. G. 2004. *Monuments, Objects, Histories. Institutions of Art in Colonial and Postcolonial India,* New York: Columbia University Press. Dharmapala

Thompson, E.P. 1967. 'Time, Work-Discipline and Industrial Capitalism', *Past and Present,* 38, 56–97.

Thorpe, T.E. 1922. *A Dictionary of Applied Chemistry,* London: Longmans, Green and Co.

Trentmann, F. 2006. 'The Evolution of the Consumer. Meanings, Identities, and Political Synapses before the Age of Affluence', in S. Garon and P.L. Maclachlan (eds), *The Ambivalent Consumer: Questioning Consumption in East Asia and the West,* Ithaca and London: Cornell University Press, 21–44.

Trivedi, L.N. 2007. *Clothing Gandhi's Nation: Homespun and Modern India,* Bloomington: Indiana University Press.

Turner, L.J.B. 1927. *Handbook of Commercial and General Information for Ceylon,* Colombo: Government Printers.

Tweed, T.A. 1992. *The American Encounter with Buddhism 1844–1912: Victorian Culture and the Limits of Dissent,* Bloomington: Indiana University Press.

VandenDriesen, I.H. 1982. *Indian Plantation Labour in Sri Lanka: Aspects of the History of Immigration in the 19th century,* Nedlands: I.H. VandenDriesen Centre for South and Southeast Asian Studies, University of Western Australia.

Ven. Phra Anil Sakya. 2008. 'King Mongkut's Buddhist Reforms: The Dhammayut Nikaya and a Pali Script', paper presented at the 10th International Conference on Thai Studies, 9–11 January, Thammasat University, Bangkok, Thailand, http://www.learners.in.th/file/asakya/King%20Mongkut%20and%20Pali%20Script.pdf.

Weerasooriya, W.S. 1973. *The Nattukottai Chettiar Merchant Bankers in Ceylon,* Dehiwela: Tisara Press.

Weidman, A. 2003. 'Guru and Gramophone: Fantasies of Fidelity and Modern Technologies of the Real', *Public Culture* 15(3), 453–76.

Wesumperuma, W. 1986. *Indian Immigrant Plantation Workers in Sri Lanka: A Historical Perpsective 1880–1910,* Kelaniya: Vidyalankara Press.

Wickramasinghe, M. 1924. '*Narak Wu piti baduna*', in *Gehaniyak*, Dehiwela: Tisara Prakasakayo.

——. 1961. *Upandasita*, Dehiwela: Tisara Press.

Wickramasinghe, N. 2003. *Dressing the Colonized Body,* New Delhi: Orient Longman.

——. 2006a. 'La Petition Coloniale. Objet de Controle, Objet de Dissidence', *Identity, Culture and Politics: An Afro-Asian Dialogue* 7(1), 82–97.

——. 2006b. *Sri Lanka in the Modern Age: A History of Contested Identities,* Honolulu: University of Hawaii Press and London: C. Hurst.

——. 2011. 'Colonial Governmentality: Critical Notes from a Perspective of South Asian Studies', *Comparative, Zeitschrift für Globalgeschichte und Vergleichende Gesellschaftsforschung* 21(1), 32–40.

Wilkins, M. 1970. *The Emergence of Multinational Enterprise: American Business Abroad from the Colonial era to 1914,* Cambridge: Harvard University Press.

——. 1988. 'European and North American Multinationals 1870–1914: Comparisons and Contrasts', *Business History Journal* 30(1), 8–45.

Wilson, K. 1994. *A New Imperial History: Culture and Identity in Britain and the Empire 1660–1840,* Cambridge: Cambridge University Press.

Woolf, L. 1963. *Diaries in Ceylon 1908–1911. Records of Colonial Administrator,* London: Hogarth Press.

——. 1974. *Village in the Jungle,* Colombo: Hansa Publishers.

Wright, A. (ed.). 1907. *Twentieth Century Impressions of Ceylon,* London: Lloyds Publishing Co.

Index